Secret Money

$ECRET MON£Y

THE WORLD OF INTERNATIONAL FINANCIAL SECRECY

Ingo Walter
Graduate School of Business Administration
New York University

London
GEORGE ALLEN & UNWIN
Boston   Sydney

George Allen & Unwin (Publishers) Ltd
40 Museum Street, London WC1A 1LU, UK

George Allen & Unwin (Publishers) Ltd
Park Lane, Hemel Hempstead, Herts HP2 4TE, UK

George Allen & Unwin Australia Pty Ltd
8 Napier Street, North Sydney, NSW 2060, Australia

George Allen & Unwin with the
Port Nicholson Press
PO Box 11-838 Wellington, New Zealand

First published by George Allen & Unwin 1985

British Library Cataloguing in Publication Data

Walter, Ingo
  Secret money : the world of international
  financial secrecy.
  1. International finance   2. Secrecy
  I. Title
  332'.042   HG3881
  ISBN 0-04-332107-0

Set in 10 on 11½ point Palatino by Mathematical Composition Setters,
Salisbury and printed in Great Britain by
Mackays of Chatham.

Contents

CONTENTS

Tables, Figures and Exhibits

Tables

Figures

Exhibits

For Jutta

Preface

This book is about global financial flows that nobody is supposed to know about – their size, their nature, their causes, and their effects. It is about the behavior of people who want to keep financial information from others and are willing to pay for it. It is about people, institutions and countries that are happy to handle secret assets and keep the information to themselves, for a price. There is demand and there is supply, and so international financial secrecy can be discussed in terms of economics. It is a veritable industry, one that produces services people want and are willing to pay for, and one that has its own players in a global competitive marketplace. It is a somewhat curious industry, however, in that it produces services that are of great value to some, yet positively bad for others – not unlike a number of highly pollutive industries like steel and chemicals – so that its players are constantly under pressure in a never-ending sequence of cat-and-mouse chases. This book attempts to describe that industry in all of its economic, political, social and personal dimensions.

As a study of a worldwide industry, secret money can be subjected to clinical analysis by economists, and economics forms the basic frame of reference used in this book. Concepts of market analysis, macroeconomics, international trade, economic growth and international finance all find application here.

So do war stories and anecdotes. I am convinced that international financial secrecy is a topic of enormous quantitative importance, yet it is one on which virtually no hard evidence is available. Like a jigsaw puzzle with many missing pieces, isolated facts and observations have to be assembled in an effort to discern the structure of the whole. And, much like the subject itself, almost all first-hand information is secret, while second- and third-hand information relies for its accuracy on those who tell the tale. Conceptualization is easy. Readers are not encouraged to go beyond the limits of personal safety in search of empirical verification.

Much of the research and writing on this book was done at the University of Mannheim, West Germany, under a grant from the Deutsche Forschungsgemeinschaft (Forschungsbereich 5), and I am grateful to both institutions for the generous and timely support. William Prado, Mabel Lung and Eduard Payen provided capable research assistance, while my colleagues Edward Altman, Ernest Bloch, Michael Keenan, Arnold Sametz, Anthony Saunders and Lawrence White read and critiqued parts of the manuscript. To all I am grateful, but none are responsible for remaining errors.

INGO WALTER
New York City
June 1985

1

The World of Secret Money

Few aspects of international finance are more fascinating than secrecy. Images flash through the mind of suitcases crammed with currency crossing national boundaries, of close-mouthed couriers slipping easily into and out of airports, hotels and banking offices, of expatriates living handsomely along palm-shaded beaches with no visible means of support, of churning money laundries and quiet slush funds. All find their parallels in the real world. But there are many other, less dramatic images as well: the tax evader skimming unreported income into an offshore account; the briber shuffling funds to the bribee; the violator of securities laws squirreling away illegal profits; the insecure politician or government official building a retirement fund abroad; the businessman fleeing his creditors; the husband fleeing his wife; the law-abiding citizen fleeing exposure to political or economic risk. All are players in the global financial secrecy game.

International financial secrecy is a subject of enduring and perhaps growing importance for the international economy, one that is well worth exploring. With a little imagination, the conventional tools of economic analysis can yield some useful insights into an otherwise rather murky subject. As we shall see, it is largely a matter of supply and demand.

The demand for financial secrecy

Who needs or desires financial secrecy? Practically everybody. The demand for financial secrecy – meaning non-disclosure of financial information that people are willing to pay for – arises from at least five more or less distinct sets of motivations: personal, business, political, fiscal and criminal. Each has a unique pattern of demand that helps define the overall structure of the global 'market' for financial secrecy.

A personal desire to keep financial affairs confidential may be a purely

1

domestic matter. Surveys reveal an amazing amount of financial secrecy between husbands and wives, perhaps to prevent 'irresponsible' household spending behavior or to avoid unfavorable property settlements in the event of divorce. Parents often keep financial secrets from their children, in the hope of inducing proper motivation and greater effort. Moneyed people withhold financial information from their prospective heirs in the hope of keeping the vultures at bay. In an employee's dealings with his employer over salary matters, or a shopper's haggling with salesmen over purchases of goods or services, it is usually worthwhile not showing too many financial cards. And there is the matter of personal preference. Individuals feel more or less strongly that personal finances are nobody else's business, that they have a basic 'right' to financial privacy. Nor is it wise to attract thieves, kidnappers, con-artists and other social parasites by unnecessary financial disclosure. Personal financial secrecy usually remains in substantial compliance with the law, and in many countries has been well served by long-standing traditions of banking confidentiality. Indeed, it is often regarded as a cornerstone of personal liberty.

Confidentiality is no less important an aspect of business affairs. Withholding financial information from competitors, suppliers, creditors and customers is a right that business people assume from the outset. Release of such information is made only in a tightly controlled manner and, where possible, only in a way that benefits that enterprise. As such, financial information is proprietary. It is capitalized in the value of a business to its shareholders. Leakage of financial information could easily erode this value, and so confidentiality and the judicious use of information is generally assumed in business as a critical component of the rules of the game in market-oriented economies. Banks, for example, may wish to adhere to strict standards of secrecy on the liability side of their balance sheets in attracting deposits, yet minimize secrecy on the asset side with respect to borrower creditworthiness if they are permitted by the regulators to do so. Beyond this, however, people in business may wish to keep financial information from employees, partners, potential acquirers and filers of lawsuits, not to mention the tax man, all the while remaining fully in compliance with the law. Again, standard confidentiality arrangements in national banking and financial systems are usually well suited to meet the need for business secrecy.

There are times, however, when people worry about their exposure to political risk. The owner of a company or a farm worries that a new regime may confiscate his assets. The government official worries about being overthrown, possibly necessitating a hasty exit to save his own life. Ordinary citizens have been wiped out time after time as governments come and go with exciting but often misguided new policies. As the years go by, they develop a deep personal distrust of 'visible' domestic financial and real assets as a reliable store of value. Meanwhile, foreign investors in a country worry about the risks of being aliens, and often seek to submerge themselves as far as possible in the host environment, possibly through the services of local intermediaries or beneficial owners. Because political risk usually extends only to a nation's borders, extraordinary value is placed on 'outside' assets kept under wraps in other, less troublesome political jurisdictions. Yet the ownership of 'outside' assets may itself be viewed at home as evidence of a lack of commitment, a telegraphing of options, and possibly as a crime, thus placing a great premium on secrecy as long as the principal – or people he or she cares about – remains behind.

Then there are the tax evaders. Death and taxes are said to be the only great certainties that face human beings. Around the world people feel that they are unfairly taxed. Some are exposed to high levels of income taxation. Others are hit by confiscatory wealth taxes or death taxes. Still others feel forced by high indirect taxes or wage and price controls to escape into the underground economy, or are encouraged by stiff import duties and other market distortions to enter the contraband business. And there are always those who are simply greedy, for whom the only 'fair' tax is zero.

There are usually ways to avoid taxes legally, for a price. There are also ways to evade taxes – illegally to escape government claims on income or assets. None is entirely risk-free, and all require varying degrees of financial secrecy to work. Once again, 'outside' assets, beyond the reach of the national fiscal authorities, can take on an extraordinary value to the tax evader.

Lastly, there are the crooks (we can leave aside for the moment tax evasion and political risk avoidance as examples of out-and-out crookedness). Drug traffickers not only accumulate huge amounts of cash, but regularly deal in a variety of foreign currencies. So do gun runners and terrorists, feeding off the political turmoil and insecurities that afflict others. And there is organized and unorganized crime – robbery, burglary, auto theft, illegal gambling, prostitution, loan sharking, protection, extortion and other forms of racketeering. All need ways to stash funds and eliminate paper trails that might be taken as evidence of criminal activity – money needs to disappear and stay that way, reappearing only in freshly laundered form. Bribery and corruption require financial secrecy no less, with slush funds skillfully set up and carefully kept from the public eye.

Whether personal, business, political, fiscal or criminal, the secrecy objective is the same. Yet the secrecy 'products' that are needed, and the willingness to pay for them, are vastly different.

The supply of financial secrecy

As with the demand for secrecy, the supply side forms a rather complex patchwork of intermediaries and assets that yield varying degrees of safety from unwanted disclosure. Supply dimensions can be classified into onshore financial assets, offshore financial assets, and physical assets held either onshore or offshore.

Onshore financial assets include bank deposits and certificates, cashier's checks, equity shares, bonds and notes of public or private issuers. All normally yield 'market' rates of return, yet provide the investor with some degree of protection from unwanted disclosure. Traditional banking practice in most countries provides for confidentiality with respect to unauthorized inquiries, which gives adequate shielding from the prying eyes of many of the institutions and individuals targeted in the 'personal' and 'business' needs for protection from disclosure. Once the law gets involved, however, either in civil, tax or criminal matters, much of this protection may be lost.

Under proper legal procedures, the state can force disclosure in the event of divorce proceedings, creditor suits, inheritance matters and tax cases, not to mention criminal actions. Although a certain amount of added protection can be obtained through 'bearer' certificates of various types, this runs the risk of theft, loss or accidental destruction. Onshore beneficial ownership — placing financial assets in the name of friends, associates or family members – can also provide greater protection, assuming the third parties can be trusted and will not themselves face legal trouble as a result. Or 'shell companies' and legitimate business 'fronts' can be used, both to hide financial assets and to launder tainted money. The history of organized crime and fiscal skullduggery worldwide is replete with cat-and-mouse chases of mind-boggling complexity. Sooner or later a rat seems to emerge, confidentiality is blown, and the jig is up. As long as secrecy is sought domestically, governed by a single more or less efficient law-enforcement process and subject to the political whims of the moment, the quality of onshore secrecy 'products' is invariably tainted.

Foreign financial assets may offer a good deal more in this regard, if only because national sovereignty halts at the border, and extra-territorial investigation normally requires disclosure terms carefully and often reciprocally negotiated between governments. Bank deposits may be held abroad in carefully selected countries, outside the political jurisdiction of home authorities, and thus deemed acceptably safe from unwanted disclosure. Foreign equities and debt instruments may provide similar security, yet may be subject to the host country withholding taxes and negotiated disclosure at the request of the home country. Things are a bit easier, of course, when the host country is also a tax haven. Bearer certificates, beneficial ownership and shell companies may provide some added protection, and certainly greatly increase the complexity of the inevitable paper chase. In all cases, the secrecy attributes of the host country – evidenced in its history, traditions and proneness to corruption – are of critical importance.

An alternative to financial secrecy sought in other countries is provided by true 'offshore' assets. These may be held in the form of bank deposits or certificates in Euro-banking or booking centers ranging from New York to London, from Singapore to Panama, from Nassau to Luxembourg. All provide substantial exemption from taxation, although secrecy may be eroded if deposits in offshore branches of home-country banks are involved (or foreign banks that do business domestically), and authorities are able to force disclosure through the domestic entity. Deposits in offshore branches of foreign banks that do not do business domestically may avoid this problem, but could be perceived in some cases as being more risky. All normally deal in large sums, so small-timers may be left out. Another form of offshore assets is provided by Eurobonds, generally available in bearer form, which can be purchased by individuals at retail, either on issuance or in the secondary market. Once again, shell companies and beneficial ownership can be used to further draw the veil of secrecy.

All sellers of financial secrecy products have an important stake in doing their best to limit disclosure as far as possible. Their business depends on it. Any form of discretionary disclosure will damage the value of what they have to sell, perhaps irreparably, given the extreme risk aversion of clients taking advantage of their services. Governmental jurisdictions responsible for the secrecy vendors tend to be on much the same wavelength, depending on the importance of the secrecy business in generating real economic gains in the form of local employment, income and taxes.

Lastly, there are physical assets, kept in the form of collectables, precious metals and stones, other forms of tangible property, or even cash (domestic and foreign), secreted away in walls, mattresses, safe deposit boxes, and holes in the ground. Hoarding is as old as mankind. People in countries ranging from France to India have, over the generations, developed a profound distrust of conventional financial assets as waves of political change, economic mismanagement and social unrest have swept over them. Again, physical assets may also be held offshore, consigned to an individual or institution to watch over with care. All such assets provide effective secrecy as long as they remain undiscovered, yet may put the owner at risk of theft, fraud, extortion or even bodily injury if information or suspicion leaks out.

Not all assets yielding the desired degree of secrecy are available to everyone, of course. While secreted physical assets and domestic financial assets are generally usable by anyone, this is not true of many of the more interesting offshore assets that are relatively safe from disclosure. Lack of information and financial sophistication, exchange controls, inertia, fear of getting caught, and size of the necessary transactions are some of the factors that inhibit people's access to the secrecy 'products' available around the world. This leads to considerable market segmentation, which in turn gives rise to both constraints and profit opportunities in the international secrecy business.

The cost of secrecy

As they say, there is no such thing as a free lunch. Like anything else, secrecy has its cost. And the higher the degree of secrecy (the 'quality' of the product), the higher the cost. Nobody expects to pay the same for a Mercedes and a Toyota, and people in the market for a Mercedes are not too likely to seek out the Toyota showroom, or vice versa. What determines the cost of financial secrecy in the international market place?

Perhaps appropriately, the cost of secrecy is a bit shadowy, and focuses in large measure on the difference between what sort of return is actually earned on the secreted assets and what *could have been* earned on a comparable portfolio of non-secret assets in the open market. Moreover, non-secret returns generally have to be adjusted for taxes, while secret returns do not. And secret assets may be more risky as well. We thus have an 'opportunity cost', one that comprises at least three differentials: returns, charges and risks.

Everyone knows that assets like gold, domestic or foreign cash and other physical property yield nothing, except for possible capital gains. Neither, ordinarily, do bank checks or demand deposits. And some income-earning assets yield a good deal more than others. The cost of secrecy attributable to return differentials is the gap between returns on the mix of assets actually held in order to achieve the desired degree of secrecy and returns on an optimum mix of assets held by the same individual *if* secrecy were not a consideration. This includes both ordinary asset-related yields and expectations of net capital gains. A numbered foreign account yielding next to nothing (or even having a negative yield), or gold bullion in a foreign bank vault, would seem to involve high-priced secrecy, but a confidential account in a local bank that yields a 'market' rate of interest would not.

Second, charges levied by suppliers of secrecy can add to the cost. Banking fees may be raised for asset-holders known to be driven by the secrecy motive. Transactions may have to be routed in clandestine ways, through narrow markets, via inefficient conduits, all the while picking up transactions costs. Foreign exchange transactions, perhaps repeated several times or involving black markets, may add further costs. People may have to be bribed. Third parties, beneficial owners and shell companies may have to be used to enhance secrecy, all of which costs money. Since many of the counterparties in such transactions know the name of the game well, they may not be shy about pricing their services.

6

Such charges must be added to any yield differential in ascertaining the cost of secrecy.

And then there is the matter of risk. Some assets are clearly a lot more risky than others. Beneficial owners may renege on their pledge. Gold and other physical assets may be highly volatile in price, and subject to theft. Fixed-rate financial instruments and foreign currencies expose the owner to interest-rate and exchange-rate risk. Deposits in potentially shaky banks, and purchases of stocks and bonds expose the owners to default risk. Country risk, in turn, exposes them to the willingness and ability of governments to honor external claims on domestic real or financial assets. And some types of assets that would make possible greater portfolio diversification and earnings stability may simply not be available to the secrecy seeker. The risk differential between a portfolio of assets yielding the desired degree of financial secrecy and an *optimum* open-market portfolio can thus be defined as an implicit 'cost' to the individual. The greater the person's aversion to risk, the greater will be this perceived cost.

So the real cost of secrecy to an asset-holder with a certain risk-preference profile is the risk-adjusted net differential in returns between an open-market portfolio and one containing the desired dose of financial secrecy. Clearly, different classes of secrecy seekers will face vastly different costs. Even within each class, cost differentials may emerge due to differences in transaction size, sophistication, risk aversion, and the like.

Does it pay to buy financial secrecy? That depends. The cost of secrecy gives half the picture. The other half is based on what may happen if the secrecy cover is blown – what economists call the 'damage function' – and the probability of this actually occurring. Damage can range from execution, exile, prison and political ostracism to confiscation of assets, incremental taxes, social opprobrium and familial tension. Avoidance of damage is, after all, what the secrecy seeker is after, and, since damage usually is a matter of probabilities, his attitude toward the risk of exposure is a critical factor in how this benefit is valued.

How much secrecy should one buy? Simple. Just enough so that the marginal cost of financial secrecy equals its marginal benefit – both sides risk-adjusted, of course. This may sound a bit academic, but it's conceptually correct. It may stretch the imagination to envisage the harried secrecy seeker carefully equating marginal costs and benefits, but he will surely know when he's bought too much (being 'secrecy poor') or too little.

The price of secrecy

When out shopping for secrecy, people thus confront a variety of products, each of which has a price. Some are 'list' prices, paid by everyone regardless of the willingness to pay, while others are individually negotiated. Both are set by the forces of supply and demand in the secrecy market.

List prices such as bank interest rates, bond yields and equity returns are established by broad market forces that extend well beyond seekers of secrecy. The returns involved may well impose an opportunity cost on the secrecy seeker, yet still be higher than what the individual would have sacrificed to achieve the degree of financial secrecy actually obtained. He thus enjoys an unearned benefit we can call a 'secrecy seeker's surplus' (SSS).

Financial products specifically tailored to the secrecy market, like all high-quality items, involve substantially higher opportunity costs and hence smaller SSS. Numbered bank accounts abroad, a jewel among available secrecy products, tend to have correspondingly high opportunity costs. Yet even these are in large part list-priced so that, despite the expense, much of the SSS remains intact.

Not so in the case of custom-tailored secrecy items whose prices are set largely on the basis of bargaining. The secrecy vendor tries to ascertain how much his product is worth, given the apparent motivations of the secrecy seeker. He adjusts his asking price accordingly, and there may be an interval of negotiation before final agreement is reached. He will never, of course, threaten to breach the confidential relationship, since this would seriously and perhaps fatally impair the value of his product. In the final negotiated price, much of the SSS may evaporate – it is drawn off by the vendor.

So supply and demand interact in the market for financial secrecy, just as they do in any other market. A hierarchy of differentiated products exists, each with its own market characteristics. The greater the demand, the higher the price. The more intense the competition among vendors, and the easier the substitutability of secrecy products, the lower the price. The rational secrecy seeker will presumably shop around, insofar as his position is not jeopardized thereby, to fill his basket with an optimum mix of products at a cost that makes the whole exercise worthwhile.

Market structure

If secrecy is a product that can be bought and sold in national and international markets and described in terms like supply, demand, cost and price, then some of the dimensions of the secrecy market itself – in terms of competitive structure, conduct and performance – should also be amenable to rational analysis.

On the demand side, we see highly differentiated characteristics among secrecy seekers, in terms of their willingness and ability to pay.

We also see widely divergent secrecy products and vendors, many of whom compete with one another. A few vendors have products with no good substitutes, so that demand for them may well be quite inelastic (insensitive to price) and their sellers are able to command very high prices indeed. Some traditional secrecy products (gold, dummy companies, holes in the ground) are easily available in some places but less so elsewhere. Others have been built up over the generations as secure repositories (Swiss numbered accounts) and can command high premiums. But high premiums also attract competitors, whose entry may alter the structure of the market. It is probably safe to say that higher levels of secrecy involve successively greater degrees of monopoly power in the definition of competitive structure and market organization.

As we shall see, the international market for financial secrecy is perhaps more competitive than might at first appear. Countries see it in their economic interest to offer secrecy products in competition with one another, and institutional arrangements that threaten to erode some of its value are often fiercely resisted.

Plan of attack

In this book, we shall explore the various facets of secret money as an international economic phenomenon. Chapter 2 outlines the principal secrecy 'products' available in the international marketplace, some of which are quite complex. This clarifies what is being bought and sold, and permits a reasonable definition of the 'market' for financial secrecy in terms of characteristics associated with demand (Chapter 3) and supply (Chapter 4). Who are the major players on the demand side, how do they behave, and what are they willing and able to pay for financial secrecy? What kind of vendors have emerged, how do they differentiate and price their services, and how do they relate to their respective governments? Both chapters form an illustrative set of real-world cases intended to substitute (albeit imperfectly) for the chronic lack of reliable data in this area.

Chapter 5 identifies and evaluates a variety of measures intended to break the veil of secrecy associated with public policy action to combat corruption, tax evasion, terrorism, drug trafficking, and various other kinds of activities that need financial secrecy to work. It discusses the principal threats to the international market for secret money.

Having carefully traced through the available evidence on international financial secrecy, can a coherent theory be devised that fits the facts? Theory is important, after all, in making sense of the whole issue, and in forecasting its future evolution. Chapter 6 outlines the principal conceptual aspects of international financial secrecy from an economic perspective. As with much of economics, no matter how useful, the discussion is somewhat arcane. Readers less interested in theory are encouraged to skip to the end of that chapter for a summary of the main conclusions.

The final chapters of the book attempt an evaluation of the broader consequences as well as the future of secret money.

2

The Nature of Secret Money

It is perhaps best to begin by discussing the 'raw material' of the secret money business – the products that are being bought and sold – as well as the relative importance of secret transactions in a broader economic context.

The underground economy

We can define the underground economy as comprising transactions that create value but are intended to escape something (taxes, revelation of bribes, bureaucractic red tape, exchange controls, criminal prosecution, etc.). It may be convenient to categorize underground economic activities in two ways: (1) transactions to avoid government-imposed impediments to the efficient conduct of business and to evade taxation; and (2) criminal transactions involving drugs, robbery, contract murder, prostitution, racketeering, and the like – basically economically motivated criminal activities. Escape means secrecy, and secrecy means that the transactions involved and the economic activity they represent are very difficult to measure – and sometimes escape measurement altogether.

There are several ways to attempt measurement of the size of the underground economy.[1] The 'fixed ratio variant' assumes that there is a monetary ratio (currency in circulation divided by gross national product) that, without the underground economy, would have remained constant over time, and that there was a 'golden' period in the past when no underground economy existed. The 'golden period' monetary ratio is compared with the monetary ratio at present to estimate the relative change in the share of underground (cash) transactions.

The 'currency-denomination variant' assumes that the underground economy is associated mainly with the use of bills of certain denominations. The estimate of the size of the underground economy is based on

11

the change in the number of such bills in circulation. At least one weakness of this approach is that large-denomination US dollar bills are used for transactions and as a store of value in foreign countries. Therefore, the increase in the number of such bills in circulation can also be due to an increase in foreign holdings rather than in domestic underground activities.

The 'currency-equation' variant assumes that underground activities are the direct consequence of high taxes, and that currency is used mainly for carrying out such transactions or for storing wealth accumulated from them out of the reach of the taxman.

The 'physical input approach' assumes a stable relationship between some physical input into the economy, such as kilowatt hours of electric power, and national output. The difference between the estimated size of the economy, based on such a relationship, and the reported GNP is attributed to the underground economy.

The 'labor market approach' originated in Italy, where the official rate of labor force participation has decreased drastically since the late 1950s, while unofficial estimates of labor force participation rates have been much higher. The difference gives some idea of the relative size of underground economic activity.

The 'gap approach' involves a comparison between income reported in the tax returns and income estimated in the national income accounts. For the comparison to be meaningful, the national income statistics must be derived from sources other than, and independent of, the income tax authorities.

The 'legal tax potential' approach defines evaded tax as the difference between the legal and the realized tax potentials. This represents the difference between the amount of revenue that would have been raised if all legal tax liability had been paid and the amount of tax actually collected.

In the 'survey approach', one obtains information on the income of the taxpayers through a survey. The income determined by the survey is then compared with the reported income in the tax returns, thereby estimating the tax non-compliance.

The 'constant tax ratio' approach applies the ratio of taxes to gross domestic product (GDP) of a 'representative' year to the GDP of the year under study, in order to arrive at an estimated tax for that year. This is not really a measurement of total tax evasion, but rather a measure of additional tax evasion, the level of tax compliance and the quality of tax administration. Another problem is the assumption of a constant tax/GDP ratio.

It may also be possible to measure the size of tax evasion by examining tax returns filed during special tax amnesties. Argentina, India and Thailand have offered special tax amnesties more than once in recent history. The US Taxpayer Compliance Measurement Program (TCMP) is an example of the use of a special audit for the same purpose. Unlike regular field audits, TCMPs are line-by-line audits performed by experienced examiners on a nationwide stratified random sample, typically of 50,000 taxpayers. The major weakness is the exclusion of people who fail to file tax returns at all. Not unexpectedly, the TCMP estimate of non-reported income is low.

Figure 2.1 gives some 'guesstimates' of the overall size of the underground economy in a number of developed and developing countries.

It is likely that there would be little in the way of an underground economy without a public sector that for whatever reason generates distortions in national markets for goods and services. Figure 2.2 gives an interesting overview of the degree of distortion in various national economies around the world, as related to the rate of measured economic growth. This relationship could well be quite different if the underground economy were included in the measures of economic performance indicated in that analysis.

It thus seems reasonable to argue that the size of underground transactions varies enormously from one country to the next, depending on the structure of incentives and disincentives, past, present and expected in the future.

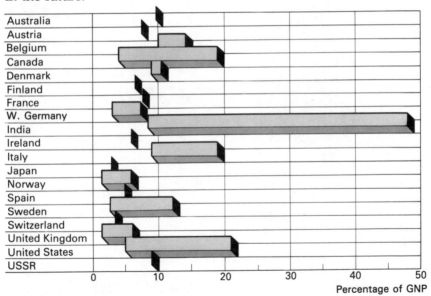

Note: These data show the ranges of estimates made for each country at different times; they are suggestive and should not be taken to be precise.

Source: Vito Tanzi, 'The Underground Economy', *Finance and Development*, December 1983.

Figure 2.1   *Estimated size of underground economy*

13

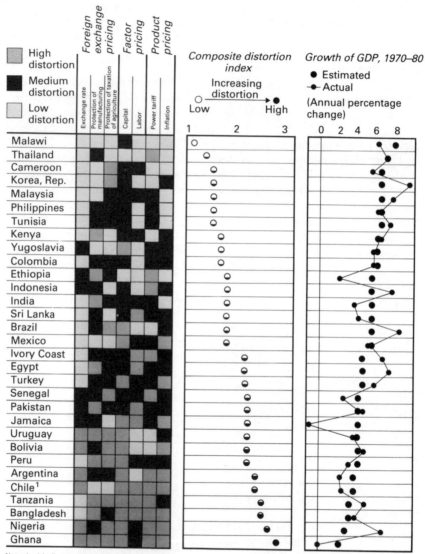

Note: In this figure, countries are listed in order of increasing degree of distortion in prices. In the first section, the color of the squares indicates the degree of distortion in the principal categories of prices. The middle section is a composite index of price distortion for each country: as a country's distortion index increases, the color of the circle changes from gray to black. In the right hand section, the small circles show the actual annual rate of growth of GDP; the large circles are estimates of GDP growth obtained by a regression relating growth to the distortion index.
[1] Price distortions for the decade were heavily influenced by the policies of the Allende regime, which ended in late 1973.

Source: World Bank, World Development Report 1983.

Figure 2.2 Price distortions and economic growth in the 1970s

The fundamental causes of underground economic activity can be outlined in detail.[2] First and foremost is *taxation*, which in some countries takes over 50 per cent of nominal income. Swiss bankers have a saying, 'There would be no tax havens without tax hells'. Obviously, as the rate of taxation increases, the cost of honesty also increases – honesty with respect not only to income taxation, but also to taxation of wealth, transfers of wealth, value-added, sales, and mandatory social insurance contributions. Expectations of what the government will do with tax receipts also affect the incentive to pay: wasteful expenditure, consumption and social insurance schemes from which the payer is unlikely ever to benefit broadly in proportion to his contribution all sap the incentive to pay taxes. Poor tax administration and inequities in tax burdens may likewise demoralize taxpayers and increase the incentive to escape into the underground economy and create black markets for labor, goods and services, and wealth. Import and export duties may be included in taxation; they lead to smuggling in international trade transactions. Tax evasion always involves financial secrecy, and often transcends national boundaries because of investigative and jurisdictional limits set for revenue authorities. International cooperation in matters of tax evasion obviously exists, but there are plenty of loopholes.

Second is *regulation*, which may fix prices, wages, returns on capital, exchange rates, etc. Each time a regulation is set, an incentive is created to evade it, along with its symptoms such as queuing, rationing, forced sales, quotas, bans, etc. In many countries, parallel financial markets (sometimes called 'curb markets') emanate directly from financial controls, as do parallel foreign exchange markets involving currency smuggling and/or over- and under-invoicing of international trade transactions ('transfer pricing'). All create economic activity that is neither taxed nor recorded in the official statistics.

Third is *prohibition*, usually associated with drugs, guns, prostitution, gambling, protection, usury, and other criminal activity. Most involve cash transactions that are difficult to trace, and all raise the question whether they add to the value of real output and income in the national economy despite their nefarious nature.

Finally, there is *corruption*, which seems to be endemic among public officials in a large number of countries. Activities include bribes on public procurement contracts, customs clearance, traffic violations, zoning ordinances and building permits, investment licenses, import and foreign exchange permits, allocation of consumption, investment and infrastructure goods that are in short supply, and a host of others.[3] Bribery is always illegal, although it may be part of the national cultural, political and economic system and tolerated with more or less equanimity by society. Actual 'markets' may exist for the right to collect illegal payments and the bureaucratic power to extort them. Corruption that

15

is clearly tolerated probably requires relatively little financial secrecy; big-time corruption, on the other hand, usually involves secrecy. In all cases, corrupt officials run the political risk of a change in regime, which, if malfeasance can be proved and often even if it cannot, may well result in severe retribution – perhaps death. For this reason the corrupt often demand the highest levels of offshore secrecy, in part to provide for a hasty exit in case of need.

As a generalization, the more intensive the distortions imposed by government on the market economy, and the larger the relative size of the government sector, the greater are the incentives to go underground. The past record of economic distortions plays a role as well, because people get into the habit of doing things 'off the books' – behavior that is often viewed by enforcement agencies as a 'victimless offense', and is sometimes even the source of pride as something of a 'national sport'. Moreover, the past is often a good guide to the future, and may condition expectations about the probable nature and severity of future distortions, thus supporting the precautionary dimension of the underlying incentive structure.

Disincentives include the probability of getting caught, the level of punishment, and the strength of social disapproval associated with tax evasion and other aspects of underground transactions. The disincentive structure may be as complex as the incentive structure, and the two together are highly specific to time and place. For example, among the developed countries, Sweden has a relatively small underground sector, and Italy has a relatively large one. Among the developing countries, Singapore and Hong Kong have relatively small levels of underground activity, and Nigeria and Mexico are characterized by relatively large underground sectors.

In 1976, the US Internal Revenue Service (IRS) estimated legal-source unreported income in America at $31.1 billion, of which unreported interest and dividend income came to $7.5–14.5 billion. Unreported income from illegal-source activities (gambling, prostitution and drugs) amounted to some $30 billion, or 1.7 per cent of the gross national product (GNP). Together, the IRS estimated the size of the US underground economy at about 3.4 per cent of GNP in 1976.[4] These estimates are at variance with others, however, which put the size of the US underground economy at between $176 billion[5] and $330 billion [6] in that year, with the latter representing about 16 per cent of 1976 US GNP. Each uses a different estimation technique. A more recent study places underground transactions at 7.5 per cent of 1981 American GNP, with growth of the underground economy, accounting for 0.1–0.4 per cent of US annual economic growth between 1950 and 1981.[7]

By any reckoning, the size of the US underground economy is very substantial indeed. Most observers in the United States today estimate that 2–5 per cent of actual GNP is attributable to criminal activity such as drug dealing, illegal gambling, and the rackets. In addition, transactions that are not recorded for tax purposes or for purposes of national income accounting have been estimated at anywhere between 5 per cent and 20 per cent of GNP in the mid-1980s.

The high estimates are based on such indicators as currency in circulation, and there is general agreement that the size of cash transactions has been growing in those sectors where it predominates – e.g. transactions of proprietorships and other small-business income. However, these same sectors as a group have been declining in relation to total economic activity, based on such non-financial indicators as employment. So the evidence remains somewhat contradictory. If we take a conservative guess of 10 per cent of GNP, however, the United States still had a domestic underground economy of about $300 billion in 1984.

Peru probably has one of the largest underground economies of all, dwarfing estimates for the US and even much higher ones for Italy. An estimated 60 per cent of Peruvian economic activity is taken underground. The reason, of course, is taxation, bureaucratic inefficiency, impenetrable regulations, and official corruption. In one experiment, a research institute '... tried to set up a legal government company without easing the way with tips. It took a lawyer and three others 301 days of full-time work, dealing with 11 government agencies, to complete the paperwork – which, when laid end to end, measured 102 feet. (One of the researchers then tried the same experiment in Tampa, Florida and finished it in $3\frac{1}{2}$ hours).'[8] Official statistics list over half of Peru's population as living in poverty and an equal proportion as being 'unemployed'. The real world, however, is quite different. Underground business hums along in a variety of sectors, ranging from manufacturing and farming to construction and bus services, and it is estimated that the average Peruvian citizen is about 50 per cent better off than the official statistics indicate – $1,300 in annual income compared to a reported $900. A four-year study found rapidly growing underground economic activity in essentially all goods and services sectors, including at least 85 per cent of garment production, bus assembly, precision tools, and manufacturing of electrical controls.[9]

As another example, the Indian government controls about three-fourths of the equity in Indian industry, either through outright government ownership or through shareholdings in private companies. Indian companies have grown comfortably lazy, backed by low-interest loans and subsidies, producing obsolete but expensive products under quotas that guarantee a market regardless of quality or price. Inevitably, black markets have flourished. World Bank economists estimate that India's underground economy could be half the nation's GNP. To thwart such dealings, the government spun ever-thickening webs of taxes and licenses, thereby creating vast new opportunities for corruption among government officials collecting taxes and issuing licenses.

Moreover, any firm or industry association benefiting from such a complex of competitive restrictions and subsidies can be expected to channel illicit funds to the politicians who make it all possible.

The existence of a significant underground economy has a number of side-effects that may create problems for economic policymaking. For one thing, actual unemployment rates and inflation rates may be quite different from those that are measured in the national statistics. This may lead to excessively stimulative or contractionary monetary or fiscal policy, not to mention policy related to the balance of payments. Moreover, the underground sector may have a significant effect, both positive and negative, on the level of efficiency in the national economy. For this reason, while measurement of the underground sector may be quite important, direct measurement is nearly always impossible.

Internationalization of underground financial flows

If domestic underground economic activities are notoriously difficult to identify and to gauge, secret international money flows provide an even greater statistical challenge. The connections, however, are clear. Domestic underground dealings have to be kept hidden by means of cash transactions or bearer financial instruments that cannot be traced. Use of the domestic banking system is difficult, and the probability of exposure depends on confidentiality rules and traditions – which will almost always lead to exposure in serious cases. International financial secrecy provides a good alternative, with domestic underground goods or services, for example, being paid for by foreign bank transfers from buyer to seller.

International secret money flows have been the focus of attempts at measurement not too different from those aimed at domestic underground economies, yet they are extraordinarily difficult to track. Every once in a while, a customs inspector finds a suitcase or package stuffed with currency. Now and then a government agency or financial institution gets caught making unauthorized or unreported money transfers abroad. The US Internal Revenue Service estimated in 1983 that $20–135 billion in illicit money flows annually from the United States to foreign secrecy centers. Much of this involves drug traffic, but an increasing share evidently involves tax evasion. In general, no one has even a remote idea of the size or direction of global secret money flows, or of the identity of those involved. It is, however, possible to speculate.

For one thing, national statistics that are supposed to keep track of international payments for goods and services simply do not add up. What one country imports, another should export, and if this includes

18

all goods, services and investment income the disbursements of one country should equal the receipts of another, and so the 'current-account' statistics in the balances of payments of all the world's countries should add to precisely zero. But, as Figure 2.3 shows, they do not. In 1983, the world's reported payments exceeded receipts by over $100 billion. Why? Unless the world as a whole had a transactions deficit of that magnitude with the man on the moon, something is wrong.

Obviously, keeping track of international payments is no easy task, and some countries have far better statistical systems than others to accomplish that task. Some countries also misrepresent their numbers. But there is no reason why the errors on the disbursement side should be systematically greater than those on the receipts side. Indeed, at least as far as international trade data are concerned (where expenditure data are collected alongside customs information), it should actually be the other way around. Even allowing for problems related to record-keeping and governments massaging the figures (again biased toward over-stating receipts and understating disbursements), much remains to be explained.

Various candidates emerge. Criminal imports (drugs, weapons) are unlikely to be reported to the international trade statisticians. Interest and dividend payments to foreigners tend to be reported by the payer to his government's authorities, but may not be reported by the recipient. Receipts of dividends and interest payments taken into Swiss ac-

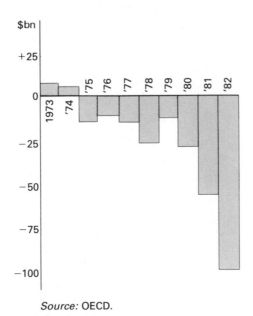

Source: OECD.

Figure 2.3 *World current-account discrepancy*

19

counts are not recorded by Switzerland in its balance of payments, since the account holders are not residents. Those who engage in international trade may overstate the value of imports and understate the value of exports in order to avoid taxes or exchange controls, thus again contributing to current-account deficits in some countries that are not counterbalanced by surpluses in others. Among other major flows that are likely to escape the statisticians are earnings on foreign-owned capital held overseas, and non-remittance of earnings of capital held abroad by residents of countries like France and Mexico – an estimated $30 billion in the case of the latter.[10]

According to the International Monetary Fund (IMF), the key items giving rise to the global current-account discrepancy are: (1) income from overseas investment and receipts from services, (2) the growing use of tax havens, accounting for an increasing discrepancy in investment income and, (3) the fact that the main recipients of investment income and payments for services that give rise to discrepancies are the OECD countries. Table 2.1 gives the IMF estimates of the size of these flows. Underreporting of current-account receipts is not concentrated in any single country or group of countries within the OECD area, according to the IMF.

Certainly not all the $100 billion or so that shows up in the statistical discrepancy in world current accounts involves secret funds flows associated with tax evasion, capital flight, or criminal transactions. But if even one-half is motivated in this way, $50 billion is still an enormous amount.

Balance of payments discrepancies can also be identified by looking at the 'errors and omissions' item in individual countries' reported balance of payments statistics. Errors and omissions have increased spectacularly in the US: over $100 billion during 1979–83. The situation is more serious due to compensating errors. There is no necessary connection between the global current-account deficit and the errors and omissions item in individual countries' balance of payments statistics. Net errors and omissions typically reflect larger errors on a gross basis that happen to be offsetting. Furthermore, the bulk of errors and omissions is believed to represent unreported capital movements. One im-

Table 2.1 *Global current-account discrepancy*

	$ bn
1977–80 average	−8
1981–83 average	−64
1984	−79
1985	−92

Source: IMF estimates and forecasts.

plication is that US borrowing from abroad has been severely understated.

An assessment of the 'errors and omissions' item in the US external accounts reveals a 'surplus' of nearly $140 billion between 1978 and mid-1984. The official view is that the bulk of these unrecorded inflows reflects capital inflows. For instance, a recent study by the Federal Reserve Bank of New York states that errors and omissions are treated as unrecorded private and official capital flows because they appear to fluctuate over time more like capital flows than like current-account transactions.

On the assumption that the bulk of the cumulative errors and omissions surplus since 1978 represents capital inflows, US liabilities to foreigners at the end of 1983 were understated by some $120 billion. This would transform the country's stated net creditor status into net debtor at the end of 1983. The implication is that the recorded positive net creditor position of the US, built gradually over the entire postwar period, would be reversed in the space of only three years (1983–5). By 1986, US external debt would thus have surpassed that of the whole of Latin America.[11]

Yet another way to try to get at the volume of secret money flows is to follow the external use of national currencies. The Federal Reserve System and other central banks around the world know with a fair degree of precision the amount of national currency outstanding at any given time. Some of that money is in domestic circulation as an active means of payment, and some is hoarded by domestic residents. We noted earlier that a number of economists have attempted to use the relationship of currency outstanding to the total money supply and to economic activity measured at the national and regional level to gauge the size of the underground economy. For instance, drug deals, the rackets, organized crime, and tax evasion are all dependent in large part on cash transactions.

In addition, however, domestic currency may be held *outside* the national economy. We know, for example, that foreign countries may from time to time become 'dollarized'. Typically, irresponsible domestic monetary, fiscal and exchange-rate policies, along with exchange controls and other market distortions, rapidly erode confidence in the purchasing power of the national currency, resulting in a growing demand for dollars or other foreign currencies that better retain their value or that can be used to acquire otherwise unobtainable products or services. Examples include Argentina, Mexico, Israel, Brazil and Poland during the 1980s. Sometimes, even domestic prices are expressed in dollars, as the mismanaged domestic currency loses its meaning as a viable unit of account. And there are some countries, such as Panama and Liberia, where the dollar is used as the currency and there is no central bank or independent monetary authority. Panama, where the US dollar and the colon exchange freely at par, is probably the most dramatic example in this category. In 1983, the country had a population of 1.8 million, $38 billion in bank deposits, and 3,000 lawyers, many of whom no doubt have found lucrative business in the secrecy trade.

Dollarized economies may play at least two distinct roles in secret money flows. First, the origin of dollars in domestic circulation is, almost by definition, clandestine (except for Liberia and Panama) as holders fail to declare them when they enter the country. Second, such countries represent a 'sink' for hiding and laundering illicit cash transactions that take place in the United States and elsewhere. It is suggested, for example, that a sizeable part of the drug money generated in the United States finds its way in cash to dollarized economies and, after complex laundry services, emerges with a new image. Large amounts of US currency apparently leave Panama and certain other countries aboard aircraft daily for the United States, to be deposited in US banks in the natural course of interbank transactions, thus enabling the proceeds of illicit transactions to enter the normal channels of payment.

Not only dollars are involved. One popular story has currency leaving France strapped to hang-glider pilots who launch themselves from a French mountain near Geneva and conveniently come down to land in Swiss farm fields on the plain below – to be met by 'clean' accomplices who take the money straight to a Swiss bank.

Secret money vehicles

Even if the vast international flows of secret money are difficult to measure, it is at least possible to pin down the vehicles that are used. As noted in Chapter 1, they range from long-standing traditions of financial confidentiality to schemes of almost diabolical complexity.

The vehicles of financial secrecy are not particularly difficult to identify. Cash is one alternative, but has the disadvantage of zero yield, ease of loss, traceability in large denominations, as well as difficulties and suspicions aroused in large-scale transactions. 'Outside cash' (the currency of other countries) may be considerably more attractive, but suffers from some of the same drawbacks. Gold, silver, stamps and collectables offer an alternative that could provide capital appreciation and desirability, but suffer in the area of security and liquidity as well as frequently low yields and large spreads between 'buy' and 'sell' prices. Bearer instruments such as cashier's checks and money orders can offer a temporary refuge, but also suffer from some of the same disadvantages and are not suitable for long-term holdings. Rather better are bearer bonds, available in some national capital markets and in the Eurobond market, which provide a (secrecy-adjusted) market yield and may be a good long-term alternative – assuming the problem of theft or loss can be taken care of.

From such relatively straightforward 'off the shelf' assets that can yield financial secrecy, we then move to products that directly involve the secrecy seeker with counterparties and hence a relationship of trust.

The privileged relationship between banker and client goes back at least to ancient Greece, and has sometimes been compared to the Hippocratic oath in medicine, which governs the relationship between physician and patient, and to corresponding privileged ties between client and lawyer that are anchored in law and practice throughout the world. Frederick the Great in 1765 formulated the relationship in a banking regulation as follows:

We forbid, on pain of royal displeasure, anyone from investigating the banking assets of anyone else. Nor shall bank employees disclose such information to third parties, whether verbally or in writing, on pain of dismissal and criminal prosecution. They must, on accepting employment, solemnly swear that any transactions that come to their attention in the course of their work will be considered the greatest secret that will be carried with them into the grave. [12]

Historically, confidentiality has been an aspect of political freedom and privacy as important in many respects as the freedom of association, religious affiliation and speech.

In totalitarian societies, where the interests of the state clearly override the interests of the individual, the right to financial confidentiality is largely absent. Confidentiality from the state can be achieved only outside the law.

Most countries, however, have reasonable confidentiality safeguards even in tax matters. For example, in 1984 the Netherlands Finance Ministry reached agreement with the Netherlands Bankers' Association to revise a voluntary set of guidelines that had existed since 1948. [13] These guidelines basically protected the right of individuals to financial privacy except when there were clear signs of fraud. However, the enforcement enthusiasm of the tax authorities increasingly breached these guidelines, necessitating a revision. The authorities now have a clearer mandate to pursue suspected tax evaders, but individual privacy safeguards have been strengthened against unreasonable forced disclosure. Similar debates on the 'reasonableness' of government access to private financial information have occurred in West Germany and elsewhere.

Wide differences exist among countries in the degree of confidentiality permitted individual bank accounts under the law in tax matters. As might be expected, Swedish tax authorities are given access to all personal and business financial information, essentially without restriction. The same is true in France, where banks also have to notify the authorities of the account holder's interest earnings for income tax purposes unless he or she agrees to a 40 per cent withholding tax on interest income. The United States likewise provides tax authorities with liberal access to financial records, and all financial institutions are required to provide account holders' social security numbers, with investigative procedures strictly spelled out under the Financial Privacy Act of 1978. Spanish banks must provide fiscal authorities with the names and identification numbers of all account holders, but not specific account information or interest earnings. Danish and UK disclosure requirements are very similar to those in the US.

The situation is somewhat more restrictive in West Germany, where tax authorities do not automatically receive account information, and gain access only under specific and relatively restrictive procedural guidelines. The same is true in the Netherlands. In neither case can the authorities go on 'fishing expeditions' in demanding disclosure of account information by banks, in the hope of frightening tax evaders.

Most restrictive in Europe are Austria and Switzerland, where the privileged relationship between banker and client is taken very seriously indeed, and where tax evasion itself is insufficient reason to break banking confidentiality. The same is true in Italy to a somewhat lesser extent, and in Lebanon.[14]

Standard domestic banking confidentiality is not, however, a principal secrecy vehicle, except when it is made accessible to foreigners who do not have comparable confidentiality at home. We can also omit domestic cash hoards, collectables and other hidden assets, whose characteristics are fairly obvious, and concentrate our discussion on foreign assets. Exhibit 2.1 lists a sample of recent legal cases in the United States that involved international financial secrecy (a more comprehensive but less detailed survey may be found in the Appendix). Scanning them, it is possible to get a rough idea of the range of secrecy products that have in fact emerged.

Banks as a group constitute the single most important vehicle in secret money operations. While most bankers do not actively cooperate in highly suspect activities, all find it difficult to distinguish between various types of secrecy seekers, and some prefer to close their eyes to the source of their deposits and thus accept variously tainted funds. Their services may include:

- allowing clients whose funds are not of foreign origin to make investments limited to foreigners;
- acting without power of attorney to allow clients to manage investments, or to transmit funds, on behalf of foreign-registered companies or local companies acting as laundries;

- participating in sequential transactions that fall just under the Government reporting thresholds;
- allowing telephone transfers of funds without written authorization and failing to keep a record of such transfers; and
- entering false foreign account number destinations with regard to wire transfers.

Banks can obviously follow careful procedures in vetting new depositors, and failure to exercise due diligence could result in serious costs to the banks themselves. But given the diversity of bank policies and practices, and the minute volume of truly questionable funds as compared to total banking volume, it is unrealistic to expect banks to devote substantial resources to any vetting procedure.

EXHIBIT 2.1

Sample of US legal cases involving international financial secrecy

VIOLATION OF SECURITIES LAWS

Securities and Exchange Commission v. Certain Unknown Purchasers of the Common Stock or Call Options for the Common Stock of Santa Fe International Corporation (1981); *Securities and Exchange Commission v. Martin* (1982) Gary L. Martin was charged with violations of the Securities and Exchange Act by fraudulently trading in the securities of Santa Fe International Corp. based on 'material non-public information' concerning the acquisition of all of Santa Fe by Kuwait Petroleum Company (KPC), wholly owned by the government of Kuwait. He received the information from a Santa Fe director who had consulted him for tax planning advice. Illegal profits totalled over $1.1 million, at least half of which were secreted in Seattle First National Bank's branch in Zurich, Switzerland. The district court issued an order to 'freeze' the assets pending litigation. Also charged with fraudulent trading based on material non-public information were Faisal Al Massod Al Fuhait, Oil Minister of Kuwait and Chairman of the Board of KPC, and 'certain unknown purchasers of the common stock of Santa Fe', trading through certain designated financial institutions named as nominal defendants, which as of the indictment date had not been identified by the SEC (with the exception of Darius N. Keaton, who agreed to disgorge all profits).

Securities and Exchange Commission v. Banca della Svizzera Italiana (1981). The SEC sought an order to compel disclosure by the Swiss bank of information about its customers suspected of purchasing, on insider information, St Joe Minerals Corporation call options immediately prior to a Seagram Corp. tender offer for St Joe stock. The court required the bank to make disclosure, although Swiss criminal law prohibited the bank from doing so. The court conducted a balancing test, considering (a) vital interests of the nations involved, (b) the extent and nature of hardship that inconsistent enforcement would impose on a person who is to perform conduct, (c) the extent to which the required conduct is to take place on the territory of the other state, (d) the nationality of person who is to perform conduct, and (e) the extent to which enforcement by action of either state can be expected to achieve compliance with that state's rule. The court held that US vital interests were involved in ensuring the integrity of its securities market and the fact that the Swiss government was aware of and expressed no opposition to the litigation warranted disclosure.

SECURITIES FRAUD

Securities and Exchange Commission v. Vesco (1972). Robert L. Vesco, chairman of the board of directors of International Controls Corporation and IOS Ltd, was charged with several counts of securities fraud and misappropriation of hundreds of millions of dollars from US corporations he directed. In a conspiracy which spanned several years and involved several co-conspirators and domestic as well as foreign entities, Vesco caused a fund he directed, the Dollars Fund (DF), to sell approximately $200 million worth of its stock, a portion of this to foreign entities he controlled, and to make investments in his foreign entities without disclosing his interests. The Overseas Development Bank Luxembourg (ODB) and Bahamas Commonwealth Bank (BCB), two banks also controlled by Vesco, were used to hold certain securities he caused DF to purchase, rather than DF's designated custodian of securities, further concealing the misuse of DF's assets. Vesco similarly caused other companies he directed, which had policies of investing predominantly in US securities, to transfer millions of dollars from their US banks to his Bahamas and Luxembourg banks in the form of investments in or high-risk, unprofitable loans to offshore entities he controlled, including several in the Bahamas and Costa Rica, to the severe detriment of these companies' shareholders, in transactions poorly calculated to achieve their investment policies. In order to deceive investors and prospective investors in these defrauded companies, he camouflaged their flagging earnings by evaluating their transactions with his foreign entities in false and misleading ways, not in conformity with general accounting principles. For example, consideration paid by his foreign entities for stock in US corporations frequently took the form of tax indemnification agreements which Vesco would subsequently have reflected in company records at their face value, despite the lack of likelihood of their materialization. The investigation into his activities is still pending, as Vesco remains at large.

United States v. Sindona (1980). Michele Sindona, an Italian financier, was convicted of a conspiracy to defraud American investors and the SEC in connection with the purchase of stock of two US corporations. First National Bank (FNB) and Talcott National Corporation (TNC). Sindona misappropriated $15 million from the general accounts of Banca Privata Finanziaria and Banca Unione, two Italian banks effectively controlled by Sindona, and placed the funds on deposit at the Privat Kredit Bank and Amincor Bank in Zurich, Switzerland. The Swiss banks then secretly transferred the funds to Sindona-owned corporations, which used them to acquire FNB and TNC. Although the Sindona corporations did eventually return the funds to the Italian banks, the transfers never took, nor were intended to take, the form of legitimate loans. In order to conceal the illegal source of the funds used to purchase the stock in the American corporations from American investors, Sindona filed false statements with the SEC, representing that the funds used to acquire FNB and TNC were his own. In 1984, Sindona was extradited to Italy to face separate charges of financial fraud [and was convicted].

TAX FRAUD

United States v. Kilpatrick (1982). William A. Kilpatrick and several co-conspirators, including the Bank of Nova Scotia, were indicted for their participation in fraudulent coal and methanol tax shelters, producing over $122 million in fraudulent tax deductions for investors and yielding $27 million in profits to the defendants. Kilpatrick-owned corporations offered investments in mineral leases producing deductions four times the amount of cash investment, the remaining $\frac{3}{4}$ of the funds to be met by loans to investors from P&J Coal Company. As P&J did not have the funds for this transaction (necessary for legitimate deductions), defendants opened several bank accounts and formed several corporations in the Cayman Islands to engage in an intricate 'checkswapping' scheme between the Cayman corporations so that a sufficient balance would appear in the accounts of these corporations at any given time. The Bank of Nova Scotia in Cayman processed these checks despite insufficient funds. The defendants also formed limited partnerships offering deductions four times the amounts of initial investments, resulting from deductible payments made by the limited partnership to International Fuel Development Corporation under a contract to conduct 'research and development' into certain methanol processes. Marlborough Investments, Ltd, a Cayman entity, was to meet the balance of the investment for the limited partnerships. As Marlborough also did not have sufficient funds for the loan, they engaged in a similar check-swapping scheme between the Cayman corporations.

TAX EVASION

United States v. Vetco, Inc. (1981). Vetco, International, A.G. (VIAG) was a wholly owned subsidiary of Vetco, Inc., an American corporation manufacturing offshore drilling equipment, charged with tax evasion. The IRS charged that the acquisition of VIAG subjected Vetco to Subpart F of the Internal Revenue Code with respect to reporting VIAG's income. Vetco allegedly avoided this treatment by shipping its products to two Swiss corporations, Weidex, A.G. and Zanora, A.G., which then transferred the goods to VIAG for sale, rather than shipping its products directly to VIAG, thus causing VIAG's income to no longer be 'derived from transactions with a related corporation outside Switzerland'. The IRS issued a summons for production of documents located in Switzerland, which Vetco argued was precluded by the Swiss–US Tax Treaty and not enforceable as a possible violation of Swiss law. The court held that the treaty information exchange provisions were not exclusive, so that summonses were appropriate means of information gathering, and that enforcement of the summons was in order as Vetco had failed to show that Swiss law would in fact be violated or that it had made good faith efforts to comply.

United States v. Hajecate (1982). Thomas M. Hajecate and Thomas H. Hajecate, owners of Uni-Oil, Inc., an oil company, and Lance Eisenberg, their tax attorney, were indicted on several counts of tax evasion. Violations stemmed from a scheme to conceal the Hajecates' interest in a Cayman bank account. To further the conspiracy the defendants filed false tax returns, failed to report financial transactions between persons in the US and foreign institutions to Customs Service, and failed to report transfers of money between the US and the Cayman Islands.

FRAUD

United States v. Carver (1981). Roy R. Carver, vice president of Raytheon Co., a concern that installed Hawk anti-aircraft missile systems in Saudi Arabia; Joseph C. Lemire, a Raytheon executive; Lionel W. Aschuck, chairman of Interconex, Inc., a shipping firm; and John T. Stephens, president of Interconex, were indicted for a conspiracy to defraud the Saudi Arabian government. Carver was charged with conspiring with Interconex executives to add-on inflated costs concealed as freight charges to several hundred units of modular housing purchased by Raytheon for the Saudi project, in return for $1 million in bribes to Carver. Proceeds were paid from secret bank accounts of offshore corporations in Liberia, Switzerland, Liechtenstein, and the Cayman Islands.

New York County v. Firestone (1982). Richard Firestone and Milton Dorison, promoters, were indicted for scheming to defraud over 200 investors of nearly $40 million in a fraudulent coal mining venture. To provide incentives for the investment, defendants arranged loans of 3 times the amount invested, to produce a tax deduction of the entire amount, from Columbus Trust Co., Nassau, Bahamas. Columbus Trust allegedly funneled $31 million through several offshore corporations, then back to Columbus, leaving the impression that legitimate loan transactions actually took place. As the loans were nonexistent and no mining was ever done, the deductions were fraudulent.

BRIBERY

United States v. McDonnell Douglas Corp. (1979). McDonnell Douglas Corporation (MDC) was charged with illegal payoffs to various officials of several government-owned airlines, 'hiking' the quoted prices to cover the sums involved, and later attempting to conceal the bribes through the use of purported 'sales representation contracts' with the same officials or offshore corporations as follows: $500,000 per aircraft to Pakistan International Airlines officials (defendants assisted in transporting funds from California to Swiss bank accounts); $3,250,000 per aircraft to Korean Air Lines officials, concealed through Jetaire, Ltd, a Guernsey Island company, and Sampaquito Investments, Ltd, a Bahamas Company; $2,000,000 to Linea Aeropostal Venzolana officials, concealed through Okemo Ltd and Luciano Chiarini and Associates, Bermuda companies; $600,000 to Air Zaire officials, concealed through Agimex, a Belgian Company.

United States v. McPartlin (1979). In 1971, the Sanitary District of Stickney, Illinois, awarded a sludge transporting contract to the Ingram Corporation after bribery of city officials, including Robert McPartlin. Payments were made in both cash and letters of credit drawn on a Swiss bank. In negotiating two of the letters, the defendants went to a bank in Vaduz, Liechtenstein, to have that bank present the LCs to the Swiss bank concerned.

LABOR RACKETEERING

United States v. Scotto (1980). Anthony Scotto, president of Local 1814 of the International Longshoreman's Association, and Anthony Anastasio, executive vice president, were convicted of labor law violations, tax evasion and accepting illegal payoffs in excess of $250,000. Scotto allegedly received $210,000 over a 3 year period from John W. McGrath Co., a stevedoring firm, in return for his help in reducing fraudulent and exaggerated workmen's compensation claims filed by members of Scotto's local. To keep the illicit payments off the company's books, the money was wired by a Philadelphia bank to Bordier & Cie, a private bank in Geneva, Switzerland, in favor of one C. C. Howard who then had the Swiss bank wire funds back to his account at Brown Brothers Harriman & Co., a private New York Bank. Howard would draw cash from the account to turn back to McGrath, which was then placed in a Chase Manhattan Bank safe deposit box.

MONEY LAUNDERING

United States v. The Great American Bank (1982). The Bank, two Florida corporations and 13 people were indicted for their participation in a money laundering scheme filtering over $96 million in illicit drug profits. Traffickers delivered large sums to the corporations and individuals involved, who then deposited the funds at the Bank, which failed to file accurate currency transaction reports with the Internal Revenue Service, with intent to conceal the illegal source of the money and true identities of the depositors. The Bank subsequently transferred funds to accounts in Zurich, Switzerland (Swiss Bank Corporation), Panama (Banco De Iberamerica), and Lima, Peru (Banco Internacional, Banco de Credito, Bank of Tokyo).

DISCLOSURE

United States v. Bank of Nova Scotia (1981). The bank was held in contempt for failing to comply with a grand jury subpoena to its Miami agent requesting the records of the bank accounts in its Bahamas branch of Robert Twist, Lesser Antilles Trading Company, and Latco Development Corporation. The bank's refusal was premised on potential criminal liability in the Bahamas of bank secrecy laws. The district court engaged in a balancing test considering (a) vital interests of each state, (b) hardship of inconsistent enforcement on the person, (c) extent to which conduct will take place in the other country, (d) person's nationality, (e) extent to which enforcement by either country would achieve compliance with that country's rule. The district court enforced the order, finding (a) US criminal investigatory interests greater than Bahamian secrecy interests, as various exceptions to the secrecy law exist, (b) the Bank made no effort to obtain consent, a Bahamian court order, or a government waiver, (c) disclosure would occur in the US, (d) nationality was insignificant in this case, (e) subpoena enforcement would insure compliance with grand jury's investigatory goal, while exceptions to the laws indicate enforcement is not an unreasonable diversion. The order was affirmed on appeal.

Source: Committee on Governmental Affairs, United States Senate, Permanent Subcommittee on Investigations, *Crime and Secrecy: The Use of Offshore Banks and Companies* (Washington, DC: US Government Printing Office, 1983).

The direct approach

To review the direct instruments of international banking secrecy, we shall go to Switzerland to open an account.[15] There are two general rules governing the practice of Swiss banking secrecy: first, minor employees of the banks need to be protected from third parties and from themselves and, second, clients need protection from bank employees.

These two rules have caused different internal practices within Swiss banks, and have resulted in different systems of numbered accounts. The contract of bank employment imposes strict adherence to secrecy practices, even when employees leave their jobs. This requirement is both legal and contractual, and is reinforced by an intricate system of numbered accounts and accounts with code names.

There are three different types of accounts generally available: (1) Mr X wants a classic account with banking secrecy but which also allows withdrawal over the counter; (2) Mr X wants a numbered account; or (3) Mr X wants additional protection under an account with another name.

A classic named account Mr X will have to fill out an 'Agreement for the Opening of an Account or Deposit' and complete his name and address, since the account is not opened primarily for secrecy. Mr X will also need to complete a sample signature card, which will allow the cashier to recognize his signature when he makes a cash withdrawal, which may be made over the counter. If Mr X also wants the bank to manage his account, he will have to sign the 'Special Clauses Completing the Agreement for the Opening of a Current Account and a Deposit'. This classic deposit arrangement is covered by extensive banking secrecy in Switzerland, and insight is strictly limited to investigations of criminal conduct defined as such under Swiss law.

A numbered account To open a numbered account, the same form will have to be filled out. However, it is stated on the form that the account is in the name of a number or a series of letters. Mr X's true signature must still be entered on the agreement. The General Conditions are the same as for a classic named account, with two differences:

- Those banks that consider secrecy seriously will require an agreement that prohibits Mr X from withdrawing cash over the counter. Some banks will permit withdrawals if the number used as a signature corresponds to that on the cashier's record. But additional confidentiality protection of the client from the bank's own cashier is offered by assigning an account manager to follow the client's affairs. The account manager will personally see the client in his office, and if cash is to be withdrawn it is done under the account manager's signature.
- A second agreement is required that is intended to indemnify the bank against any risks arising from the use of this system.

The idea of a numbered account is to permit current transactions to be performed by the bank's junior employees, who nevertheless remain ignorant of the identity of the account holder because it is under a code. The true name of the holder is known by a limited number of people, normally the bank director and the account manager. They are the only ones who have access to the files that give the identity of the account holder. The files are kept in the bank's safe. When the director or account manager wants to see Mr X's file, he must sign a dated card and provide details of the file. In addition, he can examine only one file per visit. There are various internal numbering and control procedures used by Swiss banks, but the goal is always the same – to protect customers' identity from the banks' own employees and to confine knowledge of that identity to a minimum number of individuals.

The bank also moves cautiously when, for example, Mr Y wants to transfer a sum of money to Mr X's account. The bank will take the money and tell Mr Y that Mr X is not a client, but that the money will be accepted subject to investigation. In the meantime, the bank will contact Mr X to determine whether he will accept the transfer. In the absence of instructions from Mr X, the money will be held in suspense or returned to Mr Y. Additional precautions are taken when the bank wants to communicate with Mr X. His bank statements will be sent in plain envelopes, with the recipient's name and address written by hand. In the United States, for example, the tax authorities are prevented from checking any such correspondence, even though they have legitimate suspicion of tax evasion. For this reason, the IRS from time to time has all envelopes arriving from Switzerland photocopied over a fairly extended period, and these are studied by handwriting specialists with the aid of a computer.

31

An account under a false name The main advantage of an account under another name is that, even if Mr X is found by his own regulatory authorities to possess a bank statement originating from a Swiss bank, Mr X can always claim that it is not his account, or that he is receiving the statement on behalf of a friend. Further protection (from Mr X's heirs, for example) can be afforded by combining an after-death power of attorney with the use of an open safe in another bank. *The post-mortem power of attorney* gives control over an account to a person whom the individual wishes to benefit from that account, but stipulates that the power will take effect only on the death of the account holder and on presentation of proof of death. The problem with this procedure is preserving proof of the existence of the post-mortem power of attorney so that it is available to the beneficiaries. An open safe at another bank can be used for this purpose.

Alternatives There are several ways for Mr X to obtain additional protection. For example, a joint account between Mr X and Mrs X may be opened that provides for withdrawal during Mr X's lifetime under the joint signature or Mr X's sole signature. When Mr X dies, Mrs X can operate the account on her sole signature. This is similar in effect to the post-mortem power of attorney. The concept of joint accounts is accepted in most legal jurisdictions. Alternatively, provisions may be made in a will that designate the beneficiaries of the deposits in the account, although there is a potential danger that the provisions of the will do not correspond to the 'testamentary dispositions' provisions of Swiss law.

In either case, the depositor needs to maintain proof of his wishes and assets at the Swiss bank. He now has two choices: he can put the receipt for the deposit and the agreement in a safe deposit box in another bank; or he can put the agreement in a sealed envelope and give it back to the account manager (on Mr X's statement, there would then be another item called 'sealed envelope number 00' and the date when it was deposited).

If a safe deposit box is opened at another bank, then Mr X needs to worry about where to put the key to the deposit box and the post-mortem arrangements. As far as the key is concerned, the Swiss banking system provides Mr X with a solution. He gives the key to the bank where he has his safe deposit box.The bank will then prepare another file and a stiff envelope sealed with wax. The bank and Mr X will then sign jointly. The next step is different among banks. In the most conservative banks, the cashier will want to give Mr X a receipt, which will then require Mr X to open an infinite series of safe deposit boxes to contain the receipts of other banks. Otherwise, Mr X has to rely on his confidence in the Swiss system – he will allow the cashier to keep his receipt for the key in his drawer.

The indirect approach

This description of conventional, direct banking secrecy has used Switzerland as an example. The mechanics of the arrangements differ somewhat from one bank to another, but the general principles are governed by Swiss banking law and tradition. The mechanics in other countries may be somewhat different, and this gives rise to some degree of differentiation in the 'quality' of the secrecy products involved, as discussed in Chapter 4. In particular, the services of intermediaries or beneficial owners may be required in some cases.

Examples can be found in the Bahamas and Singapore. In both cases, secrecy is guaranteed, but the identity of the beneficial owner appears at two points: (1) the central bank wants to check if the owner is a domestic citizen for exchange-control purposes, and (2) a trust agreement establishes the true ownership of shares registered in the name of one or more other people with whom the trust deed has been created. To get the maximum degree of banking secrecy under this type of structure, a depositor will use an investment company that is both non-resident and tax-exempt. This company will be free of exchange control, and subject only to an annual flat rate tax regardless of the amount of profit. Filing of accounts with the authorities is not required.

Intermediaries and beneficial owners may also be involved even in the absence of exchange control. Examples in this category include Switzerland and Liechtenstein. The name of the beneficial owner appears in the 'fiduciary' agreement, but nowhere in the records of an official body. There is no central bank check on whether the beneficial owner is a resident or not.

For example, under a classic normal trust created by a 'trust deed', Mr B is entrusted by Mr A with the trust property. Mr B is to hold the property on behalf of Mr C (an individual or a group) for the benefit of Mr C during his lifetime. Rules of trust vary from country to country, but the principles generally remain the same.

An alternative is the 'discretionary trust', under which Mr A empowers the trustee (B) to decide which of the potential beneficiaries will eventually receive the trust property. The British authorities are among those that do not accept this type of trust. In a 'disguised trust', the beneficiary (C) and the trust's originator (A) are the same person, and the trustee (B) is called a 'bare trustee'. If there is a special arrangement between Mr B and Mr A, the lawyer can remain ignorant of it under an 'alternative trust'. Under cross-examination in a court of law, however, this arrangement will not stand up if the question: 'is your client a possible beneficiary of the trust?' is asked. A more elaborate alternative trust may link the trustee (B) with a group of 'subtrustees' who will decide which group of potential beneficiaries are to receive the trust property. Mr A then has an agreement with the subtrustees that the latter will choose Mr X, who represents Messrs A, A1 and A2. There will also be a letter of renunciation of rights by Messrs A1 and A2 in favor of Mr A. If Mr A has not told the lawyer who set up the trust that he appears in the group represented by Mr X, the lawyer can swear under oath that his client has no direct or indirect beneficial interest in the property. If Mr A eventually replaces this arrangement with a completely anonymous Panama company, he will have still greater anonymity, since Messrs A1 and A2 will not know that Mr A and the owner of the Panama company are actually one and the same person.

Yet another indirect approach involves a 'protector for a virtuous trust'. Under this structure, a 'protector' is appointed who is the real beneficiary of the property – including possibly securities portfolios, real estate and trading companies. The 'protector' never appears as the owner in the strict legal sense, and could himself be replaced by an anonymous Panamanian company. The disadvantages of this arrangement are high set-up and maintenance costs, as well as extreme complexity. Alternatively, Mr A may set up a 'foundation'. This involves a permanent transfer of property, resulting in a legal entity with a name, an object or purpose, and an internal organization to effect the transfer. The true founder, who can also be the beneficiary, enters into a fiduciary agreement with a local lawyer. At this point, his name appears on the document. Again, a major disadvantage of a foundation is its very high maintenance cost.

Shell companies Anonymous 'shell' companies may be used to provide secrecy in a number of countries. All shares in such companies are issued in bearer form, and no guarantees are required from the administrators. An example of the use of this type of structure involves Panama. The state has no knowledge of who is using these structures. The user does not appear in any written agreement (not even a secret one). Local professionals who form the company under instructions given by a foreign lawyer do not even know the identity of the true owner. Panamanian administrators will give executive powers over the company to Mr _____ (the name is intentionally left blank). In return, the administrators enjoy an annual fee, without having any idea of what use is being made of the shell company or of the authority they have conferred. The user is faced with a choice of whether he should enter his name on the blank executive power, or whether he should use someone else's name. He will have to put his name to a fiduciary agreement if he chooses to use someone else's name.

Offshore captives A captive bank is an institution that exists purely for the benefit of one physical or legal person, or a group of people. This allows the owner to take advantage of substantial leverage in financing. Suppose A, B and C are companies that belong to Mr X, who also controls captive Bank X, the captive can act to fulfill the financing requirements of the companies. Furthermore, if Bank X is resident in a tax haven, the owner can realize a profit from the interest it charges A, B and C on its loans. While the interest expenses of the subsidiaries are deductible for tax purposes, the interest income of captive Bank X is tax-free in the haven.

Another advantage of a captive bank is its access to the interbank financial markets as well as possibly increased negotiating power with respect to interest rates due to the grouping of the finances of the subsidiaries. Bank X will be charged interest at interbank rates; it then will charge retail rates to A, B and C. The loans extended by the bank and the interest received by it may also be relatively free of exchange control, resulting in a more assured return.

Some captive banks are set up as offshore institutions, and are therefore excluded from local deposit-taking in the country where they are located. Offshore banks have several advantages. They usually benefit from more flexible regulations and lower reserve requirements compared to banks that take local deposits, since credit created by an offshore bank does not have any effect on the local money supply. The cost of a license for an offshore bank also tends to be lower, and it does not compete directly with local banks.

The ideal place for a secrecy seeker to form a captive bank is in a country with no meaningful banking regulations whatsoever and where all types of financial activity are allowed. Such banks, which in a number of havens nearly anyone can form for about $5,000, are really ordinary commercial companies that include the word 'bank' in their names. Their value as banks is no more than the paper on which the word is written – hence the expression 'paper bank'. The flexibility allowed sometimes has disastrous consequences in the hands of the unscrupulous.

Several conditions are necessary for the successful establishment of an offshore captive bank for purposes of secrecy. One is that it be formed in a tax haven as well as a banking haven that has tight banking secrecy laws. Second, the reserve ratios and the withholding tax on interest should not present too heavy a burden to the bank, and its operations should be completely free of exchange controls. And the true owner of the bank must be able to remain anonymous.

The problem of death

Death is an obvious problem in the secrecy business, because of the tradeoff between secrecy and the assurance that assets will indeed reach a designated beneficiary. It is not easy to make sure that secret property gets into the right hands when the principal dies. Clearly, unless careful provision is made to inform heirs of the whereabouts and avenues for obtaining access to secret assets, they may well get lost. This is obvious in the case of wealth left in holes in the ground. It is less obvious in the case of other high-secrecy assets, particularly offshore, that involve tangled legal contracts, complex and potentially weak trust relationships, and numbered accounts. Upon death, heirs may have great difficulty tracing the assets, establishing ownership, and taking possession. Indeed, under certain circumstances the bargaining power of the heirs could be very weak. The more care the individual takes prior to death to insure an orderly transfer of assets, the greater is the potential threat to secrecy through enhanced transparency of the relevant relationships. Failure to lay claim to secret inheritances may mean, of course, that the relevant assets go to the agent (bank, trustee, etc.), to the government, or to unauthorized third parties – or they are simply lost for good.

Under the direct instruments discussed earlier, the heir or executor of the estate would first need to prove his own standing *and* the death of the account holder before establishing any right to information about a secret account. The bank will normally give only current account information, and would oppose any attempt by the inheritors to trace past transactions. The account's current status is generally defined as that existing at the time of the last statement approved by the account holder.

During the account holder's lifetime, he tends to believe that the secrecy provision allows him to make any desired dispositions of his assets. It might not occur to him that his plans could come into conflict with the 'inheritors' reserve' system. In most cases, the bank would follow the depositor's instructions. But when there is a court ruling in favor of 'reserve' inheritors, the banker confronts the problem of whether he is obliged to breach financial secrecy.

In Switzerland, courts tend to consider that the right to bank secrecy passes to the heirs, especially those qualifying as reserve inheritors. However, having a separate Swiss will is dangerous because it might be considered a revocation of an earlier will, and consequently could cause a distribution of inheritance never intended by the depositor. Another problem relates to instructions left with a bank in case of death – that is, whether or not these instructions in fact constitute a will. If the instruction is intended by the depositor as a 'post-mortem' one, it would normally be considered a will in Swiss law, although a bank would still proceed very cautiously in the case of death.

When there are indirect secrecy vehicles in the presence of exchange control, there is usually no problem from the point of view of the local authorities for an investment company to be set up – based on the Anglo-Saxon type of tax haven – if the heirs are non-residents. But there will be problems if one or more of the heirs is subject to local exchange controls. To circumvent such difficulties, the beneficiaries have to avoid using a legal entity that would be subject to exchange control. Trust and fiduciary agreements could present as many problems as investment companies. Local judges might not have adequate knowledge to handle the matter, or local law might not recognize the agreements.

Where there is no exchange control, private secrecy-oriented agreements will not encounter such problems, but the same difficulties are found with respect to trust and fiduciary agreements.

Where the owner is a truly anonymous entity, such as a shell company, the difficulties related to the account having been opened directly in the name of the deceased result from administrative subtleties – for example, the problem of how to change the decisions of the administrative council if that power was vested in a person now dead.

Summary

We have seen that ordinary bank accounts provide a certain degree of confidentiality in all countries, but that access to financial information by third parties varies enormously among countries. We have discussed a number of direct and indirect instruments of banking secrecy, which differ significantly in terms of yield, cost, risk and security. In addition, counterparties can serve as trustees, owners of record or shell companies, beneficial owners of assets, etc. All require that a fiduciary relationship be exercised, which itself carries a risk.

Various secrecy vehicles can, of course, be combined into complex forms and structures, and 'layered' in ways that make them increasingly opaque. Greater complexity usually involves greater cost, but may, at the same time, mean the ability to go after higher yields, or reduced risk through greater diversification, which can more than offset the increased cost.

In the following chapters, we shall discuss the basic characteristics of demand and supply of secret money, and the organization of the market.

Notes

1 Somchai Richpuran, 'Measuring Tax Evasion', *Finance and Development*, December 1984.
2 Vito Tanzi, *The Underground Economy* (Lexington, Mass.: D. C. Heath, 1982).
3 See Thomas N. Gladwin and Ingo Walter, *Multinationals under Fire* (New York: John Wiley & Sons, 1980).
4 Internal Revenue Service, 'Estimates of Income Unreported on Individual Income Tax Returns', IRS Publication 1104 (9–79).
5 Peter M. Gutmann, 'The Subterranean Economy', *Financial Analysts Journal*, November/December 1977.
6 Edward L. Feige, 'A New Perspective on Macroeconomic Phenomenon', Mimeo, August 1980.

7 David M. O'Neil, *Growth of the Underground Economy, 1950–1981*. Joint Economic Committee, US Congress (Washington, DC: US Government Printing Office, 1983).
8 Everett G. Martin, 'Lima's Capitalists Usually are Found in the Underground', *Wall Street Journal*, 16 August 1984.
9 'Peru Economy: Hidden Cash', *New York Times*, 31 October 1983.
10 Peter J. Kilburn, 'Global Trade Mystery: A Vanishing $100 Billion', *New York Times*, 30 July 1983. See also Vivian Brownstein, 'The World's Missing Billions', *Fortune*, 22 August 1983.
11 Richard Dale, 'Unrecorded Capital Flows: Is the United States Already a Net Debtor?', *The Banker*, December 1984, p. 8.
12 'Reglement der Königlichen Giro- und Lohn-Bank', Kingdom of Prussia (own translation), as quoted in Paul Achleitner, *Das Bankgeheimnis in Österreich, Deutschland und der Schweiz* (Vienna: Österreichisches Forschungsinstitut für Sparkassenwesen, 1981).
13 'Netherlands Bank Secrecy', *The Banker*, February 1984.
14 Paul Achleitner, 'Das Bankgeheimnis in Aussländischen Staaten', *Österreichische Sparkassenzeitung*, 15 October 1981.
15 For practical guides to international financial secrecy, see Mark Skousen, *The Complete Guide to Financial Privacy* (New York: Simon & Schuster, 1983); and Eduard Chambost, *Bank Accounts: A World Guide to Confidentiality* (London: John Wiley, 1983). This discussion of secrecy mechanics is based on Chambost, Chapters 4–8.

3

Demand for Secret Money

As we have seen, there is a broad, worldwide demand for secret assets. This demand differs in intensity and complexion from one country to the next, and may vary substantially over time as well. We can categorize the sources of demand as follows:

- Ordinary business and personal confidentiality motives, totally within the limits of the law, aimed at preventing the erosion of asset values through unwanted disclosure, which may at times necessitate the placement of assets abroad.
- Capital flight, triggered by perceived adverse changes in the economic, political or social environment of countries – or the risk thereof – which could compromise the value of assets or the safety of the asset-holder.
- Bribery and corruption, involving funds obtained by corrupt public officials (and sometimes business executives) and placed abroad for security reasons, as well as 'slush funds' maintained by the payers of bribes which must also be kept away from scrutiny by home- or host-country officials.
- Tax evasion, as opposed to (legal) tax avoidance, with taxable earnings not reported to the fiscal authorities and hidden from them in financial repositories abroad. Since tax statutes are often subject to interpretation, a significant gray area exists which is sometimes called 'tax avoision'.
- Smuggling and related activities (including evasion of exchange controls) which involve contraband merchandise or financial instruments, the payments for which must be shielded from national authorities, frequently through offshore vehicles.
- Securities law violations, particularly insider trading, which is often undertaken through third parties who are much more difficult to trace and prosecute if they reside abroad and are able to undertake securities transactions using offshore funds.
- Fraud, ranging from self-dealing in banking and finance to outright

39

theft of financial or real assets, the proceeds of which must remain hidden and out of reach of the authorities in order to impede prosecution and recapture.

- Money laundering associated with illegal activities that range from gambling, prostitution, protection rackets and extortion, to gun running and the narcotics trade, many of which involve cash transactions that must be converted to bankable funds before the proceeds can be spent or invested in legitimate assets.
- Government undercover activities, generally undertaken abroad, which may be aimed at supporting terrorists (or freedom fighters) in other countries, foreign governments or opposition political groups, and other clandestine operations whose legal standing may well be ambiguous but which are considered to be in the national interest. The issues involved are often not too dissimilar from those in money laundering.

In this chapter, we shall review each of the sources of demand for financial secrecy, and in each case try to come up with a sense of the magnitudes involved, as well as the principal policy issues.

Confidentiality

Not much needs to be said about the need to keep personal and business financial matters secret. At a personal level, no laws are broken if an individual decides that an optimum portfolio of assets includes substantial foreign interests which, in addition perhaps to better diversification and improved flow of returns, shield him from the prying eyes of family or friends. In addition, depending on his country of residence, he may be able to avoid taxes and other fiscal levies, again without necessarily running afoul of the law. Moreover, foreign asset managers may well be able to provide better services than those at home.

At a business level, the inherent value of secrecy may convey significant advantages in the marketplace vis-à-vis competitors, customers, suppliers, potential acquirers, investors, and other parties. Certain types of business functions, particularly mergers and acquisitions, depend for their success on a high level of confidentiality and lightning moves that catch opponents off-guard.

Confidentiality as a legitimate business need sometimes shades into secrecy that ultimately tests the limits of the law. For example, in an effort to sell a large number of shares in the Hartford Fire and Casualty Company during the 1960s, the International Telephone and Telegraph Corporation (ITT) obtained the assistance of André Meyer of Lazard, Frères & Co. The deal had to be put over in a highly confidential manner for business reasons, and '... the transaction was a masterpiece of concealment, with its multiple layers of intermediaries and its Liechtenstein companies – all intended to obscure, from the IRS and from other pry-ing eyes, exactly where the wayward ITT stock was going.'[1] In the end, both the IRS and the SEC got involved in investigating the transaction for violations of tax and securities laws, and Lazard Frères '... had been branded in the public consciousness as the prime mover in a scheme to skirt the law, deceive the IRS and, along the way, line its own pockets and those of a few favored friends.'[2] Meyer's take from the deal: $1.4 million.

Beyond finance, business confidentiality can also shade into secrecy if trade transactions bend the letter or spirit of the law, with potentially adverse consequences for the firm. For example, during hearings con-cerning the dumping of Japanese TV sets in the US market in the 1970s, evidence emerged that the manufacturers were using secret channels to funnel rebates to American retailers through Swiss bank accounts, in direct violation of US trade laws.[3]

In 1984, a number of British labor unions availed themselves of inter-national financial secrecy to stash funds offshore with the intent of keep-ing them out of reach of court judgments levied in civil actions under that country's tough new labor laws. Although the same unions had roundly condemned capital flight in the past, their loss of immunity from civil actions prompted the National Union of Mineworkers (NUM), the National Graphical Association and the Transport & General Workers' Union to use precisely the same routes in order to spirit assets out of the country and out of the reach of the courts. Prior to its longest and most bitter strike, for example, the NUM sold about $11 million in UK government bonds, passing the proceeds through the Isle of Man, as well as banks in Ireland and the United States, to cash and bearer-bond accounts in Switzerland.[4]

In the famous 1984 Flick Scandal in West Germany, secret money was involved no less. It was discovered that an outfit called Europäische Unternehmensberatungsanstalt (European Institute for Business Con-sulting) in Liechtenstein had issued receipts for payments from dozens of German firms. The funds were then allegedly channeled into the cof-fers of the Christian Democratic Party in Germany. Under the law, West German firms are severely limited in the size of political contributions, only a small part of which are tax deductible. Front companies such as EU issuing phoney invoices for services not rendered, or phoney charities fulfilling the same purpose, thus permitted disallowed political support as well as tax evasion.[5]

Capital flight

To a large extent, private capital flows that feed the secrecy market are associated with flight capital from countries whose political or economic circumstances yield an unfavourable risk/reward relationship for asset-holders. From 1975 to 1983, over $120 billion is estimated to have been transferred to offshore assets by residents of developing countries, with $71 billion of that amount moving during the years 1981–83 alone from precisely those countries subject to the greatest difficulties in servicing their external debt – including Mexico, Argentina and Venezuela (see Figure 3.1). 1985 liquid external assets were $60–75 billion.

To produce one confidential report, a major New York money center bank combed through figures on trade and capital flows from 23 developing nations for the years 1978 to 1983. Overall, this group [of countries] added $381.5 billion to their foreign debt during the five-year period. But according to the report, no less than $103.1 billion of that sum flowed back out as flight capital....sapping local economies, draining central bank reserves and forcing nations close to or over the brink of debt moratoriums. [6]

For the same period, the Bank for International Settlements in Basle estimated capital flight from Latin America alone (except Venezuela) at $55 billion.

Total private sector assets held abroad during the period 1975–82 are presented in Figure 3.2. Note the wide differences in capital flight patterns among countries, in response to both differences and variations

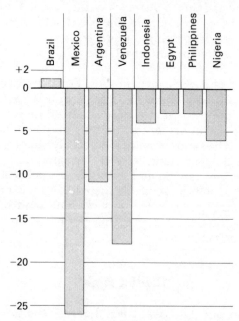

Figure 3.1   *Capital flight, 1980–82*

(a) *Total balance of payments flows, 1974–82*

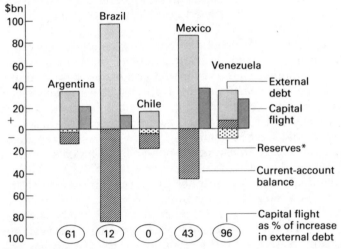

(b) *Annual increase in Latin American private sector assets held abroad*

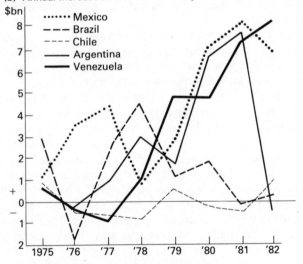

* Negative = increase in reserves

Source: International Finance Discussion
Paper, Federal Reserve Board, 1984, as cited by *The Economist*:

Figure 3.2 *Flight capital and external debt*

43

over time in economic and political outlooks as well as the severity of exchange restrictions and changes in exchange rates. For Mexico, Venezuela and Argentina, capital flight represented between 43 and 96 per cent of the funds borrowed abroad by public and private sector institutions during this period.

Flight capital has thus been especially problematic for governments in Latin America. According to some estimates, none of these countries would have experienced the severe debt problems they faced in the early 1980s if it had not been for capital flight, which essentially represented a vote of 'no confidence' in the economic and political measures designed to cope with their internal and external difficulties. Mexicans alone were said to hold some $35 billion in external assets. Unrecorded capital outflows contributed an estimated one-half of Mexico's debt problem. Indeed, former President José Lopes Portillo in 1982 publicly termed such individuals 'traitors' – rather than recognizing capital flight as a symptom, not a cause, of the country's economic problems at the time. Countries like Lebanon, Israel, France and Italy have been the scene of massive capital flight from time to time. Capital flight has been much less of a problem in Asia, with the exception of the Philippines and (for a time) Hong Kong, not because Asians don't seek safe havens and decent real returns on their assets, but because national economic and financial policies have consistently carried substantially greater credibility than those in Latin America.

The concerns of asset-holders usually center around overvalued domestic currencies, which make foreign assets such as real estate appear cheap by comparison, and which promise a substantial capital gain in local currency when an exchange-rate correction eventually occurs – as it inevitably will. They also worry about low and sometimes negative domestic real interest rates (nominal rates adjusted for expected inflation), which are kept that way by irresponsible monetary policies. And they worry about the future imposition of exchange controls, tax increases, expropriation and other measures that sometimes cause, and sometimes result from, poor economic management. In short, there develops a profound lack of confidence in the way a country is likely to be run in the foreseeable future, and its implications for real asset values. The result is a rush, sometimes a stampede, for the exit, into assets characterized by higher real returns and lower perceived risk profiles.

While most flight capital is doubtless linked to prospects for domestic economic conditions, purely political factors play a role as well. Examples are the aforementioned mass exodus of capital in 1983 from Hong Kong, faced with the uncertain prospects under Chinese sovereignty after 1997, and in 1983–4 from the Philippines, faced with economic problems and political uncertainty. According to one account at the time, 'Hong Kong investors are buying up office buildings, supermarkets, restaurants, luxury homes, and condominiums in many U.S. and Canadian cities. "The only safe place for my money is in U.S. dollars, in a U.S. bank, on U.S. soil," declares one frightened Hong Kong resident.'[7]

Private bankers, securities salesmen and real estate agents were quick to take advantage of the capital flight. Real estate operators set up sales offices in Hong Kong, 44 Edge Act (international) units of US banks joined the local banks and 33 foreign banks in Miami to tap into the Latin American market. Foreign businesses set up US subsidiaries in order to facilitate transfer pricing to move capital around exchange controls using intra-firm transactions. The dollar's great strength during this period was doubtless related to capital flight.

In the absence of exchange controls, disclosure requirements and tax regulations, much of the capital flight is, of course, perfectly legal. But even without such barriers, secrecy still plays an important role. Individuals with known foreign assets may be particularly exposed to political reprisals at home. So it may be wise to minimize disclosure in whatever way is best suited to the nature of the individual case.

Bribery and corruption

The economic and behavioral dimensions of bribery and corruption have been analyzed in some depth.[8] The bribee is generally a government official who has the power to alter his decision from one based purely on merit – to favor one supplier over another, to grant or withhold import permits or foreign exchange licenses, to approve a veterinary certificate or building permit, not to impose penalties for violations of the law, etc. In the process, the briber passes the costs along to the ultimate customers, who are then exposed to inferior or over-priced goods and services. Bribery almost always injures society, but in many countries it is a way of life, with bribees at various levels often bribing higher-ups to obtain their jobs, and with the ladder of corruption sometimes reaching into the very pinnacles of government.

Technically, questionable payments comprise at least four more or less clearly identifiable categories:

- Bribes: significant payments to officials with decision-making powers to convince them to do their jobs *improperly*;
- Grease: 'facilitating' payments to minor officials to encourage them to do their jobs *properly*;
- Extortion: payments to persons in authority to avoid damage from hostile action on the part of unions, criminals, utilities, 'renegade' troops, and the like; and

- Political contributions: payments to political parties linked to favors or threats of retribution in case of non-payment.

In many cases, such payments can be routed through 'agent's fees' to independent third parties acting on behalf of the payer.

International financial secrecy is critical for bribery and corruption to work effectively. Payment in domestic (inside) currency is often difficult for the briber and can turn out to be relatively worthless for the bribee – it often won't buy much, and may be difficult to hide in relatively poorly developed financial institutions and markets subject to government scrutiny. Much better to use foreign (outside) slush funds that can be effectively generated (e.g. using phoney invoices for fictitious services), hidden in secret accounts by the payer and then quietly transferred to an equally secret account owned by the bribee. Outside money is often worth far more to the bribee as well. It may buy merchandise, services or assets not readily available at home, and it can buy security in the form of a foreign retirement nest-egg out of the reach of national authorities should the need arise for a hasty exit.

The amounts involved can be staggering indeed. According to one report, $5–7 billion in graft and corruption was collected and subsequently sent abroad by various officials of the elected Nigerian government that was overthrown in 1983. In addition to investments in clandestine financial assets, some unusual safekeeping vehicles evidently turned up, including a solid gold bathtub in the English vacation home of one senior Nigerian official.[9] Comparable amounts have been noted in connection with high government officials in Mexico, Indonesia, the Philippines and various other countries.

The size of secret assets held abroad by political leaders, especially in developing countries, is anyone's guess. Nicaraguan dictator Anastasio Somosa is rumoured to have exported at least $500 million before his overthrow in 1979 by the Sandinistas, a substantial portion of which landed in Swiss accounts. Emperor Haile Selassie was estimated to have over $15 billion in foreign assets at the time of his death in 1975, including annual deposits in Switzerland of 500 kg. in gold bullion that eventually strained the storage facilities of a major Swiss bank. President Mobutu Sese Seko of Zaire is alleged to have placed almost $4 billion in Swiss personal accounts in the 1970s, roughly equivalent to his country's net external borrowings during that decade.[10] According to one observer, 'On the one hand, Mobutu has run out of ways to dodge [the International Monetary Fund's economic] restrictions. But he's also taken a look at his store of wealth abroad and realized that it is enough to take care of himself and his scions for centuries, if not eons.'[11]

When confronted with balance of payments difficulties, policymakers frequently resort to the imposition of exchange controls. These invariably give rise to black markets in foreign exchange. Normally, the currency trades at a severe discount on the black market as compared with the official rate. At least three issues are pertinent to measuring the size of the black market in currencies. First, transactions in the black market are unofficial, and thus it is difficult to calculate the size of the volume of those transactions. The money is not accounted for in the legal accounting processes. Second, exchange rate premiums cannot be legally declared as income. Therefore, what is not used for immediate consumption must become secret money. Third, the entire process gives rise to corruption in government as some groups try to get the scarce foreign currency at the official exchange rate. These bribes must be hidden as well. [12]

Whenever exchange controls exist, secret transfers of funds can be used by those in favored positions, or those able to bribe the authorities, to enrich themselves very substantially indeed. During the 1984 Argentine debt crisis, for example, a scheme was uncovered whereby Argentines with deposits abroad were able to use them as security in a 'self-lending' operation to borrow dollars, which were then repatriated into pesos at highly favorable 'parallel market' exchange rates. Reportedly as much as $10 billion was involved, adding substantially to an already unsustainable volume of external debt, with no productive purpose.

As in the case of bribees, the volume of transactions undertaken by bribers is no less difficult to estimate. Overseas payments became a major political issue in the United States during the 1970s. Disclosures of well over $1 billion in questionable payments by some 400 American companies under the Securities and Exchange Commission's 'voluntary disclosure' program gave rise to the Foreign Corrupt Practices Act of 1977, which made many such payments by US companies illegal. No comparable disclosures have ever been made by companies based in other countries, many of whose governments take a much more benign attitude toward foreign payoffs. So the need for secrecy in such cases seems to be less critical on the briber's side than it is on the bribee's, who faces possible retribution or claims on a share of the spoils if disclosure occurs.

Tax evasion

Governments have laid claim to a large and growing share of the economies of nations, including the developed market economies, as Figure 3.3 indicates. With high tax burdens in many countries, reinforced by 'bracket creep' (whereby inflation pushes people into successively higher tax brackets under progressive rate structures even in the absence of higher real incomes), the incentive to avoid and evade taxes may have risen significantly in recent years. And the growing com-

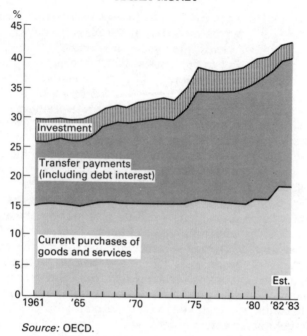

%

Source: OECD.

Figure 3.3   OECD public expenditures as a percentage of GNP

plexity of tax codes and their use for a broad range of political purposes other than revenue raising has added further to the impression of unfairness, gradually undermining tax morality and stimulating the search for escape even among otherwise law-abiding people.

Very briefly, two choices present themselves: avoidance versus evasion; and tax shelters versus tax havens. Avoidance is the legal escape from tax burdens by means of provisions written into the tax code. Evasion is the illegal non-payment of taxes either by under-declaring income or by over-declaring deductions or exemptions, usually in the face of civil or criminal penalties. Tax shelters are generally aimed at avoidance, although they may shade into evasion by taking 'abusive' forms. Tax havens may be legal or illegal, depending on the nationality and residence of the individual and the tax code of the country concerned. We are concerned here only with tax evasion, the associated costs and benefits, the available vehicles, and the chances of getting caught. Tax avoidance gets into the act because the associated cost/benefit profile of legal tax-minimization efforts may well seem to the individual vastly inferior to outright tax evasion.

In the United States, tax avoidance through shelters has become big business over the years. Oil and gas drilling, livestock, farming, speculation in commodities, energy conservation, equipment leasing, old folks'

48

homes and similar ventures can – if properly structured – produce large-scale tax writeoffs, generate large deductions for charitable contributions, or convert ordinary income into capital gains that are taxed at lower rates. 'Abusive' shelters may artificially inflate the value of donations to charity, falsely identify an asset for business use that is mainly intended for pleasure, claim excessive depreciation or depletion, engage in cross-leasing of automobiles, boats, vacation homes and aircraft, and the like. It is estimated that $8.4 billion was invested in tax shelters in the United States during 1984. As a result, Internal Revenue Service audits of tax shelters were substantially increased in frequency and intensity. The number of shelter cases before the US tax courts has accordingly multiplied.

Tax shelters can be costly, however. They tend to involve the services of smart, creative and very well paid lawyers and accountants. They are often highly promoted and sometimes over-sold, promising far more than they are worth. There is always a chance that a tax shelter project will fail, inflicting sizeable losses on the unwary investor. And there is the possibility that the shelter will ultimately be disallowed by the authorities or that the tax law will be changed. Thus the 'transaction costs' facing the tax avoider and his exposure to loss may be substantial indeed, and may induce him to step over the line into tax evasion. This is where secrecy comes in. There is no need for financial secrecy in tax avoidance. Indeed, it may well be true that more disclosure is better than less, as long as transactions remain on the right side of the law.

Many of the problems associated with legal tax avoidance are eliminated by tax evasion, which makes it possible for people to deploy their assets far more rationally (provided they don't get caught), and at much lower cost.

A case in point is Argentina, where a complex tax system, internal bank secrecy, poor enforcement, a byzantine court system and non-existent audits, as well as bribery, corruption and periodic tax amnesties, have created 'the second biggest sport after soccer', with a compliance rate of perhaps 50 per cent. It is estimated that the untaxed part of the economy in Argentina roughly equals taxable measured income and output – perhaps $70 billion in 1984.

In one Argentine case

[A] clothing retailer in a drab suburb of Buenos Aires. Of every 100 men's suits the retailer sells, 70 are sold without the required sales slip. That makes it impossible for the [tax authorities] to collect the 18% value added tax, included in the price of most goods. Of course, the wholesaler who sold him the 100 units didn't make out sales slips for 70 of them, either. Nor did the fabric merchant account for all the material he sold to the wholesaler. The government thinks the clothing retailer took in the equivalent of $300,000 [in 1983]. But the accountant who helped him prepare his tax returns says the figure excludes, of course, the $400,000 his client spirited away to a Miami bank. [13]

In another Argentine case, an executive intent on evading capital gains tax on a house he sold for $450,000 had a notary public draw up a sales contract for $200,000. The seller avoided tax on the $250,000, the buyer avoided having to account for the same amount of 'black money' he used to buy the house, and the notary received $8,000 in (untaxed) 'lunch money' for his efforts. Tax evasion has become so much part of life that nothing short of top-to-bottom tax reforms, coupled to heavy investment in information systems, auditing and enforcement, will make much of a difference. As one former Argentine tax official noted, 'If you put DDT on ants, they will develop immunity after a couple of generations. No matter what the government puts on us, we Argentines will always find a way to shake the system.' [14]

Naturally, other countries that have value-added taxes are also subject to evasion along similar lines. But computer information systems and tight audits usually make it much less egregious – as do much stiffer penalties than exist in Argentina.

In Italy in 1984, shopowners reported to the tax authorities average annual incomes of $3,579, compared with $5,694 for shop *assistants* and even higher incomes for factory workers. At least 5 million families are involved, and this makes a government crackdown exceedingly sensitive politically. According to one observer, 'There isn't any doubt that tax evasion is rampant. For the three million people either self-employed or in small businesses, evasion has been allowed. It isn't quite written in the statutes, but almost.' [15]

Even in West Germany, tax evasion seems to be growing, with otherwise law-abiding people 'forgetting' to report income to the tax collector whenever little likelihood exists of getting caught. It is estimated that roughly one-fourth of all securities, valued at perhaps DM 40 billion, are hidden from the authorities, with an annual revenue loss of DM 1.5 billion. After the collapse of the Herstatt Bank in 1974, taxmen for the first time were able to determine the full extent of evasion through a comprehensive audit of the defunct bank's books. This gave rise to later, controversial 'fishing expeditions'. In one such case, a number of dentists in the Düsseldorf area were found to be buying gold for dental fillings, booking it as a business expense and then reselling it for hidden personal gain. [16]

In the United States, tax compliance has traditionally been high. Whether because of patriotism, a sense of fairness, the need to finance functions of government generally approved of, or fear of criminal or civil prosecution, Americans have on the whole paid a significantly higher share of taxes legally owed than the citizens of most other countries. As a result, the United States relies heavily on the personal income tax, based in large measure on self-reporting and voluntary compliance, while other countries have been forced to resort to import duties, sales and value-added taxes, wealth and death taxes, and other forms of fiscal levies that are more difficult to evade.

All of this has changed. Inflation in the 1970s pushed taxpayers into ever-higher tax brackets, and the combination has in many cases (for example, the average US industrial worker) led to an actual reduction in real disposable income. Heavy capital gains taxes must be paid on fictitious appreciation attributable only to inflation – in effect partially expropriating private property. The tax code became impossibly complex, and the cost of honest compliance increased dramatically in time, trouble and expense. The Congress riddled the tax code with special provisions, loopholes and benefits aimed at selected interest groups and social engineering, leaving an impression of pervasive inequity. And as stories of tax avoidance and 'evasion' emerge in the media or in rumor-mills, impressions of inequity are amplified.

The result was a significant drop in US tax morality. In 1985, it was estimated that around $100 billion of legally owed taxes were uncollected. Table 3.1 gives some idea of the breakdown of evasion categories. Some fail to file tax returns at all. Others file late. Some are discouraged by the system's complexity. Many who are in a position to do so underreport income. Probably an even greater number overstate

Table 3.1 *The pattern of US income tax evasion (1981 estimates)*

	Shown on tax returns $bn	Should have been shown $bn	Per cent unreported
Wages and salaries	1,455.2	1,549.7	6.1
Pensions and annuities	58.5	67.3	13.1
Interest	129.1	149.6	13.7
Dividends	44.9	53.7	16.4
Estate and trust	3.9	5.2	25.8
State income tax refunds, and other income	11.7	18.9	38.0
Royalties	4.4	7.1	38.8
Capital gains	25.9	43.7	40.7
Nonfarm proprietor	53.5	106.5	49.7
Partnership and small business corporation	14.9	31.6	52.9
Rents	2.5	6.9	62.8
Off-the-book services	4.5	21.5	79.1
Farm proprietor	−2.0	11.1	NA
Total income	**1,807.0**	**2,072.8**	**12.8**

NA = not applicable (total farm income report was negative)
Source: *Business Week*, 16 April 1984, p. 89. Developed from Internal Revenue Service data.

their deductions. A 1984 poll revealed that 38 per cent of US taxpayers are believed to cheat on taxes, and that tax evasion is not generally viewed as a serious offense. A law that would have required banks to withhold tax on interest income on savings and other accounts was repealed by Congress under pressure of the banks themselves, in full knowledge that the underlying issue was tax evasion. Tax shelters have proliferated, although tax audits have declined. Criminal penalties are rare: in 1983, only 1,800 people were prosecuted for tax evasion. As one former IRS Commissioner has noted, 'If a person is an economic being and figures out the odds, then there is a very high incentive to cheat. That is, of course, putting aside honor, duty and patriotism.'[17]

According to one critical review of the IRS's efforts to close tax loopholes,

...the weakness of [its] position is that members of the general public are increasingly dissatisfied with the state's presumption that it has the right to deprive the citizen of his wealth ... [It] is quite clear that the avarice of the state in respect of its enormous claims on the private citizen's wealth has been directly connected with the mismanagement of the U.S. public sector's finances ... [T]he public authorities cannot be trusted with the public's money and ... have an incurable tendency to squander it.[18]

Even major sports figures are getting into the act. On signing a four-year, $4.8 million contract with the Boston Red Sox baseball team in 1985, a 30-year-old relief pitcher came up with one of the more memorable tax-related quotations. Said he: 'I guess I'll have to get one of those Swedish bank accounts.'

While secrecy may seem like a handy way to evade taxes, the prospects of civil or criminal penalties are never very far away. American residents, for example, must indicate each year on their tax returns whether or not they own or have control over a foreign account in excess of $5,000 and, if so, must provide details on a separate form that is likewise filed annually. Since a person's signature on a tax return warrants that the information is true and complete, misrepresentation constitutes an act of perjury and may trigger severe criminal penalties.

Of course, accusations of tax evasion can sometimes be used for political reasons as well. For example, in 1983 the Greek government moved against the Tsatsos family, owners of a successful cement business, who had supported an earlier military regime. Altogether, 13 directors and managers of the company were accused of using questionable payments to foreign subsidiaries to transfer over $100 million illegally out of the country. The action, however, was viewed by some as 'revenge' for the family's earlier political activity and as a way for the government to divert attention from Greece's persistent economic difficulties.[19]

The Marc Rich case

In 1982, the largest tax evasion case in US history came to light. It focused on the highly successful commodities trader, Marc Rich, and a number of his associates.

Three sets of allegations were leveled at Marc Rich. The first concerned evasion of US price controls on crude oil. In a fundamentally flawed program to hold down the price of oil, the United States in 1973 set in place a complicated three-tier pricing structure: 'old' oil, which already was being produced at the time of the first oil-price shock, the price of which was fixed: 'new' oil, which was found thereafter, but whose price was still limited significantly below the market; and 'stripper' oil, produced by small wells at less than 10 barrels per day, which could be sold at the free-market price. The aim was to equalize competitive access to crude oil for refiners and, of course, to ease the oil-price shock to consumers. As with any set of regulations designed to replace market forces, this scheme created enormous built-in incentives for evasion by creating 'daisy chains' of crooked oil dealers intended ultimately to relabel 'old' and 'new' oil as 'stripper' oil, and take the price gap as profit. Marc Rich was accused of being at the center of a daisy chain operation, making well over $100 million in illegal profits. As expected, all such schemes collapsed with the decontrol of crude oil prices early in the Reagan administration, but the accusations of prior wrongdoing remained.

The second allegation against Marc Rich, which is related to the first, was that US profits accumulated in a 'pot' controlled jointly by Marc Rich and the West Texas Marketing Corp. (WTM), from which funds were then drained through a transfer pricing scheme to evade the US corporate profits tax. Oil would be sold at market prices by Marc Rich AG (Switzerland) to WTM, which would then resell it at substantially lower prices to Rescor, a Panamanian firm owned by Marc Rich. The 'pot' was thus drained by the resulting accounting losses, with Rescor reselling the oil at the free-market price and booking the profits in Panama. All in all, the estimated tax evasion was $48 million, the largest such case in US history.

The third allegation involved trading with the enemy. As part of the US reaction to the events in Teheran in 1977, American firms were prohibited from doing business with Iran. In violation of that ban, the government alleged, Marc Rich's US operations aggressively purchased Iranian crude, which that country's regime was anxious to market, and sold it at high profit in various parts of the world, including the United States.

By October of 1982, a US grand jury investigation was under way into

Marc Rich's business affairs, and subpoenas were issued for thousands of documents designed to shed light on them. At the center of the investigation stood Marc Rich himself and Pincus Green, both US citizens and long-time business associates. The specific charges, in addition to tax evasion, eventually included mail and wire fraud, racketeering and conspiracy in a 51-count indictment handed up by the grand jury. A US associate, Clyde Meltzer, was also charged with 28 counts of tax evasion, racketeering and fraud. The indictments carried penalties ranging from 5 to 20 years in prison and $1,000 to $20,000 in fines, although consecutive sentencing could result in life imprisonment.

Headquarters of Marc Rich & Company AG, with a 1981 net worth of $200 million, is Zug, Switzerland, a town of 80,000 that lists 8,000 corporate headquarters. Most of these are letter-box companies that benefit from lenient local tax treatment, yet altogether contribute per capita tax revenues that are by far the highest in Switzerland. Each company must have a majority of Swiss directors – Marc Rich & Company had Marc Rich, Pincus Green, and three Zug attorneys.

Three actions were taken by the grand jury and US tax authorities: (1) a subpoena was issued for financial records material to the case, including those in the possession of the Swiss parent company in Zug: (2) a warrant was issued for the attachment of assets of Marc Rich and Pincus Green; and (3) the Internal Revenue Service filed claims for back taxes, interest and penalties amounting to over $100 million.

As expected, Marc Rich & Co. AG refused to comply with the subpoenas, claiming that as a Swiss company it was beyond the reach of US courts. That argument was rejected by the court in view of the enormous amount of business the firm did in the United States, whereupon Marc Rich's attorneys argued that Swiss secrecy laws prohibited compliance, especially inasmuch as none of the offenses involved were considered crimes in Switzerland. The US judge then imposed contempt of court fines of $50,000 per business day on the American subsidiary, Marc Rich International, which were duly paid. In July 1983 the US company was sold to Alexander Hackel, who besides Marc Rich and Pincus Green was the third major shareholder in Marc Rich AG, and renamed Clarendon. The idea evidently was that, since Marc Rich International no longer existed, the fines imposed by the judge did not apply. Shortly thereafter, the court froze all of Clarendon's US assets (amounting to over $90 million) and effectively put the company out of business.

Earlier, US prosecutors alleged, about $750 million in assets had been liquidated between March and August of 1983, threatening insolvency and the government's ability to collect back taxes. Even the company's building in Zug was transferred to ownership of the Swiss parent, and during the summer as much as $45 million was shifted to bank accounts in the Cayman Islands and the Bahamas – although it was later returned to the US under threat of further American legal sanctions. The Clarendon sale potentially added obstruction of justice charges to those already facing Marc Rich and Pincus Green.

In October 1983, the IRS filed an assessment seeking $90 million in back taxes, penalties and interest from 13 of Clarendon's banks. The banks, which had loans estimated at $130 million outstanding to Clarendon, attempted but failed to have the IRS assessment blocked, even though the debt was guaranteed by Marc Rich AG in Zug. Thereafter, bank financing of Marc Rich's US business became all but impossible, having already become increasingly difficult in the preceding months.

In August 1983 Marc Rich AG had given in and agreed to submit the requested documents, but, almost immediately following the agreement, US customs agents – evidently acting on tip – halted Geneva-bound Swissair Flight 111 on the apron at Kennedy Airport in New York and removed several large steamer trunks filled with company documents being taken as checked baggage by a New York paralegal. Marc Rich's attorneys maintained that the documents were being flown to Zug for review and sorting, to ensure that no unrelated confidential information was disclosed. They also noted that other documents had gone to Zug earlier. Unconvinced, the judge told Marc Rich's attorneys that 'The thinness of the ice on which your client stands is something you must be aware of'.[20]

Meanwhile, the Swiss authorities, apparently fearing that the Marc Rich case, because of its size and visibility, could ultimately blow a large hole in the corporate secrecy veil, went on record denouncing the 'heavy-handed' US tactics and publicly warned Marc Rich AG of serious violations of Swiss law if it complied with the US court request. Ultimately the Swiss authorities seized what were said to be the requested documents from Marc Rich AG in Zug.

The Swiss view was, in part, that turning over the documents could reveal proprietary information about companies with which Marc Rich AG did business, in violation of the Swiss criminal code on 'economic espionage'. Were the US to follow normal diplomatic channels, the documents would be turned over in due course, it was indicated, but with the names of all third parties deleted.

The US Justice Department took a hard-line approach, even though it was clear that this could alienate the Swiss authorities and jeopardize future cooperation in tax fraud cases. It was only after the Swiss government blocked disclosure by Marc Rich AG that an effort at cooperation was undertaken. It remained unclear whether the affront to Swiss sovereignty was deliberate or only normal bureaucratic bungling. The Marc Rich case came up after the Swiss had demonstrated greater willingness to cooperate in cases of tax fraud and securities laws violations, and before a scheduled renegotiation of a 1952 bilateral tax treaty. A heavy-handed, prosecutional approach that minimized cooperation and diplomacy seemed to many to be counterproductive in the Marc Rich case and certainly in successful future efforts to curb the role of foreign financial secrecy in the commission of criminal acts in the United States. On the other hand, US prosecutors saw Swiss stonewalling as a potentially critical blow to their case and, as the 'steamer trunk caper' seemed to demonstrate, susceptible to abuse by the accused. The Swiss stakes were very high indeed – especially since confidentiality with respect to third parties was involved – and their actions were entirely predictable, regardless of the merits of the case at hand. But their stakes in continued access to US markets were equally high, and this probably figured heavily in how much pressure the Justice Department felt it could exert without encountering irreparable damage to bilateral relations.

According to one Swiss official, 'The U.S. has a tendency to consider firms that are controlled by Americans but domiciled in foreign countries to be under U.S. jurisdiction. For us, Marc Rich AG is a Swiss entity under Swiss jurisdiction. That is a fundamental point.'[21]

The US–Swiss confrontation over the Marc Rich documents dragged on through the summer of 1984, even as the $50,000 per day in fines continued. The Swiss position was that the US subpoena was 'confrontational' and an impediment to voluntary and cooperative compliance. The Justice Department's view was that the Swiss had already agreed to comply and that, in any case, it was unclear whether the subpoena could in fact be dropped under US law. A major point of conflict continued to be the role of 'uninvolved third parties' who might be compromised by disclosures related to the Marc Rich case. Under Swiss law, such individuals have the right to object to disclosure; yet materials pertiinent to the case would be difficult to separate from those affecting their interests.[22] A note was sent by the Swiss Ministry of Justice to the US authorities in July 1984 indicating that documents would be released in the case of Marc Rich only if the government agreed that he could not be forced to comply with US court orders that violated Swiss sovereignty.

In July 1984, under a 1900 bilateral treaty, the US filed extradition papers on Marc Rich and Pincus Green to have them stand trial in New York for tax evasion, racketeering and fraud. The Swiss initially refused to accept the documents because they were written in English, noting that the US only accepts English-language requests. They did accept them about one month later, after translation into German, but noted that the charges on which the September 1984 trial was based were not directly covered by the 1900 extradition treaty, and any affirmative finding by the authorities could still be appealed to the Swiss Supreme Court.

Once again, there was the need to prove that the alleged offense involved commission of a crime under Swiss law. After a warrant was issued for their arrest in 1983, the Swiss consul in New York noted that '... it would be "most unlikely" that the Swiss would extradite the commodity traders on the basis of allegations of tax evasion or trading with Iran. The treaty calls for cooperation only in the case of murder, robbery, burglary, counterfeiting, forgery, embezzlement, and breach of trust involving a fiduciary.'[23] However, as one US attorney noted, 'We have every reason to believe, based on their past behavior, that Mr. Rich and Mr. Green will become fugitives from justice. As I understand it, Mr. Rich and Mr. Green are guests of Switzerland. They may become unwelcome guests.'[24] In order to make extradition more difficult, Marc Rich quickly obtained Spanish citizenship and Pincus Green became a Bolivian national, both renouncing their US citizenship – Marc Rich himself having obtained that citizenship as a child after fleeing with his family from his native Belgium to escape Nazi persecution.

In mid-October 1984, the case against Marc Rich & Co. AG was settled in New York. The company pleaded guilty to 38 counts of making false statements to federal authorities and two counts of tax evasion. The original charge had involved 51 counts of mail and wire fraud, racketeering, violating federal oil-price controls, and tax evasion. In the settlement, the company paid the government $150 million, forfeited $21 million in court fines already levied plus $24–40 million in future tax benefits, and paid $780,000 in fines and $33,000 in costs – for a total of about $200 million. Clyde Meltzer pleaded guilty to one count of making false statements to the government, and was sentenced to five years on probation and fined $5,000. The government thereupon lifted all restrictions on Marc Rich's US operations, and made possible the payment of $130 million in debt to 14 banks on the part of the parent firm in Switzerland. Marc Rich and Pincus Green still faced fraud, racketeering, tax evasion and other charges, although the likelihood of extradition from Switzerland remained remote. According to the Swiss, all of the particulars in the US extradition request 'are only violations of either currency, economic or fiscal measures, and they aren't extraditable under the US–Swiss treaty of 1900.'[25]

The Marc Rich case was a new milestone in the use of financial secrecy for purposes of tax evasion and other crimes in the country in which business is done. Its importance extended far beyond the case itself, although in some ways the degree of secrecy involved was unique. 'The reason so little is known about international trading companies is that the boundaries between the U.S. and the rest of the world are much less delineated for them. The whole area is so legally foggy and the competition so stiff that it is inherently a very secretive business'.[26] However, the US Commodity Futures Trading Commission (CFTC) has established a set of rules bearing on foreign-based participants in American markets which would ban them if they do not provide adequate information about their trading activity and profits. This, in turn, could lead to a disclosure of sensitive competitive information about trading activity both in the US and abroad.

The sensational Marc Rich case certainly seems to be an exception – and an unnecessary one at that, given the evident trading competence and profitability of the firm even in full compliance with the law. Tax evasion in most cases is far less dramatic. The rule in many countries seems to be, 'If there's a reasonable chance that income or capital gains cannot be traced by the authorities, then evasion using secrecy vehicles is fair game.' There are enough tax havens and ways of routing funds to them that, given the continuing evolution of tax hells around the world – marked by confiscatory rates, complexity, inequity, and the high costs of legal avoidance – the use of secret international funds flows for this purpose is bound to grow.

Smuggling

Besides tax evasion, the attempt to bypass other types of government distortions of competitive conditions in free markets is another major source of the demand for secret money. One such distortion is exchange control, whereby governments drive a wedge into foreign exchange transactions by forcing recipients of foreign currencies to surrender receipts to the authorities for local currency at a fixed exchange rate, and by permitting exchange allocations only for specific purposes – again at a fixed rate. Exchange controls invariably foster black markets, in which a 'free' or 'parallel' exchange rate indicates the degree of distortion built into the official rate. Those who are lucky enough to have foreign exchange are much better off keeping it that way (often illegally and hence secretly) and converting what they need into local currency on the black market. Those who require foreign exchange are likewise encouraged to use the black market, even at considerable added expense, to buy what they cannot get official exchange allocations for or to get their money out of the country. Black markets often work (despite periodic government crackdowns) simply by means of smuggled currency (foreign currency in, domestic currency out). They can also work by means of off-market pricing – over-invoicing export transactions or under-invoicing import transactions wherein the foreign partner puts the difference between the agreed price and the invoice price aside in a secret account owned by the domestic partner in the deal. Financial secrecy is necessary for the evasion of exchange control, since discovery of external accounts could destroy future evasion opportunities (or encourage extortion) and subject the individual to severe penalties.

In addition to smuggling currencies, people smuggle goods. Conventional smuggling involves evasion of import controls and duties by people who purchase goods abroad and sell them domestically at a profit equal to the domestic/foreign price differential less the cost of smuggling. Procurement of contraband normally involves secret accounts and

funding channels. Less conventional is export smuggling. This may involve stolen cars or other merchandise, products (especially farm commodities) whose prices are controlled domestically at levels below their
foreign prices, and products whose export is restricted for other reasons,
such as national security. Again, secret money is usually necessary to
carry it out.

One big-time use of international financial secrecy has been the diversion of sensitive high-technology equipment to the Soviet Union and
other Warsaw Pact countries. To a significant extent, the flow of
restricted equipment has apparently been channeled through dummy
corporations established in Switzerland, Liechtenstein, and elsewhere;
it has even involved secret return shipments to the West of defective
equipment for servicing. According to reports, several thousand East
European 'technology collection' officers are at work in the West under
various covers, responsible for assembling precise shopping lists of
equipment and components wanted in the East. Orders are then processed, sometimes through dummy corporations and sometimes using
unauthorized procedures within legitimate Western European enterprises, through an 'intricate series of post-box companies in Liechtenstein and Switzerland, forged, purchased and misappropriated
documents, and great amounts of cash.'[27] The process has continued
over decades, only coming under increased pressure in recent years as
a result of rather controversial US initiatives. One major conduit, the
Hedera Establishment of Liechtenstein, was dissolved in January 1983.
'Under corporate law in Liechtenstein, its papers suggested nothing
more about who paid for its multimillion-dollar account other than the
two Vaduz lawyers who served as the entire membership of its "administrative" board.'[28]

The use of international financial secrecy in international high-
technology smuggling was exposed at least partially in the case of a German named Richard Mueller. For years, the United States had been trying, with mixed success, to keep defense-related high technology out of
the hands of the Soviet bloc. Ordinary strategic considerations argued
for such a policy, but the issue became far more critical in the late 1970s
and 1980s when a massive Soviet military buildup of already numerical-
ly superior forces, coupled with rising East–West political tensions, put
an increased premium on qualitative weapons-system superiority. The
Soviets responded by vastly increasing their technology acquisitions
and espionage activities, and the US sought to tighten leaks wherever
it could – often with less than enthusiastic backing from its allies and its
own business community. This situation spelled big profits for middlemen who could evade US restrictions using financial secrecy and
legal inconsistencies among Western countries. As a West German
businessman noted, 'It is not against [American] law to ship U.S.
technology to West Germany and it's not against German law for a com-

pany then to ship it to Switzerland, and there are no Swiss laws against shipping goods to the Soviet Union.'[29]

Richard Mueller discovered that enormous markups were possible in the trade of restricted technologies early in the game. According to US authorities, Mueller initially operated directly out of California's Silicon Valley, purchasing components and equipment for shipment via more or less clandestine channels to Eastern Europe. Once identified as a major technology smuggler by US agents in 1976, Mueller left the US, returned to West Germany and traveled widely on a Swiss passport. The technique was to establish or acquire shell companies in countries that would have legitimate needs for high-tech US equipment, purchase the equipment from American manufacturers that complied with all US export regulations, and then spirit it on to Eastern Europe.

By 1981, Mueller was reportedly clearing over $5 million yearly tax-free, with intensive and open business contracts with the Soviet Union, East Germany, Hungary and Czechoslovakia. His German employees were paid from Swiss accounts, his companies showed no taxable profits in West Germany, and his own earnings presumably remained untaxed in Switzerland. The Mueller organization appeared to function smoothly until 1982, when he purchased control of a more substantial firm, Gerland Heimorgelwerke, a manufacturer of home organs in financial difficulty located near Lübeck. The firm would purchase US electronics equipment, repack and relabel it, and ship it through a series of other Mueller-controlled companies, often by circuitous routes, to Eastern Europe – leaving a complex and highly opaque trail. It also shipped cargoes to West Berlin by road. Some of the cargoes would simply evaporate on the passage through East Germany. The equipment orders placed with the manufacturer '... often displayed unusual features: manufacturers' offers to install the equipment were declined, extra large supplies of spare parts were sought, unusual plugs were demanded, payment was often by unusual channels.'[30] Particularly favored procurement was from Digital Equipment Corporation (DEC), whose VAX series of computers have wide military applications and one of whose former employees was part of the Mueller team.

The Gerland operation closed down in 1982, after some of Mueller's employees reported a night shipment of five truckloads of DEC equipment, on East European vehicles, that was destined for Hungary and the Soviet Union. Mueller thereupon liquidated Gerland and moved his operations to South Africa, where he had obtained a residency permit in 1980. A front company, Microelectronics Research Institute (MRI), was set up in Cape Town, controlled by Mueller through two Swiss holding companies and an intermediary South African venture. The whole thing was financed from Switzerland and a well-known South African management consultant was used as a front. On the pretext of establishing a microchip manufacturing operation in South Africa, an export license was obtained from the US Commerce Department for a complete computer-assisted microchip design system, which was fully set up and tested in a converted shoe factory outside Cape Town. These arrangements apparently had the dual purpose of preserving the MRI cover and satisfying the Soviet customer that things worked as they should.

Early in 1983, parts of the facility were dismantled and sent to the Soviet Union via Sweden using Mueller's corporate network and a Swedish accomplice who had rented space in a warehouse near Stockholm, ostensibly to establish Sweden's first microchip manufacturing facility. On 23 October 1983, the main computers and other gear were shipped from South Africa. After US pressure was exerted on West Germany and Sweden, as well as a chase worthy of James Bond, part of the shipment was intercepted in Hamburg, West Germany, and in Hälsingborg, Sweden. However, substantial amounts of other equipment are suspected to have slipped through the net. Meantime, the Swedish accomplice was arrested on tax and currency violations related to Mueller's payments via Switzerland, and Mueller himself dropped out of sight.

Mueller was described by one US official as the 'most toxic of all' technology bandits. His total take, originally estimated at about $18 million, actually appears to have been much higher. Disclosures by Swiss banks revealed over $100 million in his accounts. Although his network has been dismantled, Mueller escaped unscathed and is now evidently based in Eastern Europe.[31]

Violations of securities laws

Rules have been established over the years in many countries to assure orderly, efficient and equitable financial markets. In two respects, however, these rules have been subject to periodic violations: outright fraud and insider trading. Both are generally made possible by international financial secrecy. Securities markets lend themselves particularly well to the abuse of secrecy, precisely because successful dealings legitimately depend on the astute use of non-disclosure of information – and on moving on the basis of available information faster and more decisively than the competition. Fraud is discussed in the next section. Here we shall focus on insider trading.

Insider trading in the securities markets is a perennial problem. It involves trading by those in a position to use privileged information about factors affecting the market value of securities before that information is made known to outside investors and the general public. Such information may be acquired directly or by accident, through bribery and reciprocal tip-offs, or through financial espionage and intelligence gathering. Particularly high-stakes financial activities, such as mergers and acquisitions, lend themselves to insider trading. While insider trading in the United States is illegal under the Securities and Exchange Act, there are important gray areas concerning the definition of 'insider' and the circumstances under which particular kinds of behavior could be held illegal and subject to civil or criminal penalties. Moreover, since insider trading seldom involves a paper trail, investigations by agencies such as the US Securities and Exchange Commission (SEC) and obtaining a conviction in a court of law tend to be an arduous and often unsuccessful process.

Because the culprit will often go to some trouble to cover his tracks, the evidence may well be largely circumstantial. For example, a 1982 case involved an office manager for the prestigious New York Law firm of Sullivan & Cromwell, who originated tips on a major takeover deal for which the firm was doing the legal work.

> Thirteen persons, ranging from New York policemen to brokerage-firm officials, were charged: they were alleged to have made more than $1.2 million in profits on tips passed by the office manager, who was privy to takeover plans of the Sullivan & Cromwell clients.
>
> The SEC subpoenaed telephone records, which showed that one of the traders repeatedly called someone in a Hong Kong hotel in February 1982, just before buying the securities of one of Sullivan & Cromwell's clients. With help from British and Hong Kong law enforcement authorities, SEC officials said, they identified the Hong Kong connection as a vacationing New York brokerage-firm employee.
>
> Hong Kong phone records, in turn, showed that the brokerage employee called the law firm's office manager in Brooklyn shortly before talking to the trader. From the sequence of calls, the SEC alleged that the acquisition tip passed from the office manager through the Hong Kong vacationer and back to the trader in New York.[32]

A number of observers argue that there is nothing wrong with most kinds of insider trading – that, indeed, it is a valuable function that improves the efficiency of the capital market. They view investor mistrust as a fundamental *strength* of open financial markets, in that private initiatives designed to shield investors from the possibility of fraud and malfeasance have created a bulwark that is much stronger than regulation can ever be as the basis for public confidence and constraints on criminal activities. There is little evidence, this view holds, that anyone is hurt by insider trading; indeed, such activities help prices adjust more quickly than they would otherwise.

The positive market-efficiency attributes of insider trading are thus considered to outweigh the unfairness of important information being available to, and acted upon by, a few investors before it becomes known to the general public. Efficient markets, in turn, help insure that shareholders get what they pay for – that their asset values will not be eroded by information not yet released, but that comes to be known later and thus blindsides the investor. Insider information thus may enhance, rather than detract from, fairness. More efficiently priced stock, moreover, embodies lower risk. Hence companies should reward employees in part through inside information, on the basis of which they would act and thus trigger share-price movements in the market. Nor is it clear that outsiders lose in proportion to insiders as a result of such behavior. Some outsiders lose and some win; no one knows whether the losers would outnumber the winners, or vice versa, without strict limits on insider trading.[33]

Others argue that the equity or 'fairness' costs far outweigh any conceivable efficiency gains. If ordinary investors, including institutions, are going to be excluded from information that benefits the favored few (in terms of capital gains or capital losses avoided), then the integrity of the financial system and the usefulness of market capitalism itself can be called into question. Nobody enjoys being fleeced, and, when the sheep become sufficiently numerous and agitated, they may end up destroying some very valuable institutions.

Whatever the merits of the opposing arguments, the fact remains that insider trading is illegal in most major securities markets, including those in the United States. American insider trading laws are principally set forth in the Securities Act of 1933, which states:

> It shall be unlawful for any person, directly or indirectly, by the use of any means or instrumentality of interstate commerce, or of the mails or of any facility of any national securities exchange: (a) To employ any device, scheme, or artifice to defraud; (b) To make any untrue statements of a material fact or to omit to state a material fact necessary in order to make the statements made, in the light of the circumstances under which they were made, not misleading; or (c) to engage in any act, practice, or course of business which operates or would operate as a fraud or deceit upon any person, in connection with the purchase or sale of any security.

Essentially, the law precludes investors from buying or selling securities where non-public information is the basis of the investment decision if the investor does not first disclose that information. A Supreme Court decision has interpreted this rule as holding essentially that, for a violation of the insider trading provisions, it must be found that the investor owed a fiduciary duty to the shareholders of the corporation whose securities were traded. This decision created a clearer, but more stringent, test for insider trading liability.

Insiders and their cohorts need financial secrecy to cover their tracks, and various secret money channels are in regular use. Indeed, the channels themselves may be used as tip-offs on possible insider activities. For example, a major figure in the Wall Street arbitrage game claimed that he could benefit from insider trading even without being an insider or tippee himself. He carefully observed the stock trading activities of a number of small Swiss banks that he suspected of acting on behalf of Wall Streeters having access to inside information. Any unusual activity could indicate a deal, and he would then himself move immediately in its wake. Since it pays insiders to publicize information after they have taken their own positions, profits can sometimes be made in the short term even if the information ultimately proves to be factually incorrect or exaggerated.

A common securities fraud scheme is thus to effect securities transactions through banks in foreign jurisdictions to avoid disclosure of the purchaser's identity. The authorities' statutory responsibilities cannot adequately be met unless the Securities and Exchange Commission is able successfully to complete an investigation into the alleged misuse of insider information. To do this, account identity of participants and information regarding the transactions in question – such as the reasons for the purchase and/or sale – are vital.

The SEC's investigations of suspicious trading or transactions pointing to insider activities may be categorized into a two-fold approach. First, trading records of identified brokers and customers involved in the questioned transaction are acquired. Second, sworn testimony is taken. Both avenues are pursued on either a voluntary or subpoena basis. The SEC may subpoena witnesses for testimony and/or the production of relevant books, papers, memoranda, correspondence or other material.

Testimony is used as a fact-gathering method to elicit further information, enabling the SEC to determine whether actual violations occurred. In most cases, the testimony of customers and representatives of brokerage and financial firms are the most pertinent in the array of evidence sought during the investigations. The identity of the suspected customer is necessary, and information about his transactions are vital to determining and proving a securities law violation.

Of course, the customer may simply refuse to confirm or deny information about suspected transactions. Even this assumes that the SEC has surpassed the first hurdle – obtaining the usual court subpoena enforcement action for the customer's testimony, which is a costly and time-consuming process. The alternative is to request account information from foreign financial institutions, whose officials are likely to refuse, asserting bank secrecy prohibitions. In the end, a culprit goes unpunished and the investing public loses confidence in financial markets. The examples cited in Exhibit 3.1 illustrate this dilemma.

EXHIBIT 3.1

Examples of international financial secrecy in cases of insider trading

---

ILLUSTRATION A

Mr X, a hypothetical American citizen, resides in Zurich, Switzerland, and is a member of the Board of Directors of Solar, Inc., a Delaware corporation. On January 15, X learns at a board meeting that an engineer employed by Solar has discovered a practical and inexpensive method for substituting solar energy for gas and oil. The board decides to delay public announcement of the news until final testing has been completed.

Mr X, who at present is not a Solar shareholder, returns to Zurich planning to profit from the anticipated rise in the value of Solar stock. At the time, Solar common stock is selling for $2 per share on the New York Stock Exchange. Mr X is advised by his attorney that, under an earlier US court decision, the news of the discovery is 'material, inside information'. Therefore, Mr X is told, he would be violating the law if he were to trade Solar shares on the basis of this undisclosed information. Moreover, even if he does not purchase the stock until after the news has been disseminated to the public, but then sells the shares within six months of his purchase, he would be required to transfer to the company all profits derived from these transactions. Thus, in order for Mr X to cash in on the expected increase in the value of Solar's shares, he must remain an anonymous investor.

To ensure anonymity, Mr X instructs Geheimnis, a Zurich bank with which he maintains an account, to purchase 50,000 shares of Solar common stock on his behalf. Funds for the purchase are drawn from Mr X's savings account. Geheimnis submits the order to its broker in New York and the transaction is completed. The broker's records indicate that Geheimnis purchased 50,000 shares of Solar on January 20. The identity of the beneficial owner of the shares, Mr X, remains undisclosed.

On February 1, Solar publicly announces its great technological advance. Within one month, the price of Solar common stock soars to $20. On that day, Mr X instructs Geheimnis to sell his 50,000 shares. The transaction is completed; Geheimnis is the seller of record, and Mr X has cleared a gross profit of $900,000.

Meanwhile, the rapid rise in the price of Solar stock has attracted the attention of the SEC. The Commission discovers that less than two weeks before the announcement of the development in solar energy, 50,000 shares of Solar were purchased by Geheimnis. Unlawful insider trading is suspected and Mr X, a director of Solar residing in Zurich, is a prime suspect. The Commission is presented with a problem. It can subpoena Mr X to testify concerning his transactions in Solar stock. He will undoubtedly refuse to disclose that he purchased and sold the 50,000 shares. On the other hand, if the Commission chooses to subpoena Geheimnis for information pertaining to the account of Mr X, the bank will almost certainly refuse to comply, due to the constraints of Article 47(b) of the Swiss Banking Law and Section 273 of the Swiss Penal Code. Consequently, it is very unlikely that under these circumstances the Commission will be able to gather sufficient evidence to prove that Mr X engaged in unlawful securities transactions.

ILLUSTRATION B

Elastic, Inc. is a Delaware Corporation which manufactures rubber bands. In 1976, the corporation issued 500,000 shares of common stock at a par value of $10 per share. The stock is sold in the over-the-counter market. Two years of unsuccessful business has left Elastic close to bankruptcy. The market price of its shares has fallen to $1 by 1 January 1978.

Mr Y, a US resident, maintains an account at Geheimnis Bank in Zurich. He instructs Geheimnis to purchase 25,000 shares of Elastic for his account. The purchase is made in the name of the bank. Mr Y informs investors and brokers, with whom he is acquainted, that he has learned through sources at Elastic that the company will sign a contract with a large Brazilian rubber company. This contract, he explains, will enable Elastic to purchase large quantities of rubber at an extremely favorable price. He suggests that at $1 per share Elastic stock is a 'steal'. Mr Y then orders Geheimnis to purchase 50,000 shares of Elastic. Again, the transaction is made in the name of Geheimnis.

Mr Y's contacts become interested in Elastic as a result of Mr Y's 'tip' and the unusual trading activity in Elastic's stock. Demand for the shares increases and the price begins to rise. Mr Y continues to buy and sell through Geheimnis. The price of Elastic common rises to $25. Mr Y eventually sells all of his shares in Elastic for a large profit. The funds are deposited in his account at Geheimnis. Meanwhile, Mr Y's substantial sales cause the manipulated price at Elastic to crash, and the remaining investors are left with virtually worthless stock. Although Mr Y has violated the Securities Exchange Act of 1933, Swiss bank secrecy would most probably prevent the SEC from ascertaining the principal (i.e. Mr Y) on whose behalf Geheimnis traded Elastic's shares.

ILLUSTRATION C

Suppose XYZ Corporation plans a tender offer for the shares of ABC Corporation. Suppose, further, that either an officer of XYZ or one of its professional consultants misappropriates material non-public information concerning the unannounced tender offer, and places a purchase order for the securities of ABC through a bank in a secrecy jurisdiction. If the transaction had been conducted through a US brokerage firm, the Commission could quickly identify the individual involved. However, because the transaction was effected through a bank in a secrecy jurisdiction, the Commission would be denied access to the information necessary to determine whether a securities law violation had occurred.

Source: Adapted from *International Law and Politics*, Vol. 9, p. 417, and testimony of John M. Fedders, formerly Director, Division of Enforcement, US Securities and Exchange Commission, before the Permanent Subcommittee of Investigations of the Senate Committee on Governmental Affairs, 24 May 1983.

Fraud

Whereas the use of international fiscal secrecy for insider trading purposes is certainly controversial in terms of its effects on efficiency and equity in financial markets, its use to perpetrate outright financial fraud is a different matter altogether. Charlatans have long used human greed for their own purposes, often with great success. But ultimately the jig is usually up, and it helps at that point to have the loot safely stashed out of reach of victims and law enforcement officials, and to place oneself under the protection of a country that will not honor financial disclosure or extradition requests. Financial secrecy, moreover, is a potent device for drawing-in prospective victims who hope to evade taxes.

In 1984, for example, a case came to light in the United States involving abuse of fiduciary relationships in the presence of financial secrecy. J. David & Co. promised investors up to 40 per cent annual returns on their money and complete confidentiality, with records of transactions kept outside the United States. The opportunity attracted large numbers of wealthy investors in California and elsewhere. The investment proceeds were ostensibly to be used for currency trading operations. Much of the money evidently went into the various personal activities of the company's founder, J. David Dominelli, as well as to cover exceedingly high operating costs (six houses, three jet aircraft, over two dozen luxury automobiles).[34] Little apparently went into actual trading activities, certainly not in the volume that could conceivably have yielded the kinds of returns promised to investors. Despite suspicions of fraud, the nature of the interbank foreign exchange market made it impossible to substantiate or refute earnings claims made by the company, and transactions were routed through offshore points such as Guernsey and the Caribbean island of Montserrat.

Records kept by J. David & Co. appear to have been either sloppy or non-existent, with tax identification numbers often missing – indicating at least inferentially the intent of many of the firm's prominent clients to evade US federal and state taxes. Few people appear to have withdrawn their funds, while those who did may have been paid largely out of investments by others. The whole scheme began to unravel in the fall of 1983, when J. David's obligations began falling past due, various other signs of trouble began to emerge, and Dominelli began to scramble to cover withdrawals. Checks bounced with increasing frequency, suits began to be filed by investors, and at an early stage in the investigation only $600,000 in liquid assets could be located to cover over $150 million in liabilities.

Dominelli eventually escaped to Montserrat, where he had set up a captive shell bank for secrecy purposes. From there he flew to Antigua, where he was arrested and extradited to the United States to face the music. Suspicions arose that the affair did indeed involve an elaborate Ponzi scheme – where existing investors are paid off out of the proceeds of subsequent investments, to the extent that they withdraw their funds – or that Dominelli lost large amounts in actual foreign exchange speculation and in efforts to cover those losses. For the rather unsophisticated but greedy investors for whom a promise of a 40 per cent annual return and the chance to evade taxes seemed too good to be true, it was. Still, indications were that large numbers of investors, lured by the dual prospects of high returns and tax evasion, would rather walk away from their losses than risk disclosure of their financial affairs in court proceedings.

Then there was the case of Edward Markowitz, a government securities trader who peddled tax shelters to investors partly through what turned out to be fictitious and fraudulent trading. Some of these trades were with mysterious Cayman Islands companies, and his associates '... were unable to learn anything about the financial strength of the Caribbean entities with which Mr. Markowitz traded, or even who their owners were'.[35] In the end, he was brought up on tax fraud charges ($445 million), pleaded guilty to a number of them, and cooperated with the authorities in their investigations.

International financial secrecy can thus be used as bait in fraudulent financial dealings, as well as a way to protect the spoils by making money disappear. An interesting case in the latter category occurred in May 1983. Chase Manhattan Bank and Manufacturers Hanover Trust Company of New York had made a loan to the Colombian government in the amount of $47.2 million, for the purchase of equipment and supplies by Colombian military and police authorities. Some of the loan had already been drawn-down, but most of what was left in the Colombian current account at Chase's London office ($13.5 million) was ordered transferred to an account at the Morgan Guaranty Trust Company in New York, an account that in turn belonged to the Zurich branch of Bank Hapoalim, a major Israeli financial institution. Chase maintained that it followed accepted principles in transferring the money on instructions telexed from Bogotá bearing the name of the Finance Ministry's director of public credit and the telex number of Colombia's central bank. The Colombians argued that no record of any such telexed instructions could be found in Bogotá, and in any event the transfer should not have been made without a disbursement order from Chase's own Bogotá representative. Moreover, normal telex security precautions evidently were seriously flawed, and there were misspellings and other procedural errors. Whether Chase checked the inconsistencies is not known, but a religious holiday in Colombia in any case would have prevented immediate verification.

The Colombian government accused Chase of mismanagement in what was clearly a case of highly sophisticated bank robbery – and just as clearly an 'inside job'. Where did the money end up? The last word was that most of the funds had been transferred to the Panama branch of Bank Leumi, another Israeli bank, and there the trail ends. Domestic Colombian investigations into the case were accompanied by several suspicious deaths of people with information about the affair.[36]

Hundreds of cases of secrecy-related financial fraud have come to light over the years, but certainly the story of the decade (perhaps of the century) was the Banco Ambrosiano case.

Banco Ambrosiano

On 18 June 1982, the body of Roberto Calvi – chairman and president of Banco Ambrosiano, a major, prestigious bank headquartered in Milan – was discovered hanging from scaffolding under Blackfriars Bridge in London. Calvi was often called 'God's Banker' in the press because of his close association with the Vatican. About $1.3 billion of his bank's funds were soon found to be missing, most of it evidently extended as loans to a handful of Panamanian and Liechtenstein shell companies owned directly or indirectly by the Vatican's own bank, the Instituto per le Opere di Religione (IOR). None of the missing assets have been recovered.[37]

The Vatican's exact role in the Banco Ambrosiano affair remains a mystery, owing to the secret nature of the Holy See's finances. The IOR is best seen as an offshore merchant bank in the heart of Italy serving the Roman Catholic Church. The Vatican is a sovereign state, subject to neither exchange controls nor border checks. Money deposited in an IOR account could be sent anywhere in the world. Calvi learned from Michele Sindona, the financier who declared bankruptcy in 1974 and was convicted in the US of fraud and perjury in 1980, the means to exploit the opportunities offered by the system.

Italian legislation, framed to prevent repetition of the financial disasters of the 1930s, prevents banks from buying non-banking interests, and vice versa. The way to get around this legislation has been to establish foreign shell companies, preferably in tax havens where local scrutiny is lax. These foreign shell companies could then make the prohibited investments. Ownership of a bank offered perfect means to activate the system. Bank funds could be appropriated and, through the 'fiduciary' or trustee accounts, exported out of Italy to the shell companies abroad, owned either by the initiator himself or by his associates. In turn, these companies might pass the funds on to offshore 'investment' companies, again either owned by the initiator or by associates. The funds could then be used to carry out financial operations that would normally be illegal back in Italy or elsewhere.

Speculative assets, once bought, might subsequently be moved around a network of companies at ever-higher prices, creating 'profits' for further speculation. If the price of the underlying Italian assets seemed deficient, one's own bank could step in, pushing up the value of the shares in question by buying on the relatively thin Milan market. This brought the further advantage that one could then more easily pass the shares on to innocent third parties at an inflated price. The initiator would always retain majority control, usually concealed in the offshore labyrinth.

Roberto Calvi's elaborate and complex scheme was possible only with the consent of the IOR, which was either knowingly or unknowingly involved. The IOR was an ideal, much-respected, candidate for the role of fiduciary, or trustee. To get the IOR interested in Calvi's pursuits, the Banco Ambrosiano paid unusually high interest rates on its IOR deposits. Sr Calvi would transfer funds, or the shares of a company, to the IOR. According to the instructions received, the IOR would either hold the assets in Calvi's name, or pass them on to a specified recipient, usually outside Italy. In addition, the IOR's well-respected secrecy and offshore status made discovery of what was taking place particularly difficult for the Italian authorities.

Cardinal Paul Marcinkus, chairman of the IOR since 1971, disclaimed any responsibility for Calvi's manipulations. The IOR maintained that Calvi had taken it for a colossal ride. Its sins, if any, were those of naivety and inexperience. The question nevertheless remains: where does negligence and naivety end and collusion begin? The truth about the Vatican bank's relations with Calvi will probably never be known. Was the IOR acting on its own interest? Was Ambrosiano acting on behalf of the IOR? Was the IOR behind Ambrosiano, which in turn was behind the IOR?

The relationship between Calvi and Marcinkus dated from August 1971, if not earlier, when Marcinkus joined the board of the newly formed Cisalpine Overseas in Nassau, Bahamas. Cisalpine Overseas marked the beginning of Calvi's scheme to buy up control of Banco Ambrosiano itself, and Bahamian financial secrecy laws played a critical role. A subsidiary in the Bahamas not only fitted Calvi's image as an internationally minded banker, but it would also later permit him to conduct his most sensitive business safely away from the prying eyes of the Italian financial authorities. With Paul Marcinkus as director, the Vatican had an original shareholding of $2\frac{1}{2}$ per cent in the Nassau operation, which later rose to 8 per cent.

Banco Ambrosiano's first foreign acquisition actually occurred in the early 1960s, when it bought Banca del Gottardo, just across the border in Lugano, Switzerland. Besides Cisalpine, a second firm, Suprafin, was established in Milan in November 1971, controlled by a Luxembourg holding company called Anli. Suprafin would deal in Ambrosiano's shares, and smooth out fluctuations in the stock price.

The fall of Michele Sindona, as well as rumours about Calvi, resulted from two separate investigations of Banco Ambrosiano by the Banca d'Italia (the central bank of Italy) between 1971 and 1973. This caused massive selling of Ambrosiano's shares. Suprafin bought shares to support the price, and gradually began gaining control of Ambrosiano. Most of the shares purchased were sent to an entity called Ulricor in

Vaduz, Liechtenstein, supposedly owned by the IOR. All in all, Suprafin sent abroad 15.4 per cent of Banco Ambrosiano's outstanding shares. The recipients were shell companies, like Ulricor, consisting of no more than an entry in a lawyer's books. But all of them were in one way or another managed by Calvi and his banks. The stock purchase placed with Suprafin had come first from Banca del Gottardo, and later from Cisalpine Overseas.

In 1974 and 1975, more shell companies were set up. Besides Ulricor in Vaduz, there were Sapi, Rekofinanz, Sektorinvest, Finkus and Sansinvest. There were more distant shells in Panama, where registered companies did not even have to provide accounts, including La Fidèle and Finprogram.

Calvi evidently worked in close collaboration with the Vatican bank throughout. Besides the IOR's probable ownership of Ulricor, the Banca del Gottardo in November 1974 set up another Panamanian company, United Trading Corporation, in the name of the IOR. The United Trading Corporation established various nominees, two of them in Liechtenstein, which later purchased full ownership of Suprafin.

Besides buying control of his own bank, Calvi had his eyes set on gaining control of a newspaper as well. The purchase of *Corriere della Sera* by the Rizzoli publishing group presented Calvi with an opportunity. Rizzoli bought *Corriere* (the newspaper had been owned by the Crespi family, the oil magnate Angelo Moratti, and the Agnelli family, which controls Fiat) in July 1974 for 44 billion lira. But *Corriere* lost 12 billion lira in the first year. Roberto Calvi provided Rizzoli with much of the needed purchase price and gradually gained control as capital was added to cover the paper's financial losses. In the summer of 1977, Rizolli's capital was increased from 5 to 25.5 billion lira to keep pace with the paper's growing debt. The funds used by Rizzoli to subscribe the increased capital were put up by Banco Ambrosiano. Calvi insisted that 80 per cent of Rizzoli's shares be lodged with Banco Ambrosiano as collateral for the loan. Later, this majority interest appears to have been passed on by Calvi to the IOR. On the surface, however, the entire sum was put up by the Rizzoli family and they retained a 91 per cent share of the newspaper group.

The so-called '159' law, passed in April 1976, signified the beginning of Calvi's troubles, and eventually led to his downfall. This law turned illegal export of currency from a simple 'administrative' offense into a criminal one. Its effect on Calvi was to make it harder to operate an offshore company with impunity. Previously, if a foreign debt became a serious concern, the possibility existed of settling it by remitting lira from Italy. After April 1976, that safety valve was largely removed. Foreign debts could now only be paid off by contracting new ones abroad. Most often, the debt was denominated in US dollars, which continued to rise against the Italian lira throughout the period.

Because the law was made retroactive, Calvi's failure to describe the nature of his dealings to the Italian authorities laid the groundwork for the impending investigations and the criminal charges to come. The first was his involvement in the November 1975 purchase by La Centrale, a holding company once owned by Michele Sindona, of 1.1 million shares in Toro, an insurance company. It was later revealed that the Toro shares in question were in effect already owned by La Centrale. The transaction was merely a re-import of shares into Italy, and an illegal export of currency representing the difference between their value on the Milan market and the price actually paid – some 23 billion lira.

A second factor that eventually brought about Calvi's demise was the 1978 Bank of Italy investigation of Banco Ambrosiano. 'Not at all satisfactory' was the verdict of the 12-man task force after a 7-month investigation. It was confirmed that Banco Ambrosiano had put together a foreign network that allowed it to shift large sums without scrutiny by Italian authorities. The report also identified the chain of command within Ambrosiano itself, from Milan through the Banca del Gottardo in Lugano to the key – Cisalpine Overseas in Nassau. By then, Cisalpine had borrowed more than $200 million from Banco Ambrosiano. On the other side of its balance sheet were $183 million of assets, described only as unspecified 'financings'. And on the board of Cisalpine sat not only Calvi, but Archbishop Paul Marcinkus, chairman of the IOR, which was also found by investigators to be the owner of Suprafin, the mysterious buyer of 15 per cent of Banco Ambrosiano's shares between 1974 and 1977 – shares that had in turn been dispatched, on buying orders placed by Cisalpine through Banca del Gottardo, to the group of Liechtenstein and Panamanian companies.

What the inspectors could not prove was that various foreign entities were the property of either Banco Ambrosiano or the IOR. But they had their suspicions. The mysterious growth of $183 million in assets in Nassau might be connected with the massive purchase of Ambrosiano's shares. That is, Banco Ambrosiano had lent the money to Cisalpine to buy control of itself. Their report also remarked that 'it cannot be excluded' that the Liechtenstein and Panamanian companies were part of the Ambrosiano group. Although the Vatican bank said it had a shareholding of only 1.37 per cent in Banco Ambrosiano, it 'could not be excluded' that it owned more through Panamanian companies that had bought large blocks of stock, with instructions from Cisalpine on whose board sat the chairman of the IOR himself. The report also noted that 32 per cent of Ambrosiano's capital was in the hands of 22 large shareholders, all of them in one way or another 'friendly' to Ambrosiano. The inspectors needed to prove that Calvi and the IOR were behind these offshore companies. Besides the suspect illegal offshore activities allegedly undertaken by Calvi, the inspectors also found further breaches of Italian banking law and severe organizational shortcomings, and that Ambrosiano was severely undercapitalized.

Calvi was alarmed by the central bank's findings, but evidently had his contingency plan well thought out. In September of 1977, Ambrosiano's Luxembourg subsidiary, Banco Ambrosiano Holding (BAH), set up a new bank called Ambrosiano Group Banco Commercial in Managua, Nicaragua. During 1978 and 1979, a good part of the unspecified 'financings' by Cisalpine was transferred to the books of the new bank, which was run from Nassau by Cisalpine. Besides exemption from tax, the bank was the only one not to be nationalized by the Nicaraguan government – which is perhaps indicative of the amount of money Calvi spent to buy political support in furtherance of his scheme.

In October 1979, Calvi again transferred his business, this time from Managua to Lima, Peru, where he established the Banco Ambrosiano Andino. Filippo Leoni became the first chairman of the bank, and his deputy was Giacomo Botta, both trusted lieutenants from Ambrosiano's international group in Milan. Decisions were taken in Milan and conveyed through Banca del Gottardo or Cisalpine in Nassau. From late 1979 on, most of the loans extended to the Panama and Liechtenstein companies were transferred to Lima.

Between 1977 and 1980, a new group of companies (17 altogether), usually with a nominal capital of $10,000 each, were formed in Panama and Liechtenstein. They were registered through resident agents but were owned by Manic S.A. of Luxembourg, formed in 1971 under the nominal ownership of the IOR. The main purpose of these companies was to finance the other Panamanian and Liechtenstein companies owned by Manic, which in turn owned Banco Ambrosiano shares. Physically, the shares never left Milan, but were on deposit with Ambrosiano itself. These companies were also to serve as repositories for other Calvi activities, evidently including funds that were channeled to the secret and highly controversial P2 Masonic lodge, in which he appears to have been active.

In 1979, Ambrosiano was forced to increase its capital from 20 billion to 30 billion lira. If Calvi was to retain control and avoid the risk of a drop in Ambrosiano's share price, the shell companies in Panama and Liechtenstein would have to undertake more borrowings. Calvi's plight thus continued to worsen. In June 1980, the construction group of Mario Genghini declared bankruptcy, defaulting on a total debt of 450 billion lira, one-third of which represented borrowings from Ambrosiano. A few days later, Italian authorities finally concluded that La Centrale's purchase of Toro in 1975 was in fact an illegal export of currency. The magistrate demanded that Calvi surrender his passport. In late 1980, Calvi purchased 20 per cent of the Artoc Bank and Trust Company (based in Nassau) through Banco Ambrosiano Overseas (formerly

Cisalpine). The main attraction was the prospect of rich new financial contacts in the Arab world.

New Italian financial regulations were passed in January 1981 that further complicated Calvi's life. These regulations frowned upon Italian banks' ownership of foreign holding companies that were not themselves banks, and warned that such an interest could be permitted only under two conditions: (a) that they could be properly scrutinized by the Banca d'Italia, and (b) that they were operated in countries with a proper system of banking supervision.

In the spring of 1981, Calvi was confronted with yet another challenge. The Milan stock market's regulatory authority forced Calvi to quote Banco Ambrosiano shares on the open market. Ambrosiano had always been quoted on the over-the-counter market, which was subject to fewer regulatory controls, where financial disclosure of consolidated accounts was not obligatory, and where trading only occurred once a week – allowing Ambrosiano to control trading in its own shares easily and cheaply.

In May 1981, Calvi was imprisoned on a charge of illegal currency exports. Calvi's family pressed Archbishop Marcinkus to admit involvement of the IOR, but he refused to come forward although the ultimate owners of the companies in Panama and Liechtenstein would have been the IOR by virtue of its ownership of Manic S.A. and United Trading Corporation. However, proof could only be obtained through Banca del Gottardo, which was bound by Swiss secrecy.

While in prison, Calvi instructed two emissaries to go to the head office of Banca del Gottardo, where they ascertained that shell companies owned by Manic S.A. and United Trading Corporation altogether owed Ambrosiano's Latin American affiliates over $900 million. The main asset used to secure these borrowings was a large block of shares in Banco Ambrosiano itself. Thus, the IOR was the owner not just of its declared 1.6 per cent, but of at least a further 10.2 per cent of Ambrosiano stock. On paper, the IOR thus controlled Banco Ambrosiano.

The trial of Roberto Calvi lasted two months. He was sentenced to four years in prison and a fine of 16 billion lira. His lawyer appealed the conviction. Calvi was released on bail and surrendered his passport. The appeal was expected to be heard on 21 June 1982.

In August 1981, the Bank of Italy demanded full disclosure of Ambrosiano's overseas affiliates and a list of all of its stockholders owning 10,000 shares or more. In desperation, Calvi requested from the IOR 'letters of comfort' confirming ownership of the nominee companies in Panama and Luxembourg to which funds had been lent, on two conditions: that the letters would entail no legal liability and that the financial tangle would be resolved by June of 1982. The IOR did indeed provide two comfort letters to the Ambrosiano Group Banco Commercial in Managua, Nicaragua, and Banco Andino in Lima, Peru. Two months later, the Vatican sent more letters to Managua and Lima, providing new figures and confirming that it would not dispose of the Panamanian shell companies 'without your prior written approval'. Calvi was told that he, and not the IOR, should unscramble the financial mess that he had created. Ambrosiano's 'Vatican connection' had turned from a blessing into a curse.

Calvi tried to avoid impending disaster by inviting Carlo de Benedetti, chief executive of Olivetti, to be deputy chairman of Banco Ambrosiano. De Benedetti paid 50 billion lira for 1 million shares in the bank. With 2 per cent of its capital, he would be Ambrosiano's largest single declared Italian shareholder. Calvi's motive might have been to polish Ambrosiano's image both at home and abroad and to encourage foreign banks to resume lending to Ambrosiano. The arrangement was, however, terminated after three months during which de Benedetti encountered 'a wall of rubber' everywhere he turned. It seemed that unidentified forces were manipulating Calvi, and were signaling that de Benedetti's presence at Ambrosiano was intolerable. De Benedetti received calls at home threatening his life and his family. In the style of the Mafia, his children were referred to as his 'little jewels'.

In January of 1982, the procedure for having Ambrosiano listed in Milan's main stock market was initiated and Calvi, having resisted for several months, agreed that Ambrosiano stock should be quoted as soon as possible. The first list of Ambrosiano's main shareholders would also be disclosed at that time. In February, the Bank of Italy stepped up its demand for comprehensive information on every aspect of Ambrosiano's foreign activities. In addition, copies of the minutes of board meetings had to be sent to the central bank, and it vetoed the proposed merger between Ambrosiano Overseas and Artoc to create a single Bahamas bank with a deposit of $1 billion.

In May 1982, the Bank of Italy sent a letter to Calvi which stated that the documents thus far submitted by Banco Ambrosiano showed that the group's lending to 'unspecified third parties' exceeded $1.4 billion. This exposure was abnormally high, and was concentrated in only three banks: Banco Andino in Lima, Ambrosiano Group Banco Commercial in Managua, and Ambrosiano Overseas. Of the total, more than $650 million was provided directly by Ambrosiano Overseas and Banco Ambrosiano Holding of Luxembourg. The latter had given its guarantee for a further $300 million in loans.

A week later, Calvi tried to persuade the IOR to acknowledge its responsibility for the debt, but Archbishop Marcinkus replied flatly that there was nothing to be done. On 11 June 1982 Calvi left for Trieste, then proceeded to Klagenfurt, Austria, and finally to London, traveling with a false passport bearing the name 'Gian Roberto Calvini'. The next morning, the news broke that Calvi had disappeared. Ambrosiano's shares fell by over 15 per cent on Monday, 14 June. Three days later, Italy's leading financial newspaper published the Bank of Italy's letter of 31 May to Calvi. It was to be the last day of trading in Ambrosiano shares – the stock price was half of that of one-and-a-half months earlier, when Ambrosiano shares were first quoted on the main market.

On 16 June, an inventory was taken of the IOR's assets held in Panama:

- 5.2 million shares in Banco Ambrosiano (10.4 per cent of its capital);
- 5.5 per cent of La Centrale, held in the name of two Liechtenstein entities called Zwillfin and Chatoseu;
- 6 per cent of Banca del Gottardo;
- 5,500 shares in Suprafin;
- 2 million shares in Vianini;
- 189,000 shares in Rizzoli;
- 300 shares in Ambrosiano Overseas Nassau;
- 520 shares (52 per cent) of Sorrisi e Canzoni TV.

These were funded by a total of $1,287 million in debt.

Ambrosiano officials argued that the bank had to liquidate at least some of the loans immediately, but IOR spokesmen insisted that the debts were not theirs. A final scheme was put together. It called for the sale of Banca del Gottardo and other assets for $250 million. The IOR was to raise $1 billion through an international loan with maturity of six–seven years. When the loan came due, the IOR would repay it by selling the 5.2 million Banco Ambrosiano shares. On the following day, Cardinal Marcinkus demanded a firm promise that Ambrosiano buy the shares when the loan fell due, and argued that the Vatican could not meet the interest payments of roughly $100–150 million a year or accept the foreign exchange risk involved. On the same day, the board of Ambrosiano was dissolved. It was explained that the Panamanian and Luxembourg companies controlled by the IOR owed Ambrosiano's foreign subsidiaries, especially Banco Andino, almost $1.1 billion, while IOR owed them $200 million directly.

On 18 June, Roberto Calvi's body was found in London.

On 2 July, a meeting was held between Cardinal Marcinkus and Bank of Italy commissioners. Marcinkus continued to deny responsibility. The IOR was not generous with information, and it was assumed that Marcinkus managed to convince the Vatican Chief of Staff, Cardinal Casaroli, and the Pope that the IOR had been deceived by Calvi.

The Bank of Italy ceased assisting Ambrosiano's overseas affiliates in meeting their debts, a decision based on the 'Basle Concordat' among central banks of 1975. The Concordat only obliges a central bank to come to the aid of banks in its own territory or their branches, for which it has regulatory and supervisory authority. It does not oblige a central bank to act as 'lender of the last resort' for bank *subsidiaries* located abroad. In this case, subsidiaries such as Banco Ambrosiano Holding (Luxembourg) and their appendages would not fall under the central bank's agreed responsibilities. The Bank of Italy commissioners also hoped that this uncompromising policy would exert pressure on the IOR, since they realized full well that they were otherwise powerless to act against that institution, representing a foreign bank on foreign soil. Banco Ambrosiano Holding (Luxembourg) collapsed immediately, and the Bank of Italy set about the difficult task of reconstruction of the Nuovo Banco Ambrosiano back home.

In July 1982, the IOR announced the appointment of its own 'three wise men' to examine relations between the IOR and Banco Ambrosiano. The three investigators made clear that the IOR disowned not only the indirect borrowings through Panama 'covered' by the letters of comfort, but the direct ones as well. Although the IOR continued to insist on its innocence in events leading to Banco Ambrosiano's collapse, the Pope made an effort to help the Italian government in coming up with resources to repay Ambrosiano's domestic creditors. In November 1982, he told President Sandro Pertini of Italy of his intention to make 1983 a Holy Year – a surprising decision both because of the short notice and because it was only eight years since the last Holy Year. The secular significance of the decision was that there would be substantial expansion of travel to Rome, and consequently in tourist expenditures which would benefit the Italian economy – an elegant and indirect way to redeem the IOR's 'debt' to Ambrosiano and Roberto Calvi.

In February 1984, Pope John Paul II authorized a 'good will payment' of $230 million by the Vatican to help compensate banks for losses suffered when Banco Ambrosiano Holding (Luxembourg) failed. This payment would be part of a settlement of the $450 million in claims filed by 88 non-Italian banks against the Italian government liquidators. The rest of the money was supposed to come from the sale of Banco Ambrosiano's assets, including Banca del Gottardo in Lugano, Switzerland, which was valued at $100–130 million. Some would also come from funds that were recovered from various Swiss bank accounts controlled by associates of Roberto Calvi. The Vatican insisted that this represented a voluntary payment, and was not in any way an acknowledgement that it was at fault. Wide-ranging speculation about where the unrecovered $1.3 billion ultimately went run the gamut from international arms trading and the 'Bulgarian connection' to a major secret struggle between East and West and the financing of Solidarity in Poland.

The final settlement was signed on 25 May 1984 in Geneva, among over 50 representatives of Ambrosiano's creditor institutions, the Bank's liquidators and the Vatican. The principal sum of the settlement was about $539 million, allocated as follows:

- $406 million to Banco Ambrosiano Holding's creditors, of which

$152 million was paid by the IOR, $144 million from Ambrosiano's sale of its shareholding in Banca del Gottardo to the Sumitomo Bank of Japan, and $110 million from other Banco Ambrosiano Holding assets that retained value;

- $85 million to creditors of Banco Ambrosiano SPA, Milan, involving $50 million from the IOR and $35 million from the sale of back-to-back deposits in Latin American banks at a discount (a $40 million IOR deposit in escrow was available to make up deficiencies in assets covering payments to creditors of the parent bank);
- $8 million to be paid by the IOR to creditors of Ambrosiano's Nassau affiliate.

All claims against the bank's successor, Nuovo Banco Ambrosiano, were dropped, and the settlement represented a loss to creditors of roughly one-third of their claims against Banco Ambrosiano and its affiliates. All further claims against the IOR were likewise dropped.

The IOR reiterated its stand that its overall payment of about $44 million was made voluntarily 'in recognition of moral involvement'. However, it seemed that the Vatican was pressured into accepting this obligation by the Italian authorities and by a writ that had been prepared by the creditors for use against the IOR itself – an unprecedented action. The funds were raised by selling about $160 million of Vatican property and investments in debt and equity securities, and there were rumors that the balance was being raised through a bank loan in the United States. In April 1985 the IOR sold its 51 percent stake in the Banco di Roma per la Svizzera to the Chase Manhattan Bank of New York for about $100 million. Archbishop Paul Marcinkus, meanwhile, remained under investigation in Italy for financial fraud.[38]

While the financial nightmare had apparently been cleared up, the mystery of Roberto Calvi's death – whether suicide or murder – lingered. His financial dealings, particularly his links to the P2 Masonic lodge and its notorious underground political manipulations in Italy, continued to raise suspicions of foul play. Indeed, the story took on new life when a man named Licio Gelli was arrested in Geneva during 1982 while attempting to withdraw $120 million from a numbered account with the Union Bank of Switzerland. The account had been set up by Roberto Calvi, and the arrest brought to light a long association between the two men, as well as Gelli's own unusual past.

From humble origins in Tuscany, Gelli, an early supporter of Mussolini, rose to become grand master of the P2 Masonic lodge, whose membership of 923 included at least three former Italian cabinet ministers, senior officials in the secret service and the military, judges, police chiefs, civil servants, and bankers. Gelli himself evidently developed a significant international pharmaceutical and weapons business, which brought him into contact with Juan Perón in Argentina, and which in turn reinforced his influence in Italy. He allegedly amassed a number of confidential state documents, which were used to blackmail and cajole reluctant participants in his own and P2's causes. Among those influenced was Roberto Calvi, with Gelli protecting Banco Ambrosiano from the early investigations by the Bank of Italy that would have exposed its problems far sooner than they ultimately came to light. On 17 March 1981, a police raid on Gelli's villa near Arrezzo produced a raft of documents that, among other things, helped expose Calvi's fraud, and an arrest order was issued for Gelli on charges of extortion and sedition. Gelli fled the country, probably to South America, only to reappear later in Geneva traveling on a forged Argentine passport.

Gelli's arrest in Geneva triggered an extradition request from Italy. For nine months he was held at the high-security Champ Dollon prison, while receiving various visitors and associates from the old days. Shortly before his extradition was to take place, Gelli escaped by bribing a warden with SFR 20,000, and has not been heard from since. Accounts of the ease of his escape strain credibility, and it is generally assumed that people in high places – in government, financial institutions, and organized crime – feared nothing more than the possibility of Gelli's testimony in Italy. Such testimony might have answered a number of questions about the Banco Ambrosiano affair and the death of Roberto Calvi. Following Gelli's escape, Calvi's son, Carlo, was quoted as saying: 'It goes a long way towards backing my belief that the people who were capable of freeing Gelli were certainly capable of murdering my father.'[39]

The Banco Ambrosiano fallout continued to spread in 1984, with a loss of perhaps $300 million facing the government of Peru. That country's Banco de la Nación had acted as middleman on some $235 million in transfers to the Banco Ambrosiano affiliate in Lima, and the collapse brought law suits by foreign banks against Banco de la Nación. The suits made it difficult for the bank to operate abroad, increasing Peru's already serious international financial problems.

One of the leading characters in the Banco Ambrosiano affair, Frencesco Pazienza, was arrested by customs authorities in New York in March 1985 and held for extradition to Italy. Pazienza had been sought since 1982 to face charges of fraud and misappropriation of funds in connection with setting up dummy companies for Banco Ambrosiano and the $1.3 billion still unaccounted for in the case. He was also sought in connection with his presence in London a few days before the death of Roberto Calvi, who had hired him to help pull Ambrosiano out of the mess in which it found itself and to keep the Italian authorities at bay. Pazienza was apparently well-connected in Italy, including high-level links to the intelligence service and the Mafia.[40]

79

Money laundering

Within the overall structure of demand for international financial secrecy, the laundering of money has probably experienced the most rapid growth. Laundered funds are, by definition, ill-gotten gains.

The need to use money laundries has been necessary for US crooks at least since 1931, when the Internal Revenue Service put Al Capone behind bars for tax evasion. Whereas direct evidence of criminal activity may be very difficult to enter in a court of law, tax evasion cases may be comparatively easier to prosecute. For this reason, money laundries have become big business, involving bank employees, executives, lawyers, accountants and other professionals at all levels. According to one US attorney, government agents running an undercover drug operation '...are getting solicited with all kinds of offers from business and professional people willing to provide them with false documents to give them an apparently legitimate source of income or to avoid taxes.'[41]

Traditionally associated with organized crime involved in the rackets, protection, prostitution, extortion, illegal gambling, and so on, the real growth in laundering in recent years has come from drug trafficking. The volume of international currency movements arising out of drug trafficking appears to be enormous. A recent estimate for the United States puts the figure at $70 billion, which would place it in the top rank among US imports of goods and services. Similarly, Colombia's gross exports of narcotics (mainly marijuana and cocaine) have been estimated at $30 billion, helping that country's bilateral trade surplus with the United States to rise from $500 million in 1974 to over $3 billion in 1983.

In a typical domestically oriented money laundering operation in the United States, a cash deposit is made at a cooperating bank. In return, the bank gives the depositor cashier's checks that do not name the payee. These checks may then be exchanged a number of times in Latin America, Europe or the United States itself to cover a variety of drug-related or weapons-related transactions, for example. The funds tied up in the cashier's checks, of course, earn no interest for the holder and represent 'float' to the issuing bank, which, in addition, may charge a fee of 1–3 per cent for the service. In a 1983 Senate staff study, 24 Florida banks had over 3 per cent of their deposits outstanding in cashier's checks, generally regarded as a sure sign of money laundering. The international component of money laundering has been stimulated by greater government scrutiny of such domestic transactions.

In a typical internationally oriented operation, money is transferred physically or wired to a secrecy haven abroad, where a lawyer creates a shell corporation using standard 'boilerplate' documentation – for a fee. The funds are then deposited in a local bank, probably an offshore bank authorized to undertake transactions only with non-residents, in the name of the new corporation. The corporation next transfers the money to the local branch of a large international bank. The corporation then borrows money from this bank, secured by the deposits, for use in the owner's home country or elsewhere around the world.

The size of the cash hauls can be staggering:

> Federal agents stopped a Learjet as it taxied for takeoff from Fort Lauderdale [Florida], bound for Panama. They confiscated nearly $5.5 million in cash. A subsequent search of the home of one of the passengers yielded 62 pounds of cocaine valued at $18.5 million, 15 weapons, including a submachine gun, and $40,000 in counterfeit bills.[42]

Take the case of Eduardo Orozco Prada, who deposited over $150 million in cash with about 18 banks and foreign exchange firms, mostly in New York, for transfer to Panama, the Cayman Islands, the Bahamas, and in various accounts distributed around the United States. Most of the money apparently was from drug trafficking. The laundry operation also involved Orozco's interests in small businesses in a variety of countries in Europe, the Middle East and Latin America, as well as major currency exchange businesses in Colombia and several other countries in the region. Described as a '... well educated, sophisticated, highly intelligent professional, with all the trappings of a legitimate businessman',[43] Orozco enjoyed the support of many legitimate business people and senior-level Colombian politicians.

Once established in New York, Orozco set up a company called Cirex International at 120 Wall Street, which in retrospect was clearly a money laundering operation. Over a four-month period, he placed $2.3 million in cash deposits with a Swiss bank until it refused to take any more, and subsequently with the Marine Midland Bank & Trust Company and the Irving Trust Company, both in New York. The cash evidently came from his own exchange houses in Colombia, either via Miami or via Panama using couriers and occasionally planes of the Colombian Air Force – on average about $3 million monthly. Cash transport was difficult and risky, but necessary to avoid FBI surveillance of South Florida banks and to avoid the cash-deposit fees charged by some of them. The deposits were then transferred after varying periods of time to accounts in other banks by wire, and were thus effectively laundered.

Apparently the laundering operations were highly sensitive to the investigative activities of the federal authorities. In 1980 and 1982, Orozco was doing substantial business with the currency exchange house of Deak-Perera in the name of Interdual, a Panamanian affiliate, and Dial Securities. Unlike other laundry operations that find ways to avoid filing the US government's Currency Transaction Reports on domestic deposits and withdrawals or Currency or Monetary Investment Reports on international cash and securities movements (see Chapter 5), Orozco's transactions always were in compliance with the law, yet difficult or impossible to trace because of the use of other people's names and never making a cash deposit himself. Intermediaries were evidently paid 25 cents per $100 cash deposit, with possible further payments to bankers to see that funds were transferred without delay. By mid-1981 his deposits at Deak-Perera were running at $10–12 million a month and were beginning to attract an unusual amount of attention.

In his search for yet another bank, Orozco fell into a Drug Enforcement Agency trap. Subsequent fund movements through third parties were tracked – mostly deposits of $10 and $20 bills, totaling $15 million over an 18-month time span. Tape-recorded conversations confirmed that most of it was drug-related money, with a 3 per cent laundry commission probably earned by Orozco and possibly large additional gains from acting as a principal in the drug trade itself – yet he never physically came into contact with the drugs. In 1983 Orozco was found guilty of drug law violation and sentenced to one year in prison and a $1 million fine; he was immediately released on $2 million bail pending appeal.[44]

Money laundering also played an important part in the 1984 'pizza connection' case, a multimillion-dollar Sicilian-run heroin operation that used pizza parlors as fronts in various parts of the US well outside the established crime centers, and employed orders for various pizza ingredients as codes for narcotics trafficking. Funds were mainly transferred through Swiss accounts, and law enforcement officials became suspicious when one of the central figures was moving far more money than was justified by his bakery in New York.[45] According to a US attorney,

He was, for a guy in the bakery business, depositing a tremendous amount of cash [representing] a highly sophisticated means of investment and money laundering. Multimillions of dollars were transferred from the United States to Switzerland and Italy for payments of past and future heroin shipments, and for investment in legitimate and illegitimate enterprises there.[46]

Money laundering has attracted large numbers of otherwise respectable people who evidently see nothing wrong in being accomplices to crime. Take the case of Richard McConnell, a former trial attorney in the US Justice Department's Tax Division from 1967 until 1971, and subsequently in private practice in Alexandria, Virginia. On behalf of a client named Julian Penell, McConnell used his firm's escrow accounts to deposit large sums of cash, which were withdrawn in short periods and paid to newly established US corporations or trusts set up in the Cayman Islands. In this way, over $30 million of Penell funds were moved during a seven-year period without filing federal currency reports. These funds, it turned out, came from marijuana and hashish operations in which 20 people, including Penell, were charged and later convicted. McConnell, charged under a racketeering statute, claimed he was 'used', and that the Cayman trusts were intended to help Penell's heirs (his age at the time was 38) avoid estate taxes in the US. He, too, was convicted, along with another lawyer in the case.[47]

Lawyers appear confident of using their privileged relationships with clients to shield themselves from prosecution in such cases. Bankers can hide behind dense layers of bureaucracy and blame misconduct on lower-level employees. But once the activity becomes large and greed gets the better of caution, defenses may fall by the wayside. Another lawyer named Nathan Markowitz, previously an SEC attorney, paid the officers of a Los Angeles bank to take in large cash deposits without the required federal currency reports, funds that were subsequently wired to Bermuda trust accounts controlled by Liberian companies and re-lent to US corporations established for his clients. The loans, as laundered funds, were used for payment of salaries, pensions and other expenses. In a tape-recorded conversation offered in evidence by the government, Markowitz offered drug-related services directly on imports from South America: 'I can give you buys, if you have to buy it down there ... I can give the airstrips. I can give you guys that, press it, package it. I can give you the street [dealers] ... I've done it for those people for years.'[48] His bullet-riddled body, with over $50,000 in cash in his pocket, was found in a Los Angeles parking garage on 3 April 1981. Even for lawyers, the laundry business can be hazardous to health.

In the United States, money laundry activities have clearly been concentrated in Florida, where forgery, bad checks, credit card fraud and highly questionable banking practices are by-products of clandestine cash flows and a go-go environment that has attracted 'scoundrels' from all over the world. A report of the US Comptroller of the Currency confirmed that Florida can lay undisputed claim to having by far the largest number of bank crimes in the United States. An estimated 75 per cent of narcotics enters the US through Florida, perhaps as much as $50 billion annually, with net contributions to the Florida economy of over $10 billion a year – all in cash, which is either counted by high-speed machines or simply weighed (300 lbs of $20 bills = $3.6 million). Sloppily dressed Latin couriers have regularly deposited shopping bags full of small denomination bills in smaller Florida banks, commonly known as 'Coin-O-Washers'. On one occasion, '... the teller questioned a shopping bag woman about the source of her money, which reeked of fish. She dropped the bag and ran, leaving $200,000 behind.'[49] Estimated violations of federal currency reporting requirements in Florida ran to the tune of $3.2 billion in 1981 alone.

The South Florida drug and money laundering business has also given

83

rise to enormous demand for legal services, including 25 or so top drug lawyers who practice mostly in Miami and defend individuals accused of narcotics-related crimes. In 1982 the federal court in Miami handled more cases than the federal courts in Boston, New York, Philadelphia, Chicago and Washington, DC combined. Business for the lawyers began to pick up in the mid-1970s, when the narcotics business was increasingly taken over by Colombians, and kidnapping, murder and related offenses were added to drug charges, smuggling and money laundering – at one point the Miami morgue had to rent a refrigerator truck to handle the overflow. Legal defense in such cases is highly lucrative, visible and creative, sometimes involving constitutional issues argued before the US Supreme Court. It is also dangerous if the client is promised too much or the lawyer is not performing up to expectations – in 1980 Miami attorney George Gold was gunned down in a still unsolved case, possibly by one of the Colombian hit men who are available for only $500 a contract (plus expenses).

Legal tactics rarely produce an acquittal, but endless technical and procedural motions to suppress evidence or wear down the opposition often pay off. A client of Miami attorney Joel Hirschhorn '... was arrested after an airplane loaded with hundreds of pounds of cocaine touched down at a rural Florida airport at 3 a.m. and taxied to his car. He was charged with conspiring to import cocaine. His first trial ended with a hung jury. The jury in the second trial found him guilty. Mr. Hirschhorn then persuaded the judge to set the verdict aside on grounds of insufficient evidence.' In another case, '... a Miami prosecutor recalls watching Mr. Hirschhorn move a jury to tears over a murderer. It was an airtight case, he says, but he began to worry when the jury was crying, the defendant was crying, and Joel was crying.'[50] That case nevertheless ended in a conviction.

A fascinating look into the financial aspects of drug trafficking emerged in early 1984, in connection with a Bahamian Royal Commission inquiry into official corruption. High officials in the government were accused of receiving bribes of over $100,000 a month in order to 'overlook' an elaborate drug smuggling base complete with aircraft hangars and maintenance facilities, helicopters, speedboats and armed guards. Although the charges were vehemently denied, it seemed unlikely that they were entirely groundless in a country that is highly dependent on the drug trade and related financial flows.

In 1983 and 1984, the President's Commission on Organized Crime held hearings throughout the United States, and naturally developed a strong interest in money-laundering channels. Acting on the suspicion that the Deak-Pereira Company, a major foreign exchange dealer, had laundered over $100 million since 1969, an effort was made to obtain testimony from the firm's chairman, Nicholas L. Deak. He refused to testify, and the Commission had no subpoena powers at the time. Some organized crime members did testify, however, and disclaimed any knowledge of money-laundering activity. For example, 70-year-old Aladena (Jimmy the Weasel) Fratianno of Los Angeles said he knew little – organized crime chiefs 'don't keep no records' but instead 'rely on front men they can trust'.[51] Nevertheless, Commission investigators turned up a number of money-laundering cases by big-time criminals, including $95.7 million brought by one individual to a Manhattan Deak-Pereira office in May 1981 in the form of small denomination currency notes packed in cardboard boxes.

The activities of fugitive US swindler Robert Vesco appear to be made possible by secret money flows as well, in connection with an alleged drug-running and trade-sanctions-busting business jointly operated with the Cuban Intelligence Service.

Vesco helps arrange for shipments of heroin, cocaine and marijuana from South America to Cuba, has it transferred to smaller boats and planes there, and delivered to the U.S. and Canada. The money is laundered through offshore banks, and the Castro government is said to get payments per large boatload of drugs. Vesco also helps Castro get American goods, which the U.S. prohibits selling to Cuba. In exchange, [he] gets safe harbor in the workers paradise, living quarters at a yacht club and in a beach house near Havana, and his profit.[52]

International undercover activities

Governments need regular financial channels to implement foreign policy, some of which must necessarily be kept secret. National policy may dictate the financial support of a friendly government abroad, yet the existence of that support may be an embarrassment (or worse) to its recipient. Alternatively, national policy may require financial support of groups seeking to promote change in another country or even to overthrow the established government of a sovereign state with whom the home country may or may not have diplomatic relations. Intelligence services need money to finance their activities and to pay local operatives around the world. In all such cases the financial transactions involved, which may be highly complex and involve multiple currencies and intermediaries, must be kept from the public eye. Geopolitics and regional conflagrations, superpowers and surrogates, purchases of embargoed weapons and salaries of contract mercenaries, financial resources of dissident groups – the need for secret money covers a broad range of players and games.

An interesting case that wound its way through the 1960s and 1970s in Switzerland involved Algeria.[53] In the course of less than ten years, and through a labyrinth of facts and legal proceedings, a war chest of approximately 40 million Swiss francs that was built up by the Algerian National Liberation Front (FLN) evaporated.

In June 1962, the FLN created a provisional political bureau to operate until a government would be appointed by a proper assembly. Mr X was Secretary General of the provisional bureau, with full responsibility of the FLN's finances. In October 1962, Mr X opened an account in his own name with the Banque Commerciale Arabe SA (BCA) in Geneva. By signing the agreement with the bank, Mr X acknowledged that the legal relationship between himself and the bank would be governed by Swiss law. In addition to opening an account, Mr X also signed the account agreement twice – as the person solely authorized to dispose of the account, and also as the person in whose name the account was held.

In April 1963, Mr X resigned from the position of FLN Secretary General, but indicated a willingness to retain his financial responsibilities. In September 1963 the new Algerian constitution was adopted, and the FLN's finances became the property of the Algerian Republic. Mr Y became the new Secretary General of the FLN. He subsequently sent a letter to BCA in Geneva, notifying the bank that he would now be the 'sole person legally entitled to dispose of the funds and revenues of the FLN'. In March 1964, Mr X changed the account opened in his name with BCA to a numbered account – BP 510. He also asked to have all correspondence retained at the bank. A new FLN political bureau was formed in April 1964, which no longer included Mr X. Instead, Mr Z was given responsibility for finance.

On 12 June 1964, Zouhair Mardam Bey, the administrator of BCA, met with Mr Z and agreed that some account details should be altered. Between 18 June and 1 July 1964, Mr X withdrew 99.6 per cent of the funds in his account at BCA. Curiously, starting on 22 June 1964, four numbered accounts related to the case were opened at BCA by one or more unknown clients. On 6 July 1964, Messrs Y and Z sued Mr X and the BCA administrator for a breach of trust. A civil sequestration order was placed on account BP 510, and two days later the civil order was replaced by a criminal one. In November, the court ordered Zouhair Mardam Bey to hand over the files relating to the four numbered accounts. The latter, standing on Swiss banking secrecy, refused to comply with the court order. He also refused to cooperate with any investigation that would prove the existence of these accounts even if the anonymity of the account holders would be respected. Mr X was assassinated in Madrid on 3 January 1967.

In February 1971, the Swiss Court of First Instance ruled that the defendants in the case should pay the Algerian Republic the sum of SFR 39,246,851.80 with interest at 5 per cent from July 1964. The court determined that the FLN alone was the depositor and that Mr X acted only as a representative. The repayment to Mr X was viewed as the bank's error. The defendants appealed to the Court of Justice of the Canton of Geneva. In June 1973, this court confirmed the judgement of the Court of First Instance. In July 1974, the Swiss Federal Court annulled the decision of the Court of Justice and rejected the demands of the Algerian Republic.

Three key questions were asked by the Federal Court in arriving at its verdict: (1) Was Mr X the account holder, or was he acting on behalf of the FLN under the terms of agreements that the bank should have observed? (2) Given that the bank was not unaware that the money really belonged to the FLN, was it able to accept instructions from Mr X? and (3) Should the existence of a dispute between Mr X and the FLN have led the bank to oppose Mr X's instructions?

There is a legal device in Swiss law known as the 'third party open account'. This states that the person represented (in this case the true owner of the money – the FLN) has no claims against the bank. If the bank was unaware of Mr X's political problems, it could not, and should not, have refused to follow his instructions. Under the Swiss law, Mr X had full power over the funds involved, and could use or alter the account as he wished. The purpose of the meeting between Mr Z and the BCA administrator on 12 June 1964 should have been taken as a verbal revocation of Mr X's power. If a civil or criminal sequestration order were used, proceedings against Mr X would have been possible. Although both civil and criminal sequestration orders were used in this case, Mr X withdrew the money before they became effective. The Federal Court therefore found that BCA was not only able to return the deposits to Mr X, but was also obliged to do so.

A rather different case involved the now-defunct Australia-based banking group, Nugan Hand. In its heyday, over $1 billion reportedly passed through Nugan Hand each year.[54] Bank executives were evidently engaged in major weapons shipments to certain forces engaged in the Angola civil war, sale of a US intelligence vessel to Iran, extensive dealings with heroin syndicates, and related deals. Suspicions also emerged that Nugan Hand was heavily involved with clandestine dealings for the CIA – suspicions reinforced by the number of ex-CIA and US military officials who were employed by the firm or who had extensive dealings with it. The Nugan Hand group collapsed (with losses of over $50 million to depositors) shortly after its chairman, Frank Nugan, was found shot to death in his car on a deserted Australian road in 1980 – an apparent suicide – and his partner, Michael Hand, fled the country.

In February 1985, the government of Ireland seized a Bank of Ireland account valued at $1.65 million, allegedly containing IRA money obtained through bank robberies, kidnappings and death threats, as well as donations from IRA sympathizers in North America. There were reports that the IRA intended to use the funds to complete a large international arms deal. Fearing that the funds would be transferred outside the Republic's jurisdiction, an emergency law was enacted to permit the Dublin government to seize the funds. The money had allegedly traveled from Ireland to Switzerland and then back to Ireland. If the funds remained unclaimed for six months, they would revert to the Irish state. Sinn Fein, the political wing of the IRA, denied that the account contained IRA money. More generally, it was feared that the seizure would cause a fresh round of bank robberies, kidnappings and extortion demands designed to replenish the IRA resources.

Testimony by former IRA members, during a 1983 Brooklyn gun-running trial, also confirmed that the IRA regularly moves secret money between the US and Ireland. Since 1970, the Irish Northern Aid Committee of New York City (NORAID) has channeled $2–3 million – collected in the humble surroundings of Irish pubs and testimonial dinners – through An Cumman Cabhrach, a relief organization in Dublin. The testimony revealed that most of the funds found their way into the hands of the IRA, and that at least half of the money was sent back to the US to purchase weapons.[55]

Summary

The examples cited in this chapter should suffice to convey an impression of the level of complexity imbedded in the demand for secret money. Tax evasion is almost a mortal sin in some countries, severely punishable in others, and a national pastime in still others – while the incentives to evade are equally varied. Capital flight is no less complex in terms of its motivation and consequences facing individuals and countries alike. Neither tax evasion nor capital flight is likely to wither away as economic incentives, ingenuity and human nature continue to clash with the machinations of politicians frustrated by authority that stops at the national border. Both require secrecy that provides effective shelter from taxation under the law of sovereign states abroad, shelter that is likely to remain rather durable.

Bribery and corruption, fraud, the drug trade and other criminal uses of international financial secrecy likewise have their own unique demand patterns, which attract often vigorous law-enforcement attention and considerably greater cooperation among countries. Yet they continue to thrive. The levels of secrecy they require command a high price, and, where such demand emerges, supply cannot be far behind. Still, while the direct perpetrators are often hardened criminals who raise major law-enforcement challenges for the authorities, the money launderers are quite different in how they do business and in their attitude toward risk, and this may provide an effective indirect route for the application of pressure on the criminals.

Each class of secrecy customer demands, and is willing to pay for, a unique class of secrecy products that carry different price tags. The characteristics of suppliers of these products will be explored in the following chapter.

Notes

1 Carl Reich, *Financier: The Biography of André Meyer* (New York: William Morrow & Company, 1983).
2 *Ibid.*
3 William H. Davidson, *The Amazing Race* (New York: John Wiley & Sons, 1983).
4 'The Unions' Desperate Move to Stash Funds Offshore', *Business Week*, 17 December 1984, p. 50.
5 Peter Gumbel, 'West German Bureaucrat Who Blew Whistle on Flick Scandal Had to Fight His Superiors', *Wall Street Journal*, 27 March 1985.
6 Lenny Glynn and Peter Koenig, 'The Capital Flight Crisis', *Institutional Investor*, November 1984, p. 304.
7 'An Exodus of Capital is Sapping the LDC Economies', *Business Week*, 3 October 1983.
8 See Thomas N. Gladwin and Ingo Walter, *Multinationals under Fire* (New York: John Wiley & Sons, 1980), chapter 5.
9 See *New York Times*, 19 January 1984.
10 'Sensible Lotsen', *Der Spiegel*, No. 20, 1984.
11 Lenny Glyn and Peter Koenig, *op. cit.* (n. 6), p. 305.
12 Michael Newak, 'Black Markets in Foreign Exchange', *Finance and Development*, March 1985. See also Chris Sherwell, 'Indonesia Cleans up its Ports and Customs', *Financial Times*, 12 June 1985 for an account of bribery and corruption in that country's ports and terminals, and the Indonesian government's recent efforts to deal with it.
13 Lynda Schuster, 'Argentines Find Tax Avoidance an Untaxing Job', *Wall Street Journal*, 21 August 1984.
14 *Ibid*, p. 9.
15 'Italian Shopowners Dodge Effort to Curtail Rampant Tax Evasion', *Asian Wall Street Journal*, 28 November 1984, p. 6.
16 'Härtere Gangart', *Der Spiegel*, No. 34, 1984, pp. 68–9.
17 Alan Murray, 'Cheating Uncle Sam', *Wall Street Journal*, 10 April 1984.
18 'Tax Havens and Funk Money', *International Currency Review*, Vol. 15, No. 2, pp. 15–35. See also Walter H. Diamond and Dorothy B. Diamond, *Tax Havens of the World* (New York: Matthew Bender, 1984).
19 'Greeks Join the Chorus', *The Economist*, 1 October 1983.
20 *Newsweek*, 22 August 1983.
21 Felix Kessler, 'Legal Tug of War over Marc Rich & Co. Centers on Small Swiss Town of Zug', *Wall Street Journal*, 15 November 1983.
22 Dan Baum, 'U.S.–Swiss Accord on Marc Rich Papers is Snarled Over Terms of Pact', *Wall Street Journal*, 3 July 1984.
23 *New York Times*, 20 September 1983.
24 *Ibid.*
25 'Marc Rich and Firm's Other Top Officer Won't be Extradited to U.S. Swiss Say', *Wall Street Journal*, 13 December 1984, p. 30.
26 *Business Week*, 5 September 1983.
27 John Vinocour, 'A Trail of Western Technology is Followed to the KGB's Door', *New York Times*, 25 July 1983.
28 *Ibid*, p. A6.
29 Quoted in Joseph Fitchett, 'High-Tech Smuggling Risks are Slight', *International Herald Tribune*, 22 May 1984.
30 *Ibid.*
31 Joseph Fitchett, 'Technology Bandit Led Ring for Russia', *International Herald Tribune*, 5 February 1985.

32 'Information Greases Mergers, Challenges Courts and Media', *Wall Street Journal*, 2 March 1984.
33 Henry Manne, *Insider Trading and the Stock Market* (New York: John Wiley, 1966).
34 Frederick M. Muir, 'Can Investors Get any of $150 Million back from J. David & Co.?', *Wall Street Journal*, 21 March 1984.
35 'House of Cards', *Wall Street Journal*, 29 October 1984, p. 20. See also Arnold H. Lubasch, 'Promoter is guilty in $445 Million Tax Fraud', *New York Times*, 26 April 1985.
36 'Colombia Battling Chase over Missing Money', *New York Times*, 15 November 1983. See also 'The Chase is on for a Telex from Bogota', *The Economist*, 13 April 1985.
37 For a detailed discussion, see Rupert Cornwell, *God's Banker* (London: Victor Gollancz, 1983).
38 Alan Friedman, 'Ambrosiano Settlement Signed by Bankers', *Financial Times*, 26 May 1984.
39 As quoted in *The Sunday Times*, 14 August 1983, p. 11.
40 E. J. Dionne, 'New Hope for Clues in Italian Scandals', *New York Times*, 25 March 1985.
41 Robert E. Taylor, 'Laundry Service', *Wall Street Journal*, 25 July 1983.
42 Shirley Hobbs Scheibla, 'Where Hot Money Hides', *Barrons*, 11 July 1983.
43 *Ibid*. See also 'Chasing the Peso Leaves Argentines Breathless', *Business Week*, 10 June 1985.
44 James Cook, 'Everybody's Favorite Laundry Man', *Forbes*, 5 December 1983.
45 'An American Connection', *Newsweek*, 15 October 1984.
46 'Mafia Portrait: Aging Leaders and New Competitors', *New York Times*, 4 October 1984, p. B12.
47 Robert E. Taylor, *op cit*. (n. 41).
48 *Ibid*.
49 Penny Lernoux, 'The Seamy Side of Florida Banking', *New York Times*, 5 February 1984.
50 Thomas E. Ricks, 'Drug Lawyer', *Wall Street Journal*, 25 June 1983.
51 Selwyn Raab, 'Financier Declines to Testify in Cash-Laundering Inquiry', *New York Times*, 15 March 1984.
52 'Partners in Crime', *Forbes*, 24 September 1984, p. 42. See also Gladwin and Walter, *op. cit*. (n. 8), chapter 7.
53 See Eduard Chambost, *Bank Accounts: A World Guide to Confidentiality* (New York: John Wiley & Sons, 1983), chapter 9.
54 Jonathan Kwitney, 'Nugan Hand Acted in Covert Operations of U.S. Government', *Wall Street Journal*, 21 August 1983.
55 'IRA Funds Seized', *New York Times*, 18 February 1985.

4

Supply of Secret Money

In the financial secrecy business, demand creates its own supply. People have always hidden wealth – from their neighbors, from thieves, from their rulers. Mattresses, caves, loose bricks in basement walls, hollow tree trunks, and holes in the ground have provided financial secrecy services for centuries.

With the advent of sovereign states, and the ability to transfer financial resources between them, came the possibility for secrecy seekers to solicit protection offshore. The principle of sovereignty of states insures that foreigners will have limited insight, strictly controlled by domestic law and policy; anything more is politically unacceptable. So the likelihood of disclosure to private parties in the asset-holder's home country is minimal, while disclosure to home-government authorities in civil and criminal cases is a matter for intergovernmental negotiation and treaties. Since countries differ widely in their political and economic systems, and in their interpretation of what constitutes unacceptable behaviour (within their own borders and abroad), there is ample opportunity for the provision of financial secrecy in the international environment.

While it is clear that national sovereignty is the foundation of international financial secrecy, it is equally clear that some countries are well known as secrecy 'havens' whereas others are not. Some are quite willing to accommodate investigations by foreign governments, whereas others fiercely resist them. And some actively solicit the secrecy business. Why? The answers are found in international differences in law and policy, and in perceptions of economic costs and benefits.

Elements of supply

Some countries have more onerous tax systems than others, perhaps because of a strong social aversion to differences among people in income and wealth, or because of a powerful preference for the state over the private sector in the allocation of resources. The tax system is used as a vehicle for implementing such policies, and taxes drive a wedge between risk and return, between effort and reward as faced by individuals in society as a whole. Symmetry may exist at the level of society, but it is certainly lacking at the level of the individual.

The feeling in many countries is that their governments cannot be held responsible for the consequences of the taxation systems of others. And if they stand to benefit in the process of simply safeguarding their own sovereignty, so much the better. So tax investigations launched in one country may well be received in others with a singular lack of sympathy or cooperation, unless two countries have comparable tax arrangements or other forms of reciprocity and have negotiated mutual financial insight. Tax havens thus abound in virtually all parts of the world. Table 4.1 provides a listing of countries regarded as tax havens by the US Commissioner of Internal Revenue. Given the global reach of the American tax system as far as its own citizens are concerned, this listing is likely to be quite comprehensive.

Going beyond tax matters, countries that supply financial secrecy in criminal cases have a somewhat more difficult time justifying their actions on grounds of national sovereignty. As we have seen in the

Table 4.1 *List of countries or territories regarded as tax havens*

Caribbean and South Atlantic	Europe, Middle East, Africa
Antigua	Austria
Bahamas	Bahrain
Barbados	Channel Islands
Belize	Gibraltar
Bermuda	Isle of Man
British Virgin Islands	Liberia
Cayman Islands	Liechtenstein
Costa Rica	Luxembourg
Falkland Islands	Monaco
Grenada	Netherlands
Montserrat	Switzerland
Anguilla	
Netherlands Antilles	*Asia-Pacific*
Nevis	Cook Islands
Panama	Guam
St Kitts	Hong Kong
St Lucia	Maldives
St Vincent	Nauru
Turks and Caicos Islands	Vanuatu
Uruguay	Singapore
	Tonga

Source: Letter from Roscoe L. Egger, US Commissioner of Internal Revenue, to Sen. William V. Roth, Jr, 2 November 1981. Tax havens are defined as having little or no income tax and high levels of banking and commercial secrecy.

previous chapter, the criminal dimensions run from securities law violations and fraud to the rackets, gun running and the drug trade. However, a crime may not be considered a crime unless it is committed on the territory of the host country, which makes financial disclosure associated with criminal offenses committed abroad difficult to justify under virtually any circumstances. An alternative position is that disclosure is warranted *only* if a crime committed abroad is also defined as a crime in the host country. Here a case has to be made that the appropriate domestic due process and the associated legal tests are satisfied, which may not be easy in many instances and impossible in cases such as bribery and corruption, exchange control avoidance, securities law violations and antitrust infringements. Of course, arm-twisting can be exercised if the country where the crime has been committed has sufficient bargaining leverage. Host countries have on occasion been known to bend their own rules.

Patterns of secrecy supply

Secrecy is basically supplied by countries in two ways. One is domestic bank secrecy laws, which bar insight by national and foreign authorities alike. The other is blocking statutes, which effectively prevent the disclosure, copying, inspection or removal of documents located in the host country in compliance with orders by foreign authorities. Moreover, legal depositions may not be taken on national territory in connection with judicial proceedings being undertaken abroad. A variety of countries other than those usually identified as tax or secrecy havens have comprehensive blocking statutes to guard their sovereignty from the extraterritorial reach of foreign authorities. These include the UK, France, South Africa, West Germany, Australia, Norway and Canada.

Beyond the 'passive' supply of international financial secrecy by simply enforcing national laws and regulations, a number of countries have become very active sellers of secrecy services. Why? Predictably it is largely a matter of economics.

Countries with very small, open economies have often embraced the financial secrecy business as a way of promoting economic development. With some notable exceptions, these countries tend to be geographically isolated, with narrow production bases concentrated on a few major commodities, usually destined for export. This tends to make them vulnerable to adverse climatic conditions and international market developments. It also limits their ability to produce efficiently for the domestic market, invest in adequate infrastructure, attract foreign direct investment, and gain access to a diversified mix of export markets and import suppliers. Such economies face extremely restricted choices in mapping out a viable development strategy, choices that generally focus on geographic location, weather conditions, and human resources. Tourism is one example of an industry that such countries often turn to in the search for economic development.

Efforts to become a financial center can take two forms. One is to become a 'functional' center, where transactions are actually undertaken and value-added is created in the design and delivery of financial services. Examples of functional centers include London, Singapore, Bahrain, and Hong Kong. The other is to become a 'booking' center, where transactions are recorded but the value-added involved is actually created elsewhere. Examples in this category include the Bahamas, Cayman Islands, Seychelles, and Vanuatu. In order to attract financial booking business, one prerequisite is a highly favorable tax climate alongside a benign regulatory and supervisory environment. Clearly, strict financial secrecy or blocking statutes can play an important part in determining a country's attractiveness as a financial booking center. The benefits include induced employment, fiscal contributions, and positive linkage effects to firms and industries that service the financial sector. Unfortunately, the size of these benefits in most cases appears to be quite small.[1] However, if the marginal cost of creating a favorable secrecy environment is equally small, the number of such centers is bound to remain significant and may grow.

Of particular interest is the supply of financial secrecy for criminal purposes, which characterizes some (but not all) of the major vendors. According to one US study,

> Africa, Central America and the Caribbean Islands are the areas most vulnerable to involvement in politically corrupt or direct criminal matters where suitable control is not exercised by headquarters [of US banks]. Of these three regions, the Caribbean Islands are characterized as the most vulnerable in the world. That appraisal conforms ... to our impression of gross inadequacies, improper influence, and reported criminal involvement in the Caribbean involving some banks, local officials, assorted travelling highwaymen, narcotics traffickers and the like.
>
> Headquarters standards vary depending on the company and the homeland's central bank. Variations occur within the same banking company among its branches in offshore locations. For example, in the Caribbean, one major Canadian international bank has a consistent reputation for encouraging dirty money. One shell branch of a UK bank in the Bahamas is held suspect for its own manager's discretionary tolerance in accepting questionable funds. In the Caymans or Panama, the majority of banks are said to accept suitcase currency.[2]

One relatively new example is Vanuatu, a tiny Southwest Pacific

94

island nation, formerly the joint French–British colony of New Hebrides. With a population of 125,000 scattered across some 80 islands, Vanuatu has attempted to promote itself as a financial center by selling political stability, the lack of exchange controls, the absence of estate, death and income taxes, adequate communications, and limited financial disclosure. Lately it has made a special effort to attract capital from Southeast Asia, the Caribbean, and especially Hong Kong by allowing shareholders of registered companies to remain anonymous, with no requirements for character references or checking of Interpol criminal suspect lists. Annual financial audits are optional, as are notifications of ownership changes as long as the enterprise does not conduct business in Vanuatu itself. This does not apply, however, for banks, insurance companies, trust companies, and securities dealers.

Or take the Kingdom of Tonga, which passed an offshore banking act in 1985 providing for *pangike fakapulipuli* (secret banking) and thus joined Vanuatu, Nauru and the Marshall Islands as a Pacific haven located about 2000 miles east of Australia. With only 270 square miles of territory and a population of 87,000, Tonga's finance minister was quoted as envisaging offshore banking as 'the fastest and easiest means, even surpassing tourism' to enhance foreign exchange earnings.[3]

Many of the countries that sell financial secrecy can be described more or less in these same terms. Secrecy is simply good business in an environment where alternative routes to economic growth are severely limited. This applies to a much lesser extent, of course, to countries like Switzerland and Austria, although the underlying economic incentives are much the same. To illustrate, we can briefly survey the patterns of secrecy in a number of countries around the world.

Switzerland

Financial secrecy in Switzerland is an outgrowth of that country's long tradition of personal and individual privacy – a tradition that dates back at least as far as the age of feudalism. The legal foundation of Swiss bank secrecy is based on the personal rights established in the Swiss Constitution, the Civil Code and the Code of Obligations, supplemented by provisions in the Criminal Code. There is, in addition, the Banking Law of 1934, which was enacted partly in response to the financial crises of the early 1930s, but also as an attempt to deal with the Nazis' investigations into Jewish accounts in Switzerland. It provided for severe criminal penalties for violators of disclosure prohibitions, and made Swiss secrecy laws among the toughest anywhere. However, the Banking Law of 1934 did not include a definition of bank secrecy. Instead of narrowly defining secrecy by legal statute, definition is left to custom and practice, and to judicial discretion.

The origins of Swiss federal laws to protect the silence of bankers themselves can be traced to 1916, although utmost discretion on the part of the Swiss banking community vis-à-vis foreign authorities extends much further – certainly to capital flight associated with the Edict of Nantes and the French Revolution. In the 1930s, Swiss bankers were insisting that their privileged relationship to clients should be on a par with clergymen, physicians and lawyers. The 1934 law basically accepts this view by making it a federal crime to breach the confidential relationship between client and banker. Such action, willful or negligent, on the part of any present or former bank employee is subject to a fine of up to SFR 50,000 and imprisonment of up to six months. Those who induce such action, or attempt to do so, face a fine of up to SFR 30,000. Revision of the Swiss Banking Law in 1982 dropped this last provision, and eliminated negligence as a basis for prosecution of bank employees under the law. It is worthwhile pointing out that there has been no negligence case brought before the Swiss courts in decades. 'Inducements' related to political or economic espionage are covered under other sections of the Swiss penal code.

Specifically, Article 47 of the Swiss Banking Law provides that:

1. Whoever divulges a secret entrusted to him in his capacity as officer, employee, mandatory, liquidator or commissioner of a bank, as a representative of the Banking Commission, officer or employee of a recognized auditing company, or who has become aware of such a secret in this capacity, and whoever tries to induce others to violate professional secrecy, shall be punished by a prison term not to exceed six months or by a fine not exceeding 50,000 francs.
2. If the act has been comitted by negligence, the penalty shall be a fine not exceeding 30,000 francs.
3. The violation of professional secrecy remains punishable even after termination of the official or employment relationship or the exercise of the profession.
4. Federal and cantonal regulation concerning the obligation to testify and to furnish information to a government authority shall remain reserved;

Moreover, Article 273 of the Swiss Penal Code provides, in part:

Whoever makes available a manufacturing or business secret to a foreign governmental agency or a foreign organization or private enterprise or to an agent of any of them, shall be subject to imprisonment and in grave cases to imprisonment in a penitentiary. The imprisonment may be combined with a fine.

Unless waived by the client, or by the application of a treaty, these provisions are generally strictly enforced, even against disclosure requests by foreign law-enforcement agencies.

Moreover, Swiss authorities in general take a very dim view of any kind of unauthorized disclosure of business information, even when 'whistle blowing' is clearly in line with the country's own international commitments and obligations. Take the case of Stanley Adams, a former executive with Hoffman-La Roche, the Swiss pharmaceutical firm. As manager of Roche's international vitamins operations, Adams discovered an array of company tax-avoidance schemes involving transfer pricing, as well as price-fixing arrangements in EEC countries that were in direct violation of the Community's competition law – to which Roche was accountable under a 1972 Swiss–EEC trade agreement. Based upon Adams' disclosure, Roche was indicted and convicted in a court action brought by the Community's antitrust division. Once his disclosures came to light, Adams himself was jailed in Switzerland for industrial espionage. Informed that her husband faced 20 years' imprisonment, his wife committed suicide while he was being held without formal charges. The EEC eventually provided bail, and Adams fled first to Italy and then to the UK. In Switzerland, according to Adams, 'whatever affects big business affects the state'.[4]

A 1984 example of the sensitivity of the Swiss system to possible disclosure involved the Wozchod Handelsbank, the Soviet Union's principal gold trading vehicle, operating in Zurich. The bank's chief trader and foreign curency dealer (a Swiss) was accused of fraudulent activities that cost the bank anywhere between $36 million and $350 million in losses, eventually resulting in the bank's liquidation and its replacement in Zurich by a branch of the Soviet Foreign Trade Bank. He was dismissed and charged with criminal mismanagement. However, given the size of the fraudulent operations it was clear that a number of the bank's other employees were involved as well. All were fired, but the matter of potential disclosure was considered sufficiently sensitive that no criminal charges were brought against them.

Since the body of laws covering secrecy is rather loosely defined, Swiss banks and their employees generally exercise extraordinary caution, and do not release information unless explicitly required by judicial act. Moreover, Swiss secrecy laws apply not only to bank–outsider relationships, but also to bank–government and bank–bank relationships. For example, the acknowledgement of the *existence* of an account is a direct violation of the law, even if it is between employees of two different banks.

The opaque nature of Swiss banking creates weaknesses as well, which surfaced in the Chiasso affair in April 1977. The Chiasso branch of Crédit Suisse failed in its fiduciary responsibilities. Instead of investing clients' funds in the Euromarket with top-tier financial institutions, the manager of the branch lent heavily to an Italian wine and food group, whose profits were quickly eroded by high interest rates and depreciation of the lira. The resultant losses were covered by Crédit Suisse itself, backstopped by the other two major Swiss banks. This case nevertheless pointed up the 'moral hazard' to which each of them was exposed by virtue of the degree of secrecy embodied in the system.

The question was how to enhance the safety of Swiss banking without sacrificing the attributes, including secrecy, that give it strength. The outcome was a *Vereinbarung* (gentlemen's agreement), which signaled a tightening of control over banking operations and an end to simple self-discipline as the major guiding force in Swiss bank treatment of customers. In addition to a passport, depositors interested in a Swiss account today should be prepared for a fairly exhaustive series of interviews. At Union Bank of Switzerland, for instance, there's an initial screening followed by a lengthy chat with an investment counselor who will seem to be evaluating the depositor's investment philosophy, but who will also be trying to find out whether there are reasons for concern about his legitimacy.[5] Moreover, the Federal Banking Commission has increased the number of bank audits, instituted a wider range of monitoring activities, and issued guidelines on how banks are to manage fiduciary funds.

Given the nature of Swiss personal banking, people choose to deposit funds in Swiss banks for several reasons, some having nothing at all to do with secrecy laws:

- the well-known competence and integrity of Swiss bankers and their standing in the international banking community;
- the 'financial supermarket' nature of the vast range of services that Swiss banks can provide for a client;
- the ability of the depositors to place liquid assets in Swiss francs or other currencies as a hedge against inflation and currency fluctuations;
- the freedom from exchange controls, government regulations and interference in banking activities; and
- virtually unparalleled political stability.

For example, an American wishing to avoid the US gift tax on amounts exceeding $10,000 may legally do so by making that gift abroad, and Switzerland is probably as good a place as any. Moreover, Swiss banks may execute transactions on the basis of telephone instructions and, unlike some other banks, can offer a broad range of trust, investment and related services. Swiss accounts can be opened by mail, although the establishment of a relationship through personal contact or formal introduction appears to be more common. Swiss banks maintain that they do undertake background checks in cases where questions arise, but the frequency or depth of such checks is unknown.

Despite periodic lapses such as the 1977 Chiasso affair and a few others, Swiss banking – based more than other systems on self-regulation by bankers of their own affairs – has a track-record of careful and prudent management, perhaps at some cost to short-term earnings. For example, Swiss banks stayed largely clear of the international debt crisis of the early 1980s by limiting exposure in developing countries, concentrating on short-term trade financing and loans guaranteed by the Swiss government. In part, their cautious behaviour may have been attributed more to strict capital ratios than to self-discipline, and in 1984 the Swiss banking authorities imposed on them the requirement to disclose their international exposures semi-annually on a consolidated basis by domicile of the borrower and guarantor (if any). Additional data will also have to be provided on international assets and liabilities with respect to both banks and non-banks, as well as on their foreign exchange operations and forward commitments.

From the point of view of secrecy seekers, the Swiss image may benefit as well from the elaborate precautions the country has taken for the possibility of nuclear war. The objective is to provide a modern nuclear fallout shelter for every resident of Switzerland, in cities, towns, villages, even farms, by the year 2000. Since 1970, Switzerland has spent over $2.5 billion on its shelter program, far more than any other country on a per capita basis, and all new homes (including vacation chalets) must have fallout shelters. The government pays half the cost. A large standing military, mandatory conscription, and high level of civil defense preparedness completes the Swiss readiness effort.[6] The idea is to give Swiss citizens a better than average chance of survival in the event of nuclear war, which perhaps not coincidentally bolsters its image as a safe haven for outsiders' funds. What would be left of the real assets backing Swiss deposits in the event of catastrophe is of course open to question. On the other hand, large numbers of depositors certainly would no longer be around to collect.

Secrecy laws, of course, provide an important additional incentive for people to place funds with Swiss banks. The use of numbered accounts, *Aktiengesellschaften* (stock companies), personal holding companies, and 'base' companies are a few of the available vehicles. And the location of Switzerland itself, with outstanding transportation and communication facilities, makes it easy to slip funds into and out of the country without attracting undue attention. Much of the business remains in the hands of the 'Big Three' – Crédit Suisse, Union Bank of Switzerland, Swiss Bank Corporation – although numerous smaller players obtain a respectable share. Competition among them appears to be 'gentlemanly'.

There is a close connection in the supply of financial secrecy between Switzerland and Liechtenstein, a small principality of 65 square miles with a population of 22,000 permanent residents. Bank secrecy in Liechtenstein rests on the Company Law, enacted in 1926. This allows for the formation of several kinds of corporations such as the *Aktien-*

gesellschaft, the *Stiftung* (family foundation), the *Anstalt* (establishment) and various kinds of trusts. Most such forms of corporate organization are openly referred to as 'dummy' or 'paper' corporations, used to hold or transfer assets while at the same time protecting them from tax liabilities.

The *Anstalt* is the most popular form of corporate association and is unique to Liechtenstein. These are non-share corporations, which have a limited liability and initial capitalization of at least SFR 20,000. Once the corporation is formed, the capital can be immediately repatriated to the owners. Many *Anstalten* are set up in Switzerland by a Swiss banker, who arranges the formalities through a Liechstenstein banker or lawyer. They are always listed in the Public Register, but this does not require disclosure of the name of the *Anstalt*'s owner. Only the Swiss banker, and possibly the lawyer in Liechtenstein, know the owner's true identity. In addition to the bank and legal fees, a tax of only $\frac{1}{10}$ per cent of the initial capitalization is levied in Liechtenstein. This Liechtenstein–Switzerland connection or relationship is often described as the best and possibly cheapest means of securing privacy and anonymity for an international investor.

'If you've got $10,000 or $20,000 go to Citibank', one Swiss banker has noted. 'We can't help you and you can't help us.' While the major Swiss banks say they do not have a formal minimum for opening a numbered account, most discourage deposits under $50,000 and interest develops only well into six figures. Minimum deposits in Swiss accounts can be substantial. As of 1984, for example, the minimum deposit at Bank Leu was $10,000. Current accounts bear no interest at all. Deposit accounts yielded $3\frac{1}{2}$ per cent in 1984, with withdrawals of up to SFR 20,000 monthly without notice and two months' notice required on larger withdrawals. Investment accounts yielded 4 per cent with up to SFR 10,000 in withdrawals possible every six months, and six months' notice required on larger amounts or subject to a penalty charge of 1 per cent. Comparable US accounts at the same time yielded between two and three times as much. Obviously, exchange-rate expectations must be taken into account in comparing returns, as well as the likelihood of future interest-rate changes. It is sometimes forgotten, for example, that Switzerland imposed severe penalties on foreign account holders in the mid-1970s in order to discourage capital inflows – only the first SFR 50,000 of deposits were eligible to earn interest, and accounts in excess of SFR 100,000 incurred a negative interest of 40 per cent. Swiss deposits are also subject to an interest withholding tax of 35 per cent, of which 30 per cent will be rebated if the account holder is not a Swiss resident.

In 1983, the 564 banks in Switzerland had SFR 626 billion on their balance sheets, of which about SFR 200 billion of deposits were foreign-owned. In addition, they had SFR 181 billion in fiduciary accounts off the balance sheet, of which SFR 167 billion were foreign-owned.[7] However, private banks are not required to publish balance sheets if they do not advertise their services, and their deposit balances are not included in these totals – nor are their fiduciary accounts. Moreover, the figures on the size of fiduciary accounts in general are highly suspect, and may in fact be much larger. No information is available by country of origin or by geographic region of account holders.

Overall, Swiss banks retain a very strong competitive position in international private banking. This has resulted from time to time in massive capital inflows, far out of proportion to the size and performance of the Swiss economy. A large part of these inflows is placed directly in foreign and offshore financial markets, with the Swiss banks acting as financial intermediaries for their clients. Net income from these activities made possible fifteen uninterrupted years of Swiss current-account payments surpluses, ending in 1980.

Portfolio management activities contribute positively to the Swiss economy in several ways, including the increased leverage in world financial markets by Swiss banks. In 1981, the assets of the top 71 banks in Switzerland were valued at $200 billion, more than twice the Swiss gross national product. Commissions on portfolio management accounts supplement income derived from traditional lending business. Bank fees are earned on fiduciary, discretionary and non-discretionary accounts, in addition to ancillary fees for brokerage commissions, cable transfers and other services that are normally for the account of clients (and sometimes irk them). There are also gains from ancillary services, such as real estate, hotel accommodation, transportation and the like. While banking employs only about 13 per cent of the labor force, the services sector as a whole employs over half. The local availability of bank secrecy, moreover, discourages hoarding by Swiss citizens, who are free to avail themselves of the banks' services.

Still, the Swiss regard themselves as a much broader financial center (*Finanzplatz Schweiz*), rather than merely as a tax or secrecy haven. For one thing, Switzerland does not charter offshore companies. Swiss-registered companies pay taxes on income, and must have local directors. As noted earlier, Switzerland levies a flat-rate 35 per cent withholding tax on dividends and interest (mostly rebatable to non-residents), the highest of any nation, and there was a proposal to tax fiduciary accounts at a flat rate of 5 per cent withheld at the source (now defeated). To the dismay of the Swiss, it is in areas of finance *other than* private banking that Switzerland has steadily lost ground as a world-class financial market to the greater dynamism and innovativeness of London and New York, as well as to the rapidly evolving centers of the Far East.

Financial markets have changed dramatically in the past decade and the Swiss have been slow to keep up. While bankers in London, New York and Tokyo have been developing new services, Switzerland has continued to rely on its traditional strengths of security and secrecy. For example, the Swiss have had a difficult time figuring out how to court a new type of international investor, pension funds. Although the Swiss never had the most competitive rates, they adroitly catered to wealthy foreigners who wanted safe investments kept away from the local taxman. 'They were happy if you got them a room at the St. Moritz Palace Hotel,' commented one financier. This approach has been rather ineffective with pension funds.

Switzerland has lagged in developing futures and options trading, as well as in the application of computer systems to banking operations. Although there has been a plan to develop options and Eurofranc futures, it was not scheduled to be in place until 1986. Analysts have felt that this is much too slow.

Swiss financiers also blame their declining relative importance on the government's decision to tax a wider range of securities transactions. This has put Switzerland at a disadvantage in competition with other world financial markets. In the international bond market, for example, where the Swiss were dominant just 15 years earlier, there has been a shift of activity to London, where 80 per cent of new international bonds were underwritten during 1984. Switzerland underwrote only 12 per cent.

It is feared that the long-running tussle with the SEC and other foreign authorities seeking to crack Swiss financial secrecy (see Chapter 5) will remain a problem in future years. Switzerland's high profile and international reputation, it can be argued, attract more attention than smaller centers, so that those who seek secrecy will increasingly seek it elsewhere.

Swiss financiers have responded to these challenges by building up operations outside of Switzerland. For example, Union Bank of Switzerland has greatly strengthened its activities in London as the only way to be a major force in the Euromarket. And Swiss portfolio managers have moved some of their business to London as well as the Cayman Islands and other havens.[8]

Increasingly, Switzerland's niche in the international financial scene is indeed based on private banking and management of financial assets. Recent scandals like the failure of Leclerc & Cie in Geneva (1977), Weisscredit in Ticino (1977), Crédit Suisse (Chiasso) in 1977, the involvement of Banca del Gottardo (Lugano) in the Banco Ambrosiano affair (discussed in the previous chapter), and Banca della Svizzera Italiana (affiliated with the Irving Trust Company of New York) in 1984 have failed to make a major dent in the Swiss reputation for sober banking behavior, good sense and high-quality service.

However, the massive inflows of capital have also had some adverse effects on the Swiss economy. The most obvious disadvantage is the periodically severe overvaluation of the franc. Swiss real estate and

securities became very expensive for foreigners, and domestic inflationary pressures have intensified from time to time. The competitiveness of Swiss exports has thus been impaired, only partially offset by the
reduced cost of imports.

Although illegal funds (other than tax evasion and flight capital) probably constitute only a minuscule fraction of foreign holdings in Swiss
banks, they have become a hot political issue. The Swiss are obviously
sensitive to international criticism of their system and its alleged role as
an important 'facilitator' of criminal acts committed worldwide.
Although Swiss banks certainly cannot be considered guilty of encouraging or advocating the underlying illegal activities, the available supply
of financial secrecy still leaves the country open to charges of aiding and
abetting illegal operations through scrupulous protection of all banking
transactions, regardless of their nature.

Swiss banks' 'guidance' of political flight capital is, indeed, alleged to
be substantial, particularly through Panamanian branches. According to
CIA estimates, over 150 wealthy Brazilians were thought to have moved
about $14 billion into Swiss accounts during periods of economic
difficulty in that country in the early 1980s. President Julius Nyerere of
Tanzania publicized a proposal from one Swiss bank detailing how he
could best shift his financial resources to Switzerland. Overall, it has
been estimated that the amount of flight capital in Swiss banks was
around SFR 100 billion in 1984.[9]

Swiss bankers object that really dirty money has no place in
Switzerland, since either the client himself or his Swiss lawyer must be
known to the bank, and since secrecy is not airtight in cases of investigations of offenses that are defined as being criminal in nature under Swiss
law. They point to Austria as offering much greater anonymity (not even
a passport is required to open an account). As for tax evasion, Swiss
bankers point to excessive taxation in other countries as the primary
cause, and also maintain that they do not actively solicit funds that are
involved in evading taxes or currency controls. Besides, they argue,
there is no obligation for them to collect other people's taxes.

Following President Mitterrand's election in France in 1981, large
amounts of funds began to flow into Geneva's banking community.
Estimates of the French share of funds under management by Geneva
banks range from 50 to 80 per cent, although some put it much lower.
Others suggest that French capital flows into Geneva during the two
years after Mitterrand's accession exceeded all comparable flows during
the seven years of President Giscard d'Estaing's rule. Overall, the
amount of French funds in Swiss accounts has been variously estimated
at between $3.75 billion and $60 billion.[10]

The French reaction included an enormous beefing-up of manpower
on the Swiss border, especially around Geneva, including 800 new
customs officers and the assignment of a number of fiscal operatives to

Switzerland itself, even though a good deal of the funds transfers are undertaken not in person but rather via commercial transactions.

In 1983, the French fiscal authorities let it be known that they had cracked the computerized account data codes of the Union Bank of Switzerland (UBS), and had identified about 5,000 French citizens holding Swiss accounts in violation of French tax and foreign exchange regulations. UBS vehemently denied this, and suggested that the disclosure was a French bluff to elicit admissions of currency smuggling under promise of leniency. In a statement, a UBS deputy director general emphatically maintained that 'The lists are false or fabricated by French customs because we do not keep records of account holders by nationality'. The French State Secretary for the Budget replied, 'The French Customs Service has existed for 250 years. It is not in the habit of fabricating false evidence. There are no forgers in the Government ... The Customs Service has its methods. We have computer experts who know their job.'[11]

The information ostensibly came to the attention of the French authorities in the form of computer print-out, with military cryptographers taking the lead in decoding, yielding the account number, the amount, and the name of the account holder. The French Finance Ministry then ran the names (not identified by nationality) through its computerized income tax files.

However, since tax dodgers may request that any correspondence be held at the Swiss bank, to be picked up personally, it seemed unlikely that the French claim to be able to trace addresses was entirely accurate. Indeed, the official story – as opposed to the press accounts – put the amount of money involved at only $22 million, with 300–400 named account holders ferreted out in part by fiscal agents who physically followed French citizens across the border and, in one case, were arrested and spent two months in a Swiss jail before being released. Even the Greeks got into the act. On the basis of information about the infamous French 'list', the Greek government evidently made overtures to acquire the names of Greek citizens with Swiss accounts.[12]

Besides the perennial issue of tax evasion, Swiss financial institutions have also been cited in connection with the export of restricted high-technology products from the US to the Soviet Union. In 1983, for example, a US court ordered Crédit Suisse to provide information on the financial affairs of an American client accused of illegal exports. Crédit Suisse appealed on the grounds of Swiss secrecy provisions, but the US courts denied the appeal, citing that the alleged crime was neither tax evasion nor a political offense, but rather an outright criminal action involving forged bills of lading and an evasion of American export control legislation.[13]

Swiss authorities and Swiss bankers argue that a large number of conventions for cooperation in legal matters have been concluded between

Switzerland and other countries since World War II, and that this indicates their desire to eliminate abuses of bank secrecy by criminals. But, as noted, any such cooperation is predicated on the concept of 'bilateral culpability', which means the activity under scrutiny must be a crime in Switzerland itself to fall under the terms of applicable legal assistance conventions. Unfortunately for other countries' authorities, many of the offenses committed by their citizens using Swiss accounts to hide illegally obtained funds are not in fact illegal in Switzerland, including tax evasion and securities law violations.

The Swiss have no desire to become involved in law enforcement on behalf of the rest of the world, and have taken a strong position that appropriate enforcement activity at home would discourage illegal use of Swiss accounts. They also argue that it is unfair to criticize or condemn Switzerland when other nations permit similar kinds of banking activity, and that increased disclosure in Switzerland would simply encourage the use of other secrecy havens.

Unlike their stonewalling efforts to obtain cooperation when the laws of other countries are involved, the Swiss are very agile indeed in defending their own interests abroad. Richard Keats was accused in 1982 of dealing in and transporting counterfeit US securities with a face value of over $5.5 million, and later was also accused of placing millions in counterfeit US and foreign bonds with European banks. In Switzerland he was accused of borrowing about $5 million using counterfeit bonds as collateral. When he was finally located in Malaga, Spain, the Swiss were the first to successfully seek his extradition, and also extradited two of his cohorts from other countries. One European detective noted that 'It was clearly a case of them beating the U.S. to the punch. They are very good about getting things done when their own money is involved'.[14]

In the aftermath of the 1977 Crédit Suisse scandal, a Convention of Diligence (*Sorgfaltspflicht*) was signed by all of the major Swiss banks, and by all except three of the smaller ones. The Convention, a private agreement between the Swiss National Bank and the Swiss Bankers' Association, prohibits signatories from doing business without knowledge of the identity of the counterparty – whether such business involves accepting cash or securities deposits, fiduciary activities, or the use of safe-deposit boxes. It was extended in 1982 to cover withdrawals by clients of amounts in excess of SFR 500,000. Clients may still avoid registering their names with a bank by having a professional lawyer, notary or certified auditor do it for them, but this individual must declare that he knows the principal personally and is not aware of any abuse of financial secrecy for criminal purposes. Only banks, and not the bankers themselves, can be punished under the Convention, with fines up to SFR 10 million. Alleged violations are brought before a three-man committee that meets in Lausanne, and can impose fines of up to SFR

10 million. These fines are paid over to charity, and the cases heard by the committee are not made public. As of 1983, 30 cases had been quietly brought under the Convention, with the largest fine being SFR 500,000.[15] A proposal has been made to extend the fines to bankers as well.

The Swiss banks fought the Convention vehemently prior to its 1977 enactment, but subsequently have used it as the major justification for not deeming additional legislation to be necessary, representing it in effect as a certificate of morality.

Nevertheless, the same 1977 Chiasso scandal induced the small Swiss Social Democratic Party to introduce a formal *Bankeninitiative* (bank initiative) which would have, through referendum: lifted bank secrecy in certain tax evasion cases, whether at home or abroad, and in evasion of exchange controls; broadened disclosure in bank financial statements, which would also be extended to hidden reserves, and allowed discussions of these statements in parliament; limited bank ownership and control of non-banking enterprises; and instituted insurance for savings deposits. Under the *Bankeninitiative*, foreign fiscal authorities would have been permitted to examine Swiss bank records in cases of tax evasion and currency violations.

The Social Democrats had been calling for reforms in the Swiss banking law for more than a decade, but this did not receive significant public support until the Chiasso affair, followed coincidentally by the rapid and economically damaging appreciation of the franc. In the aftermath of the scandal, the party leadership argued that the Swiss currency was chronically overvalued because of secrecy-seeking capital inflows, and that the country had become a haven for the ill-gotten gains of corrupt foreign dictators, criminals and tax evaders from all over the world. Although the Swiss population appeared to accept only part of this argument, public confidence in the banking industry did seem to be called into question.

The Social Democrats' *Initiative* was opposed by both the government and the Swiss parliament, but was nevertheless scheduled to be put to a referendum vote in the summer of 1984. No previous Social Democrat *initiative* has passed since 1917, although many of the ideas embodied in them have eventually found their way into law.

In June 1984, after over five years of discussion, Swiss voters rejected the *Bankeninitiative* by a 3–1 margin. To some extent the *Initiative* had been pre-empted by the tightening of regulatory and supervisory controls over Swiss banks, and by the banks' leading role in bailing out domestic recession- and competition-plagued industries such as watchmaking. But besides that, a major exportable service was clearly at stake, one the average Swiss was not about to let slip away.

The Swiss banks mounted a massive public relations campaign, variously estimated to have cost around SFR 15 million, to defeat the

106

effort – including such tactics as comic books aimed at preschoolers to convince them of the value of Swiss banks. Even knowing that not more than half of Swiss voters usually turn out for referendums, and then usually vote 'no', the banks wanted to achieve at least a 60 per cent vote against the proposal to prevent the issue coming up again anytime soon. Their arguments included that erosion of secrecy would limit human rights, increase unemployment, trigger a crash in the stock market, and threaten the prevailing low interest rates on home mortgages. The banks maintained that they had no interest in retaining 'dirty money', variously estimated during the campaign as comprising SFR 8–100 billion – not including funds attributable to tax evasion, capital flight, evasion of exchange controls, and other motivations that are not considered illegal in Switzerland. They also maintained that a significant tightening-up of the Swiss banking system, including disclosure of more detailed financial information to the Swiss National Bank and the implementation of a self-financed deposit insurance scheme to cover savings and salary deposits, was already under consideration before the *Initiative* was put on the agenda.[16]

Following the defeat of the referendum, the chairman of Crédit Suisse was quoted as saying that the banks' opponents had actually '… rendered a valuable service not only to the Swiss banking industry, but to the whole economy and to the future of our country.' Bankers' expectations appeared to be that substantially greater inflows of funds would result, including those of institutional investors seeking 'to be safe from indiscretion and surreptitious or malicious prying', and an uncharacteristically competitive battle seemed to be heating up among the major Swiss banks for institutional business.[17]

For their part, the Social Democrats continued to press their case even in defeat, fearing that the outcome of the referendum would be considered a license for Swiss banks to promote tax evasion and flight capital around the world. One approach appeared to be inclusion of the aforementioned code of conduct agreed by the Swiss National Bank and the Swiss Bankers' Association, which expires in 1987, in a revision of the 1934 Banking Law. Such proposals seem likely to continue, especially in the light of apparent dissatisfaction with 'loopholes' allegedly existing under the voluntary arrangements, dissatisfaction expressed by the Swiss National Bank itself.[18]

An interesting alternative explanation for the *Bankeninitiative* emerged as well. It goes as follows: contrary to popular impression, the Swiss themselves are fairly heavily taxed, especially on earned income (salaries and wages) and on wealth – a particularly sensitive issue when yields on assets denominated in Swiss francs have generally been very low. Consequently, many Swiss are themselves tax evaders through the country's own system of banking secrecy. Those supporting the Social Democrat's initiative were really after their own countrymen rather than

107

the foreigners or the bankers. This is why the initiative received as much support as it did. Otherwise, the theory goes, to shoot oneself in the foot through a concerted attack against a major export industry makes no sense.

It thus seems clear that the referendum is hardly the end of the story with respect to debates in Switzerland on bank secrecy in both its practical and moral dimensions. The Swiss bankers' traditional complacency and arrogance may have been shaken a bit in the debates, and in the doubt they may have raised in the minds of ordinary citizens about flagrant abuses of bank secrecy. Certainly continued friction with other governments will keep the issue very much alive. Nor will the problem of secrecy rules in tax, exchange control, and similar cases go away. The agreement not to actively encourage capital flight and exchange-control evasion and to take reasonable care in client identification will in all likelihood be subject to pressure for further strengthening and perhaps for greater formalization – as will disclosure practices concerning the financial condition of the Swiss banks themselves.

Indeed, the reform of Swiss banking practices through voluntary action by the banks themselves may be coming to an end. Markus Lusser, the general manager of the Swiss National Bank, indicated in 1984 that '... he felt more could be done to stop Swiss banks from aiding and abetting capital flight from abroad. The monetary authority wants to see the banks draw up some kind of code and intends not to renew the existing good-conduct agreement with the Bankers' Association when it expires in 1987.[19] More strongly, the Minister of Finance called for a categorical ban '... on active support for transfers of this kind, saying that bank secrecy should not become a carte blanche for tax evasion' and advocated 'a possible strengthening of the links between the Swiss Banking Commission and its foreign counterparts'.[20]

Caribbean and South Atlantic

Over the years, the Caribbean has become an area abundantly supplied with secrecy havens. The reasons are several. Proximity to the United States is one consideration, supplemented by political risk constrained by vital US interests in the region and the ease of communication with the rest of the world. Geographic location is also important for attracting Latin American flight capital, as is its fortuitous positioning astride one of the world's major drug routes. And there is the matter of economic development, with most of the Caribbean countries being very small island economies dependent on tourism and primary products, plagued by a lack of options to promote economic growth. Under the circumstances, the financial secrecy business has a great deal to recommend it to planners seeking economic progress. Some examples follow.

Antigua

Antigua has become independent, but is still within the British Commonwealth. It is heavily dependent on tourism, lacks natural resources, and has a substantial amount of external debt. No registration requirement is imposed on the establishment of new banks or companies. No assets must be on deposit, and there is no vetting or screening of applicants. An attorney simply presents registration papers and fees, and within a few days the new enterprise has been officially formed.

Antigua has no explicit secrecy provisions, but the government does not know who the beneficial owners of registered companies and banks are because of incomplete or non-existent records. The lawyers involved may know only who forwarded the fees to them, and not on whose behalf they have acted. Moreover, there is no supervision of licensed banks. Antigua has been considering adoption of formal offshore banking legislation with secrecy provisions, and faces a choice of competing with the Cayman Islands for US secrecy business or cooperating with the US authorities. It is felt that, with reasonable US commitment to developing Antigua's banking and company law and general economic development assistance, the country would cooperate in inhibiting criminally tainted funds flows, and in revoking licenses for offshore companies engaged in criminal activities. Antigua may also establish its own central bank through a conversion of the East Caribbean Currency Authority.

Bahamas

The Bahamas lie only 50 miles from the US shore. Tourism contributes about 70 per cent of GNP. There is no significant local market economy, and $6 out of every $7 of national income is spent on imports from the US. Distribution of income is highly uneven, with high per capita incomes only in Nassau. There is a large underground economy, primarily engaged in narcotics traffic to the US.

Eurodollar assets held in the Bahamas exceeded $100 billion in 1982, with 330 banks and trusts licensed to do business. Between $2 billion and $5 billion in trust business was administered out of Nassau, 95 per cent of which represented accounts of foreigners. The importance of banking to the Bahamas is primarily defined in terms of the local employment it creates. Between 1,200 and 2,000 Bahamians are engaged in the financial services industry, and the banking sector accounts for 13–15 per cent of GNP. It provides training, as well as the introduction of high-technology data processing and communications facilities.

For about $1,000, any attorney can create a company quickly and easily in the Bahamas. The attorney has no obligation to evaluate the applicant's credentials, character or motives, although reputable

109

lawyers and bankers supposedly will not accept applicants without prior evaluation. The law does not require screening or any reporting of company assets. The Bahamas central bank functions well, but does not engage in the supervision or regulation of financial institutions.

Bank secrecy has been covered by criminal law in the Bahamas since 1979, although Bahamian law does provide for the lifting of bank secrecy when an attorney petitions the Supreme Court for a court order to release requested documents. Conditions under which such documents may be released are:

- the foreign authority must show that a crime has been committed, proof of which hinges on the requested documents;
- a crime is suspected, proof of which rests on the requested documents; or
- criminal proceedings are already under way abroad.

These conditions pose a dilemma for prosecutors. If enough evidence existed to indict, there would be no need for the requested documents.

The United States government has periodically complained about lack of Bahamian cooperation in criminal information requests. The Bahamas response has been that:

- US agencies are ignorant of the means easily available under Bahamian law through which lifting of bank secrecy can be allowed;
- very few US requests for information are made, and, since the requests are so few, there is no evidence of American criminal involvement in the Bahamian system;
- the US is exporting the responsibility to the Bahamas for its own failures in prevention, detection and prosecution of domestic crime; and
- US banks and firms sometimes vouch for American parties engaged in Bahamian financial business.

The Bahamian government has somewhat changed its policy on foreign tax matters, and now requires that foreigners engaged in the 'tax haven' business obtain local work permits. These are granted sparingly, and the result has been a shift of some banking and other business from the Bahamas to the Cayman Islands.

Bermuda

Overall, Bermuda has a very low crime rate and no notable corruption. The major offshore business is insurance, followed by trust-like personal investment companies. These activities together account for about 40 per cent of GNP. Tourism is also important as an income source, but

110

planning for future economic development focuses more on the expansion of financial activities.

A good relationship with the US and other countries is recognized as being fundamental in Bermuda's success. Accordingly, Bermuda makes every effort to prevent any use of offshore financial activities by criminal elements. It screens new applicants for offshore business and personal investment companies. The screening is done via referrals of major banks, law firms and insurance companies internationally, supplemented by monetary authority supervision. Like Switzerland, Bermuda has no criminal law governing tax evasion, nor will it violate confidentiality in tax cases.

There are 5,500 offshore trading companies registered in Bermuda, each of which must have local directors who are Bermudans responsible to local authority. Exempt companies must be audited, and directors are held responbile for due diligence in supervision. Management of personal investment companies must also be local, although actual ownership can be foreign.

There is no secrecy law in Bermuda backed by criminal sanction, although a wrongful disclosure statute exists. Confidentiality rests largely on the statutes governing how companies are formed. In either local or exempt companies, nominees may hold shares on behalf of others, and both banks and law firms do in fact hold such shares. Shareholders are obliged to have personal knowledge of beneficial owners, and, in the event of any change in beneficial ownership, the monetary authority must be notified. The monetary authority in turn is obliged, except under court order, not to disclose the names of beneficial owners of record, and it requires all applicants for exempt company status to be recommended by well-known foreign banks and institutions. Small private bank references are not acceptable, since the authority knows that the applicant himself may be the concealed owner of the recommending bank – as can occur with St Vincent, Anguilla or Montserrat banks. The authority also has a computer file of information on all past applicants and on all present owners of exempt companies. Companies in which the applicant has had an interest are on file as well.

Cayman Islands

The Cayman Islands, 475 miles south of Miami, probably represent the prototypical tax haven. The local economy is quite stable, and there is an absence of racial tension, poverty and high unemployment. The bank secrecy laws appear on the surface to be more stringent than even Swiss law. A person can be jailed for inquiring about a bank customer's private holdings and financial activities. No one is allowed access to account information, or the identities of depositors, unless a court order is issued on the basis of suspicion of criminal activities.

111

Montserrat

Montserrat is a British colony. The government has had a balanced budget, and the country is socially stable, without significant unemployment. The economy focuses on tourism, customs and excise taxes, property tax, stamp sales, light assembly plants, offshore companies and banking. The government hopes that future development will be focused in the agricultural and industrial areas. The relationship between local officials and foreign law-enforcement personnel is characterized as mutually cooperative, with generally free exchange of information on all criminal, bank and company matters.

Montserrat has three commercial banks, 66 offshore companies operate as banks, and various other offshore companies act as trusts. Licensing fees contribute 5 per cent of annual government income. Montserrat's offshore banks do not perform the usual interbank Eurocurrency or trust functions. Instead, they are caricatures of Eurobanks – unregulated, anonymous, international, and private. Local officials are aware that their banks are used for tax evasion, criminal fraud, and other illegal activities. Nevertheless, it is claimed that the licensing of questionable offshore facilities is a short-term measure that is needed to raise fiscal revenues. If substitute funds were available for budgetary purposes – for example, the development of the agricultural or industrial sectors, or financial assistance from abroad – local officials have indicated that Montserrat would immediately shed its offshore banking industry.

A 1976 banking statute was enacted to bring a semblance of bank licensing and control to Montserrat, at least in terms of language and administrative procedure. Since that time, a series of patchwork amendments have been added to the statute. There are no bank secrecy laws as such, nor is there a general body of coherent banking legislation. English common law provides for financial confidentiality, and a confidential information statute holds that communication between clients and professionals is privileged. However, this statute does not apply to information in the possession of the government, including that submitted by lawyers and banks.

In theory, the government should have at its disposal all information about beneficial ownership and activities of all companies and banks. Although the statute implies that information can be disclosed only with the assent of the Attorney General, a foreign authority can request information directly from Montserrat government records, and there are no statutory constraints on the Montserrat government that restrict transmittal to the requesting authority.

However, in Montserrat, what the law says and what really happens appear to be quite different.[21] Confidentiality is actually guaranteed in Montserrat by inefficiency and lack of record-keeping and enforcement instead of by secrecy laws. There are further difficulties in getting information because of a lack of competent personnel and investigative resources. The nature of the situation comes through in the following quotations from local officials:

> One is not even able to serve notices on anyone ... [and] since we do not even have the addresses of the companies ... a company may exist without any connection whatsoever with the government of Montserrat, not even an address.

> The annual [information] requirement applies to banks as registered companies, but in fact no annual returns have been submitted for many years, either for local or for offshore companies, in this territory. Furthermore, with respect to companies registering upon application, in principle the names of all shareholders must be submitted. However there are many cases on file where the names submitted are in fact the local lawyer acting on behalf of an unidentified applicant ... No-one knows who in fact the shareholders or owners are, and there is no apparatus for checking or enforcing ...

> Local banks do not need to publish their balance sheets. The government has no proof of assets of any kind.

> Whatever the requirement may be under the law, bank owners have sold banks without informing the government, so that one may not, in fact, know who a new owner is.

> No-one knows who is supposed to know who the beneficial owners are and, in any event, there is no-one to look.

> The mechanism does not exist to ensure that a person named as a beneficial owner is, in fact, the beneficial owner.

> Notification is required upon change of 25% or more ownership, but this is theoretical since there is no enforcement ... There is no department or individual responsible for processing licence applications.

> Far from being a haven with respect to secrecy, Montserrat is entirely open concerning the language of the confidentiality law ... But confidentiality is guaranteed by inefficiency.

> No-one has any idea what banks are engaging in trust business. The best that can be said is that by making it a matter of statute, it will appear that one has tried ... We are in despair of the law here ever meaning anything. Regarding banking law, the whole thing is a shambles. Not a single banking company in Montserrat is lawfully constituted. Companies and banks are out of control. No-one knows who they are, or what they do.[22]

Netherlands Antilles

One of the most active Caribbean tax havens is the Netherlands Antilles. Under a 1948 tax treaty between the US and the Netherlands (later extended to the Antilles), 'residents' were exempt from most of the 30 per cent US withholding tax on interest income paid to foreigners, until its repeal in 1984. A US borrower could therefore establish a Netherlands Antilles 'paper' corporation, undertake borrowings from foreign lenders, and remit the proceeds to the parent corporation. Interest payments were then made by the US parent to the Antilles captive finance company, essentially free of withholding tax, and subsequently remitted to the ultimate lender – likewise free of all but minimal local taxes and registration fees, which amounted to less than 1 per cent.

From 1974 to 1980, $18 billion in Eurocurrency debt was raised by US corporations in this manner. In 1981 it was $7 billion and in 1982 $14 billion. Of the 30,000 corporations registered with the Curaçao Chamber of Commerce, 25,000 were owned by foreigners in 1983, including such giants as Citicorp, Sears Roebuck and General Motors. The benefits of the reduced interest costs were passed on to the firms' shareholders and to consumers in the form of higher returns and lower prices. Even the US Federal National Mortgage Association proposed a Euro-financing through the Netherlands Antilles 'window', but this was blocked by former Treasury Secretary Regan in March 1983. In 1981, a total of $1.4 billion was paid by US residents to entities in the Netherlands Antilles, exceeding by far that paid to any other country. This is estimated to have grown dramatically in 1982 and 1983, and probably understates the actual amounts by a wide margin.

While the role of the Netherlands Antilles, with a population of 250,000, has loomed large in US corporate finance because of a legal anomaly – one that was removed once the US scrapped withholding taxes on interest paid to foreigners in 1984 – the real concern is its use as a conduit for criminal funds and tax evasion by American residents. Drug traffickers, organized crime, tax protestors, and promoters of abusive tax shelters have been named in this connection. And foreign residents can invest in the US and repatriate earnings through the Netherlands Antilles without paying American taxes.

Prominent among the objects of such transactions are foreign-owned land holdings in Florida. Curaçao corporations may be owned through 'bearer shares', and a tiering of shell corporations linked to the tax treaty can produce a dense smoke-screen:

When the U.S. Agriculture Department wanted to know who owned 1,437 acres [about 575 hectares] purchasesd in Orange County, Florida, for example, it wrote to the Curacao International Trust Co., which was managing the company listed as buyer, Debco, N.V. In reply, the Department was told through a Houston lawyer that Debco, N.V. was a 'wholly owned subsidiary of Pathway

Investments, N.V.', which in turn was described only as 'a corporation organized under the laws of the Netherlands Antilles'.[23]

Whereas the Netherlands Antilles government has accommodated US requests for financial information concerning American citizens, it has been unwilling to yield on disclosures regarding foreigners, making it especially difficult to track criminal financial flows.

Panama

Although it is sometimes grouped with the Caribbean countries in discussions of the suppliers of international financial secrecy, Panama's growing importance merits separate treatment as the only true 'Latin American' secrecy haven.

Panama has embarked on an ambitious policy of national development, with the financial services industry as the keystone.

There are three relevant activity centers in Panama: the banking and business community, its elected government, and its military police, the National Guard. The financial and business community essentially dictates banking and company legislation. The government seeks to accommodate itself to the business élite and to a growing middle class. Its interests are much the same as those of the banking community, encouraging Panama's role as a financial center. The National Guard must be dealt with whenever foreign authorities seek cooperation in criminal matters. It is said to be 'corrupt', in that offenders such as drug and arms traffickers can be assured protection from arrest if they have paid an appropriate 'safe conduct' fee.

The financial sector represents 9 per cent of GNP, with an annual growth rate of 22 per cent as opposed to an overall national economic growth rate of 3.6 per cent in 1982. Assets of the banking system in 1985 were about $35 billion in 120 Panamanian banks, mostly branches of established international institutions of which $30 billion represented foreign holdings. Conditions that make banking in Panama attractive include geography, the security afforded by the US military presence and the strategic importance of the Panama Canal, and bank secrecy legislation and statutes facilitating secret registered companies. A special treaty that established the US dollar as legal tender on a par with the Panamanian colon also helps explain that country's success in becoming a widely used financial haven. Panama particularly attracts Latin American capital seeking political safety and offshore tax and exchange-control advantages. It also attracts criminal funds because of its role in the Colombia–US drug trade and arms traffic, where Panama may also be regarded as a key Asia–Europe transshipment point.

Examples abound. Take the case of Ramón Milan-Rodriguez. On 4 May 1983 he was arrested aboard a private Learjet about to take off for

115

Panama, along with $5.4 million in cash. In testimony, it developed that Mr Milan-Rodriguez had run $150 million to Panama over an eight-month period, and that his earnings from this service amounted to over $1 million per year.[24]

Another case of drug money moving to Panama involved Inair Cargo Airlines, a Panamanian-registered carrier making regular runs to Miami. In June 1983, two top airline executives were indicted for conspiracy to ship US currency abroad without declaring it to customs authorities. Particularly interesting in this case was the apparent complicity of the Panamanian National Guard. One $2 million shipment in cartons was evidently guarded by the Panamanian authorities from the time the aircraft landed in Panama City at 4:30 a.m. to the time banks opened at 7:30 a.m. One piece of evidence introduced at the Inair trial was a laminated business card of a member of the National Guard general staff with the following message handwritten on the back: 'The bearer ... is a personal friend of your superior. Whatever cooperation, I authorize and appreciate.'[25] With such connections, it is little wonder that funds transfers into and out of Panama, even in bags and cartons stuffed with $20 bills, are relatively safe and easy.

Registered companies proliferate in Panama. The exact number is unknown, even to the government. Registered companies can be created within a few hours, and are held already formed and 'on the shelf' by local and foreign law firms. An existing 'mature' company can also be bought for a small transfer fee. Attorneys form and hold these 'vintage' shells and, as with good wine, one pays for the age. A registered company costs $600–1,000 to form and about $250 annually to maintain.

There are genuine efforts in Panama to follow strict bank licensing procedures. Panama prefers to license only major international banks already headquartered in responsible foreign countries. It will reject applications from banks headquartered in the Caribbean, as well as from major banks' subsidiaries if those subsidiaries in turn are in the Caribbean. The Panamanian requirement of $250,000 paid-in capital precludes brass-plate banks.

Despite a serious intention of insuring stable and respectable banking, the Panamanian system has profound flaws that make it an ideal conduit for secret funds flows. For one thing, the central banking authority is denied, by secrecy laws, any right to audit bank deposits. A bank, once licensed, may therefore engage in extensive laundering, fraud and looting, at least for a time, with impunity. The strict licensing requirements for new banks indeed have not prevented already licensed banks from criminal involvement.

Nor is there any mechanism for policing offshore activities by Panamanian-registered companies. Any inquiries or complaints about an offshore company can be brought to the Ministry of Commerce, which will only reveal the name of the local agent of that offshore company. There can be no release of information if crimes are not committed in Panama itself. Thus, the bank secrecy law in Panama and the fundamental territorial thrust of its criminal law protect account holders from disclosure and prosecution.

American bank examiners, over 100 in number, annually travel to more than 20 countries to conduct examinations of US banks doing business abroad. However, Panama closed off that possibility in the late 1970s in order to raise the level of secrecy associated with banking in that country, although the National Banking Commission created to provide substitute local supervision evidently leaves a great deal to be desired. As noted, Panama does not permit 'shell' banks. Still, 130 banks were operating in Panama in early 1983 with assets of $49 billion – about one-third of which were of Latin American origin. Prior to the creation of an offshore banking center in 1970, 241 'banks' operated in Panama; this was initially cut down by the authorities to 20 essentially reputable institutions, and then began a dramatic resurgence in the number of banks. Because of US concern with the safety and soundness of Panamanian banks, regulators have been reluctant to permit US institutions to participate in new Panamanian banks – a concern that was heightened by the collapse of the Banco de Ultramar in late 1983.

Laundering of drug money in Panama has been aided by a number of developments. The fact that it is Hispanic – so that Latin drug runners and their launderers can deal with other Latins, whose language and ways of doing business are familiar – reduces both complexity and inconvenience, as well as risk, compared with business done through the Bahamas or the Cayman Islands. There is also the fact that the dollar is in effect used as the national currency, so that enormous cash shipments of dollars can be legitimately made by Panamanian banks for deposit in the US Federal Reserve system without problems or questions: in 1982 Panamanian banks shipped about $1 billion in cash in this way, mostly in $20 bills. Panama's bank secrecy legislation helps as well. After a Panamanian lawyer has set up a shell corporation that can make a cash deposit in a secret account, that account can be accessed by the authorities only through a Panamanian court order showing that a crime has been committed. Panama has no exchange controls, nor any form of registration requirements or restrictions on currency shipments into or out of the country.

Panamanian banks suspected of being used in money-laundering operations profess innocence about where the hundreds of millions of dollars in banknotes are coming from; in any case, they assert that they are not responsible for tracing the source of any such deposits. But, as one US law-enforcement official notes, 'You can't tell me that when a large amount of cash is brought into the bank in suitcases and cardboard cartons, bank officials assume it's a legitimate transaction.'[26]

Other factors favoring Panama include pressure on the Bahamas, Cayman Islands and Switzerland by US officials with respect to the use of bank secrecy in laundering of drug money (see Chapter 5), so that more questions may be asked and there is a greater likelihood of a criminal investigation that could lead to a lifting of bank secrecy. Then there is the aforementioned crackdown by federal authorities on South Florida banks, which has made domestic money laundering operations much more risky and expensive.

Over 8,000 people are employed in the Panamanian banking industry – an important contribution in a country of chronically high unemployment and few other areas of international competitive advantage. The trends appear to be such that '... in ten years much of the European and Western world's criminal money will reside in Panama'.[27] This has both costs and benefits for the country. On the negative side, it may frighten away not-so-criminal money, concerned that a Panamanian connection will be taken as presumptive evidence of criminal activity. It may concentrate criminal funds flows so as to make them easier to monitor and possibly attack by law-enforcement agencies. It will also place a greater burden on the Panamanian authorities to restrict the use of shell companies and phoney financial statements to defraud investors abroad. Whether Panama has the ability or the will to clean up its act even partially remains to be seen.

For the present, foreign authorities that are seeking information about the Panamanian business activities of offenders are faced with two possibilities. They can use their own embassies in an approach to the Attorney General, although, as noted, nothing can be done if a crime has not been committed in Panama itself. They can also approach the National Guard, which will, from time to time, show its goodwill by providing assistance when a fugitive has not paid his local dues.

Other havens

As identified in Table 4.1, there are a number of other secrecy havens. The New Hebrides is a tax haven in the South Pacific. It has attracted investors from Asia, Australia and the West Coast of the United States. The most popular form of corporation in the New Hebrides is the 'exempt company', which conducts all business outside of the islands and is protected by strict secrecy laws.

Austria has a tradition of bank secrecy dating back to the Austro–Hungarian Empire. This tradition was reinforced by a 1979 law codifying bank secrecy. It allows a depositor to open an account without revealing his or her name or true identity, and the account remains anonymous as long as the depositor wishes – a form of total privacy unavailable even in Switzerland.

118

And there are more. In countries such as Luxembourg, France, West Germany, Great Britain and the United States, banks are bound either by law or by a code of discretion to maintain secrecy. Luxembourg, for example, attracts a great deal of secrecy-oriented business, especially from West Germany. However, the degree of privacy and anonymity afforded a client in most cases is hardly comparable to that available from the real heavyweights in the secrecy business.

Among US financial institutions, the supply of international secrecy services has perhaps been most closely associated with Deak & Co. and its affiliates. Besides accusations of laundering drug money, including $7.6 million deposited by middle-aged and older women working as couriers, '... the company has long provided the anonymous and convoluted transactions prized by people trying to shield their money from coups, tax collectors, and police departments.'[28] This included the attraction of large mail deposits from Latin America, especially Argentina. It also included running funds for Lockheed to Asia to use in bribing Japanese officials during 1969–75 to influence aircraft procurement. 'In 15 deliveries, Deak & Co. moved $8.3 million to Hong Kong, where a Spanish priest representing Lockheed took the cash and carried it to Japan in a flight bag or in cardboard boxes labeled "oranges".'[29] According to a Deak spokesman, 'Lockheed Corporation came in and asked us to make a payment. We made a payment. The fact that the money was used later for bribes is Lockheed's shame, not ours.'[30] And in 1978 Deak & Co. was accused of taking a deposit of $11 million by two Philippine businessmen without filing the required federal reports. All this notoriety attracted so much attention that a substantial number of secrecy-seeking clients seem to have pulled out, leading to a liquidity crisis that added to already existing business problems and caused Deak & Co. to file for bankruptcy late in 1984.

Deak & Co. estimated its debts at about $60 million. The company announced that it would repay depositors by selling off a number of its healthier subsidiaries. However, beginning in December 1984, hundreds of creditors lined up, and it appeared not only that debts exceeded $60 million, but that the proceeds from the sale of assets might not cover them. Two groups of large depositors emerged with substantial claims: the Committee of Unsecured Creditors in the US and the Hong Kong Creditors' Committee in Hong Kong.

At one time, Hong Kong creditors were apparently under the impression that their money was deposited locally, or maybe across the Pearl River estuary in the unregulated banking center of Macao. The only thing clear was that $26 million in depositor funds were missing. Funds transferred by Hong Kong to the Deak office in Macao apparently never reached their destination. The Hong Kong creditors also discovered that neither Deak-Perera Far East in Hong Kong nor Deak & Co. Macao Ltd were licensed to accept deposits. The Macao office told creditors it had no records of the deposits from Hong Kong. With no proof that they were depositors, Hong Kong creditors were fighting to be recognized. A further complication was that Deak's US operations regularly borrowed from the Hong Kong subsidiary whenever New York ran short of cash. The amount thus borrowed was pegged at $15 million.[31]

Taken together, the problems motivated Deak's Hong Kong management to close the office doors. Under pressure from local creditors, the Hong Kong banking authorities intervened by assigning a provisional liquidator to find whatever assets remained and sell those that might lose value over time. The action came too late, however, as Deak insiders estimated that only $9 million of the creditors' original $26 million in cash remained in Hong Kong. Finally, in January 1985 Lark International Ltd, a Hong Kong conglomerate, purchased Deak-Perera Far East's operations for $385,000, which will go to Hong Kong creditors. Confusion still remained about which assets belonged to which of Deak's worldwide affiliates.

In order to keep track of tax reporting on interest income, the US government ended the availability of domestic bearer bonds (previously issued mainly by municipal governments) on 1 July 1983. Old bearer bonds immediately increased in price slightly to reflect the increased value of their confidentiality, even though they traditionally sold a fraction below registered bonds of the same quality because of the virtual impossibility of tracing them if stolen and the resulting differential in warehousing risk.

In 1984, the US repealed a 30 per cent withholding tax on interest paid to foreign purchasers of domestic bonds. Withholding has traditionally made such bonds less attractive than those issued in jurisdictions that have no such provisions (such as the Netherlands Antilles) or in the Eurobond market, and in jurisdictions that rebate most or all of the tax (such as Switzerland). Repeal was designed to put the US capital market on a par with these foreign and offshore financial centers and reposition that market more favorably, while at the same time giving US private and public sector borrowers better access to foreign capital.

One sticky point emerged, however, on the matter of secrecy. Whereas bonds in the US can be issued only in registered form (with interest payable only to the registered owner), the bearer bonds that are common abroad (interest payable to anyone presenting a valid coupon) are obviously more attractive to investors intent on secrecy for tax evasion and other reasons.

Bearer bonds have long been attractive to those on the run from taxes or adverse political developments. According to Hans-Joerg Rudloff of Crédit Suisse First Boston Ltd (the leading underwriter of Eurobonds), 'We in Europe have been through civil wars, revolutions, world wars and the confiscatory policies of socialist and communist governments.

Whoever saves and has capital wants to protect himself from these events.'[32]

Table 4.2 indicates the rules applying to withholding of tax on bond interest in a number of major issuing countries, for both residents and non-residents. Interest withholding repeal coupled to bearer securities could make the US the largest and most attractive tax haven of all for non-residents, with the potential of greatly increasing the $86 billion of foreign capital inflows recorded in 1983. One motive (more or less unspoken) was to gain still greater access to foreign savings to finance a large US budget deficit and help keep the lid on domestic interest rates.

Naturally, there were howls of protest from foreign governments, including some whose markets have traditionally been used as tax and secrecy havens. The most telling objections to the prospect of bearer securities emerged at home, however, with the possibility that such

Table 4.2 *Withholding tax on bond interest*

Country	Interest payable to	Eurobonds	Other corporate	Public sector
USA	Residents[1]	0 or 20%	0 or 20%	0 or 20%
	Non-residents[2]	0 or 30%	0 or 30%	0 or 30%
Britain	Residents	0[3]	30%	30%
	Non-residents	0[3]	30%	0 or 30%[4]
West Germany	Residents	0	0	0
	Non-residents[5]	25%	0 or 25%	25%
France	Residents[6]	0 or 10–12%	0 or 10–12%	0 or 10–12%
	Non-residents[5]	25%	25 or 45–50%[7]	25%
Switzerland	Residents	0 or 35%	0 or 35%	0 or 35%
	Non-residents[8]	35%	35%	35%
Holland	Residents	0	0	0
	Non-residents	0	0	0
Belgium	Residents[9]	0 or 25%	0 or 25%	0 or 25%
	Non-residents[9]	0 or 25%	0 or 25%	0 or 25%
Japan	Residents	0	0	0
	Non-residents	20%	20%	20%

Notes:
1. back-up witholding tax until taxpayer identification
2. no tax on 'portfolio' interest
3. with certain restrictions
4. no tax on interest on designated issues
5. exemptions announced/being considered
6. possible tax of 10–12%, except on government bonds and bonds issued by French companies abroad
7. tax on negotiable instruments 25%, non-negotiable 45–50%
8. no tax on interest on bonds issued by non-Swiss borrowers
9. exemption for interest paid to certain companies and if funds are not used in a Belgian business

Source: The Economist, 27 October 1984, p. 81, from data compiled by Price Waterhouse.

securities could be used by US residents (for example, through purchases by third parties) for purposes of tax evasion and money laundering. Shortly after withholding repeal, the New York firm of Salomon Brothers announced a repackaging of $1.7 billion in US Treasury securities in the form of Certificates of Accrual on Treasury Securities (CATS), fully backed by the securities themselves held in trust and sold at discount to investors.

The Treasury was caught in a bind. Issuing bearer bonds would clearly foster tax evasion by residents of the United States and was unanimously deemed unacceptable by a non-binding Senate resolution and threatened future legislation. Yet issuing registered bonds would make them unappealing to foreign investors. So a compromise solution was devised that pleased no one. The 'special registered securities' require buyers to certify that they are not US citizens, and the investment house must provide recertification each time interest is paid, yet without revealing the identity of the bondholder to the Treasury. This created a potential tax liability for securities dealers in the case of erroneous certification – prompting them to ask investors for more information than actually needed and potentially alienating them – as well as a large amount of paperwork. Swiss banks in particular filed strong objections on both grounds, as well as the likelihood that the Treasury's requirements would conflict with Swiss secrecy laws. Resale of such securities could be made more difficult, and in particular resale in the US domestic bond market automatically precludes their further resale offshore.[33]

Summary

The motivation underlying the supply of financial secrecy in the international environment is clear – economic gain. Whether it involves individual vendors, lawyers, accountants and other intermediaries, or entire countries, secrecy-related financial services can be provided at a substantial 'markup' over their actual cost. The quality of those services is rather diverse, as we have seen. It depends on the professional competence, honesty and integrity of the vendor, as well as the legal safeguards and economic/political risks associated with his country.

The previous chapter clearly indicated the degree of diversity that exists in the pattern of demand for financial secrecy. The same degree of diversity exists in the pattern of supply. Risk-averse tax evaders will prefer some secrecy havens over others. Crooks will be similarly selective. Geographic location, language and related factors enter the picture as well.

Where there are gains there will be competition, and this is no different in the secrecy game. Individual vendors compete, and so do their governments. Secrecy attributes are vigorously protected, since their erosion will quickly drive money out. New and innovative secrecy attributes are eagerly sought after, although in most cases they cannot be created overnight and marketing them can pose a difficult problem. A competitive hierarchy clearly exists, with very significant gains going to the pre-eminent, established secrecy centers, notably Switzerland, and rather limited benefits accruing at the more highly competitive 'booking' end of the market.

Notes

1 Benito Legarda, 'Small Island Economies', *Finance and Development*, June 1984.
2 Permanent Subcommittee on Investigations, Committee on Governmental Affairs, United States Senate, *Crime and Secrecy: The Use of Offshore Banks and Companies* (Washington, DC: US Government Printing Office, 1983), p. 73.
3 'Watch Out Switzerland, Here Comes Tonga', *Institutional Investor*, March 1985, p. 24.
4 Thomas N. Gladwin and Ingo Walter, *Multinationals Under Fire* (New York: John Wiley & Sons, 1980), chapter 10.
5 Philip Revsin, 'Swiss Accounts Don't Match Exotic Image', *Wall Street Journal*, 21 February 1985.
6 Felix Kessler, 'Neutral Switzerland, without Enemies, Spending Millions on Fallout Shelters', *Wall Street Journal*, 21 December 1983.
7 'Taking the Secret out of Swiss Banking', *The Economist*, 16 July 1983.
8 George Anders and Margaret Studer, 'Stuck on Tradition, Swiss Banks Discover their Role is Waning as a Financial Center'. *Wall Street Journal*, 21 March 1985.
9 'Sensible Lotsen', *Der Spiegel*, No. 20, 1984.
10 Paul Lewis, 'Cracking a Swiss Bank's Code', *New York Times*, 23 September 1983.
11 *Ibid.*
12 'Greeks Join the Chorus', *The Economist*, 1 October 1983.
13 *International Herald Tribune*, 13 June 1983.
14 Matthew Winkler, 'Switzerland Beats out U.S. in Extradition of Richard Keats in Bogus Securities Case', *Wall Street Journal*, 29 October 1983.
15 'Taking the Secret out of Swiss Banking', *The Economist*, 16 July 1983.
16 Maile Hulihan, 'Swiss Vote on Bank Secrecy Curbs after Battle for Hearts and Minds', *Wall Street Journal*, 18 May 1984.
17 As quoted in *International Herald Tribune*, 17 August 1984, p. 1.
18 John Wicks, 'Swiss Bankers' Code Should Become Law', *Financial Times*, 30 May 1984.
19 John Wicks, 'Swiss Banks on the Up and Up', *The Banker*, July 1984, p. 43.
20 *Ibid.*
21 Richard A. Gordon, *Tax Havens and their Use by US Taxpayers – An Overview* (The Gordon Report) (Washington DC: Internal Revenue Service, 12 January 1981), p. 123.
22 *Ibid.*
23 Edward Cody, 'US Seeks to Reduce Loss of Revenues in Fiscal Fuzz of Caribbean Tax Havens', *Washington Post*, 15 June 1983. See also Alan Murray, 'We Find it Very Hard to Believe that J. P. Morgan Began this Way', *Wall Street Journal*, 4 April 1985.
24 Stanley Penn, 'Top Spot to Deposit Illegal Narcotics Profits', *Wall Street Journal*, 16 October 1983.
25 *Ibid.*
26 *Ibid.*
27 *Ibid.*
28 'How Deak & Co. Got Caught in its Own Tangled Web', *Business Week*, 24 December 1984.
29 'Collapse of Deak & Company', *New York Times*, 10 December 1984.
30 *Ibid.*, p. D4.

31 Sarah Bartlett and Dorinda Elliott, 'The Mess at Deak & Co. is Worse than Anyone Thought', *Business Week*, 11 February 1985, p. 20.
32 'Braking in the Fast Lane', *Newsweek*, 27 August 1984.
33 See 'Why the Treasury's Plan to Sell Debt Overseas May Not Fly', *Business Week*, 22 October 1984, p. 129. See also Matthew Winkler, 'U.S. Change in Rule on Withholding is Reshaping Eurodollar Bond Market', *Wall Street Journal*, 20 June 1985, and Bob Hagerty, 'Japanese Snap up the Bulk of Special Treasury Issue', *International Herald Tribune*, 3 June 1985.

5

Combating International Financial Secrecy

Given the discussion in Chapter 3, it is little wonder that governments around the world have put a high priority on finding ways to control international financial secrecy. In doing so, they often seem to confuse cause and effect, disease and symptom.

Secret money itself is not the root-cause of anything. But it makes things possible – it *facilitates*. Governments' inability or unwillingness to do very much about the underlying causes of financial secrecy perforce drives policymakers to attempt to deal with the symptoms. Yet in some cases this may be the only viable option. Funds spent combating money laundering may produce far better results than an equivalent expenditure on the direct enforcement of drug laws, for example.

Like the market for secret money itself, policies to control it can be attempted on both the supply and demand side. With respect to the supply of international financial secrecy, it may be possible to convince foreign governments to facilitate disclosure, or to crack down on secrecy vendors within their borders – or at least to encourage them to exercise self-discipline. Or it may be possible to reach bilateral accords, even multilateral ones, that would contain substantial disclosure or investigative provisions. All such efforts require the exercise of power (bargaining leverage, intergovernmental arm-twisting) or cooperation – more likely the former. Regarding demand, it may be possible to crack down on secret financial flows by increasing penalties, reporting requirements and enforcement efforts, and by raising the probability of getting caught and the pain associated with punishment. But, like water, secret money will always find a way around attempts to control it as long as the underlying incentives are there. It can be temporarily dammed-up, diverted and made more costly but it will invariably resurface. In this chapter, we shall outline some of the dimensions of controlling secret money, and evaluate their prospects for success.

Self-control

It would, of course, be nice to think that financial institutions and other intermediaries in the secrecy business will adhere strictly to the law, and even exercise a certain amount of discretion that goes beyond the law. To a considerable extent, they do. It is not good for business for financial institutions to be named in newspaper exposés of narcotics trafficking, child pornography or egregious political corruption. For most of the world's major financial institutions, abusive financial secrecy clearly constitutes a tiny fraction of their overall activities, and the possibility of contamination of legitimate business is anathema to senior management. Such institutions would be expected to stay well clear of any dealings that might be tainted – or at the very least have one or more intermediaries provide the necessary 'insulation'.

However, self-control is easier said than done, particularly in a very competitive financial environment and within often decentralized institutions. It requires a viable system of highly centralized management information and control of domestic and international branches and affiliates, as well as a consistent and unambiguous supervisory environment on the part of the regulatory authorities. These conditions are not always met.

For example, we know from Chapter 2 that the creation of trusts, other than direct transfers, is used to place funds offshore primarily for tax avoidance or evasion. One major US international bank, when accepting trust accounts for administration in a higher-yield Euro-branch, stipulates that its clients consent in advance to disclosure, and the bank reserves the right to provide information to authorities as it deems necessary. This waiver supersedes any client rights under local secrecy laws abroad. For deposits held onshore, there is no need for contractual waivers. In the United States, federal authorities may approach a bank for access to information under the Right to Financial Privacy statutes.

The majority of banks in tax havens are subject to control by their parent banks. These in turn are supervised by their own central banks and other regulatory authorities. Not surprisingly, one finds great variation in rules among haven banks as well as bank headquarters regarding secrecy and acceptance of currency deposits of dubious origin. There are also policy variations among offshore branches of the same bank. As Chapter 4 noted, in the Caymans or Panama the majority of banks, whether domestic or foreign-owned, are said to accept suitcase currency.

Central bank or other regulatory controls are probably most strict among banks headquartered in the major trading nations. However, some banks are suspected not only of being negligent with regard to their offshore branches' policies, but also of tolerating greater laxity in standards on the part of local managers with respect to their dealings with suspect clients. Expatriate managers' direct involvement in criminal activities, as well as questionable relations with local officials, do not seem to be uncommon. Besides the obvious incentive to become involved in criminal activities, local managers could find that they are actually punished for honesty. There have been instances where parent banks removed competent offshore managers for their refusal to participate in highly questionable financial activities.

According to a US Senate staff study, Africa, Central America and the Caribbean were the areas most vulnerable to bank involvement in politically corrupt or direct criminal matters and where suitable controls might not be exercised by headquarters.[1] Of the three regions, the Caribbean (including Panama) is said to be the most vulnerable of all. Conceptually, external control of foreign branches should probably come from home-country central banks. The supervision required, however, is not an audit of books but an audit of conduct.

Besides internal control and audit problems – and a heterogeneous external regulatory environment – there is also the problem of diverse views on the legal and moral status of secret money. The US or British tax evader who puts his money in Switzerland is welcome there. As long as he has not committed an act of fraud, he has broken no Swiss law. The Mexican businessman concerned with economic stability at home is welcome to place his assets in the United States, even though he might be considered a traitor back home. In the secrecy game, the gray areas are enormous, which makes it very difficult or impossible to define the 'correct' action on the part of the financial intermediaries, particularly those physically present in a number of different countries.

There is also the omnipresence of 'see no evil' operators who may be on the fringes in terms of overall financial significance but who may also carry disproportionate weight as intermediaries and middlemen in questionable transactions. The apparent voluntary cooperation of some of these banks in money laundering has been impressive. According to one US investigator posing as a courier, 'The banks were delighted to deal with me when I was "dirty". Bank guards were always willing to carry crates of money into a back room with the counting machines. Cash reporting requirements never hindered the banks, since they could afford to pay the fines if caught.'[2]

According to the testimony of a pilot before the President's Commission on Organized Crime,

When depositing money at Miami banks ... the clerks obligingly broke his large deposits into several smaller ones so he could avoid Federal [reporting] regulations .... When the volume of cash increased, [he] banked in the Bahamas. He recalled flying to a Bahamian bank carrying a large plastic trash bag full of bills. At the bank he sat talking with a bank official, the garbage bag of bills between his feet, and bargained over the banking fee. The banker finally charged a 1 percent 'counting fee' to accept the deposit. Eventually he had to buy an expensive money-counting machine.[3]

Diversity and inconsistency in the legal and behavioral picture, coupled to competitive, regulatory and control difficulties (both internal and external) limit governments' reliance on financial institutions themselves as levers in any crackdown on illegal activities giving rise to secret money flows. Rather, the majority of efforts have tended to run the other way – measures to deal directly with the flows themselves, which in turn impact on the institutions involved.

Unilateral action

There are a number of things governments can do within their own borders to try to affect, directly or indirectly, the secret money business. Even without international flows, such action will never be entirely effective. For example, someone who wants a payment by check converted to cash can get it done (for a fee) through a check-cashing service, which assumes the risk of non-payment, or by cashing it at his bank and waiting until it clears or having a 'hold' put on sufficient funds maintained in an account to cover the principal amount. Alternatively, in the United States 'money orders' can be purchased in blank form from a number of vendors, which can then be used to make payments without significant identification of the payer. Still, things can be made more difficult and more expensive for the secrecy seeker, by countries acting on their own.

The Bank Secrecy Act

One example is the US Bank Secrecy Act – the popular name of the Currency & Foreign Transactions Reporting Act of 1970. Under this legislation, the federal government has the authority to monitor large cash transactions and the export and import of large amounts of currency by means of reporting requirements imposed on banks and individuals. Although these requirements were intended to disrupt the laundering of cash for criminal purposes, effective enforcement was recognised as being difficult. A criminal already breaking the law would obviously care far less than law-abiding citizens about compliance with reporting requirements. However, a significant purpose of requiring the filing of these so-called CTR reports was to provide the Department of Justice with a means to obtain court convictions in criminal cases. This is because it is much easier to establish a criminal violation when a report is not filed than to prove the person's criminal activities. The penalty for failure to file a CTR report is either a year in prison or a fine of $1,000, or both. If failure to report is linked to other criminal activities, a much stiffer penalty is imposed – five years in jail or $500,000 in fines, or both.

With respect to financial institutions, the Bank Secrecy Act mandates that all depositors of over $10,000 in cash must be identified by name and source of funds except for volume depositors like retail outlets which may be exempted, although exempt lists must also be reported to the government. The same is true of telex transfers in excess of $10,000.

The Act imposes on the Secretary of the Treasury the responsibility for assuring compliance. The Secretary may then delegate responsibility to various bank regulatory agencies – the Comptroller of the Currency and the Federal Reserve Board.

Both the Comptroller and the Federal Reserve accorded low priority to the transaction reporting requirement in their respective bank examinations. To them, the bank examination process is defined conventionally, focusing principally on the determination of the institution's financial condition and whether it is operating in a safe and sound manner. Neither seems ready to expand its role to cover closer offshore supervision – nor are they prepared to deal with criminal activities offshore that may be related to US banking activities. Both agencies have also noted a legal impediment: the Right to Financial Privacy Act of 1978. This legislation significantly restricted government agencies from transferring financial records or information of bank customers to other agencies or departments.

Within the Treasury Department, the Drug Enforcement Administration (DEA) is subordinate to the FBI and is on the front line with respect to investigations of the flow of money through offshore accounts. The prevalence of narcotics cases, however, is not proof that drug money constitutes the largest element of crime-related offshore financial activities. It may simply reflect the intensity of the enforcement effort because of the moral, social and political concerns associated with narcotics. Also within the Treasury, the US Customs Service was given expanded search authority under the Bank Secrecy Act, with respect to both departing and incoming travelers. However, a 1981 survey found that few departing passengers bothered to fill out the CTR forms – one or two per week at JFK International Airport in New York and two or three per month at Chicago's O'Hare – although a far larger number of incoming passengers filled them out, apparently because the CTR requirement is listed on the mandatory customs forms while no forms are required to be filled out by passengers leaving the country.

An analysis of 1981 CTR forms relating to Panama showed $139 million of cash deposits, $6.5 million of withdrawals, and $9.7 million in other transactions, for a total of $155.2 million, with 86 per cent of those funds identified as being related to drug laundering operations.

In fact, the great percentage … is money from the streets of US cities which was deposited into accounts of alleged currency exchanges using Panamanian addresses. The exchanges have been found to be owned and operated by Colombians who are in the business of laundering drug proceeds for other Colombian drug traffickers.[4]

Such information, of course, reflects only a tiny fraction of the actual funds flows, the vast majority of which never get anywhere near compliance with the government's CTR reporting requirements. In one experiment, the Federal Reserve Bank of New York marked large numbers of $100 bills, which were then put into circulation locally. Within a fairly short period of time, a sizeable proportion of them turned up in Miami, having been caught up in the wash of currency to South Florida ultimately destined for domestic and offshore money laundries.

The volume and complexity of money-laundering operations so far appear to outstrip the sophistication of enforcement efforts. In Operation Greenback, begun under a 1980 US Treasury Department attempt to break the money laundries, three outfits in Florida and one in New York were in fact put out of business, yet only two officers of one small Florida bank were convicted. Pinning responsibility on banks is one thing. Marshaling more than circumstantial evidence that will bring a conviction in a court of law is quite another. However, by the end of 1984, Operation Greenback had in fact led to 211 indictments, 63 convictions, $38.5 million in dirty money seized, and $117 million in bank fines mainly in Florida and (in 1985) in Puerto Rico.

Still, a decade and a half after its passage, the US Bank Secrecy Act and its administration had failed in two important respects. First, the Act did not slow down or stop movements of illegally obtained currency from the US. Second, while some prosecutorial successes did provide an inkling of the 'big money' involved in these movements, the Act failed to yield sufficient data about onshore and offshore money laundering. Insufficient data, in turn, hindered the formulation of policy and the development of appropriate legislative, administrative and diplomatic remedies.

For their part, bankers continued to argue that it is not an appropriate role for them to police financial transactions. Even failure to meet government reporting requirements is laid to the action of individual bank employees, rather than the systematic practice of the banks themselves. Yet according to Rudolph W. Giuliani, United States Attorney in Manhattan,

The law placed the responsibility on banks to obtain and report concerning domestic and foreign transactions. And similarly, irrespective of legal ramifications, any bank that allows itself to be used as a conduit for drug money is in danger of severely damaging its image and its reputation for prudence and integrity. At the same time, it is exposing its employees, who have to deal with many sensitive situations, to being tempted to involve themselves in crime.[5]

The Bank of Boston case

In early 1985 it was revealed that, in direct violation of its reporting obligations under the Bank Secrecy Act, the Bank of Boston had failed to report to the government 1,163 currency transactions amounting to $1.22 billion, mainly with Swiss correspondent banks. It was fined $500,000. In addition, the bank had undertaken an apparently unrelated string of cash dealings with the Angiulo family, reputedly the leading organized crime group in Massachusetts, involving the sale of large-denomination cashier's checks without filing the required CTR reports. William Brown, chairman of Bank of Boston Corp., claimed that the bank had failed to report both the domestic and international currency trans-actions as required because its officers were not familiar with the law. However, Treasury officials pointed to the Bank's repeated violations even after having been notified, and wondered how a large bank could have been totally oblivious to the widely publicized regulation. Several weeks later, the bank revealed an additional $110 million in unreported cash transactions, mostly with Canada and Haiti.[6]

In March 1985, to the Reagan administration's embarrassment, Comp-troller of the Currency C. Todd Conover told a Senate committee that his agency had made the same mistake as the Bank of Boston officers. The Comptroller's bank examiners missed the irregularities during a special investigation conducted at the Bank of Boston in 1982. The Treasury expressed fears that the Comptroller's admission could pro-vide ammunition for banks seeking immunity from prosecution if they disclosed that they, too, had failed to report currency transactions as required under the Bank Secrecy Act. Almost immediately, several banks did in fact seek immunity.[7]

As far as government officials were initially able to determine, the Bank of Boston violations were mainly due to 'systems failure'. That is, most of the employees involved failed to comply with the CTR reporting requirement out of ignorance, and their failure was not picked up by bank officers up the line. Nevertheless, suspicions had been aroused that at least some were actively involved in money laundering – suspi-cions reinforced by instances in the past of bank managements' non-reporting in return for kickbacks from criminals and their associates. The Garfield Bank and the Pan American International Bank serve as examples. Garfield was hit with $2.3 million in fines, penalties, back taxes, and interest. Pan American fines were smaller, but its former vice chairman was sentenced to prison.[8] As long ago as 1977, Chemical Bank in New York fired 24 employees for cooperating in money-laundering schemes and paid more than $200,000 in fines. In 1983, Republic National Bank admitted it had not reported $165,000 in cash business from cocaine dealers and paid a $15,000 fine. The Rockland Trust Co., a small bank in Plymouth, Massachusetts, and officers of the Ansonian Credit Union in Boston, were indicted in 1984 for failing to file currency reports. Overall, by early 1985, 21 banks had been penalized for failing to report currency transactions of more than $10,000.[9]

The Justice Department investigation of the Angiulo family in Boston also uncovered connections with the brokerage firms of E. F. Hutton and Cowen & Co., as well as the Provident Institution for Savings. The Angiulos bought $520,000 in cashier's checks from the Provident and the Bank of Boston, payable to Cowen. Cowen claimed that one of its retail managers inherited the Angiulo accounts from a colleague at E. F. Hutton and brought them with him when he transferred to the firm in 1980.

Several additional banks confessed violations not long after the Bank of Boston case. The Shawmut Bank of Boston failed to report over $190 million in large cash transactions with foreign banks and improperly exempted 27 customers from the currency reporting rules. The Bank of New England admitted to two sets of unreported cash transactions. Chemical Bank of New York admitted 857 unreported cash transactions worth $25.9 million since 1980, most of which were reportedly with US foreign exchange brokers. Irving Trust Company of New York listed 1,659 unreported cash transactions with foreign banks worth $292 million, while Manufacturers Hanover Trust Company listed $140 million covering 1,400 international currency transactions – both cited oversights and 'systems failure'. Smaller amounts were reported by Bank of America and First National Bank of Chicago. No unreported cash transactions at all were found in audits carried out by Citibank, Morgan Guaranty Trust Company, and Marine Midland, among others.[10]

That most of the revelations of unreported cash transactions involved reporting errors seems beyond doubt. Nevertheless, in June 1985 Chase Manhattan, Chemical Bank, Irving Trust and Manufacturers Hanover were each fined between $200,000 and $400,000 in a settlement with the Treasury, and action against other banks was pending. Even so, the fines were criticised in the Congress as merely a 'pittance'.[11]

The E. F. Hutton case

Banks have not been the only financial institutions implicated in US money laundering related to organized crime and narcotics trafficking. The brokerage firm of E. F. Hutton accepted more than $13 million in cash during a five-month period in 1982, most of it delivered by Franco

Della Torre, one of 38 people indicted in the $1.65 billion 'Pizza Connection' heroin case (see Chapter 3). The money eventually was placed in accounts, registered in the names of Traex, Acacias Development Corp. and P. G. K. Holding, opened at Hutton's office in Lugano, Switzerland, controlled by Della Torre associates. In Switzerland, the money was handled by men who acted as professional money launderers for Giuseppe Bono, an alleged Mafia boss arrested in the Milan area in 1983. Much of the money ended up invested in Northern Italy.

Hutton was not charged with any violations of law because it had in fact complied with the Bank Secrecy Act by filing CTR reports for all of the cash transactions exceeding $10,000. However, the FBI and the US Customs Service remained perturbed by indications that Hutton's actions supported and protected the alleged money launderers. For example, the company arranged personal security for Della Torre from his hotel to the financial institutions in which the money was deposited. In addition, the amount of the deposits should have caused alarm, as they did at Merrill Lynch, where Della Torre had earlier made questionable cash deposits of $4.9 million and which had declined to accept further funds and closed the account. Della Torre then went to Hutton.

Further confusion about Hutton's role emerged in October 1982, when the firm was served with a federal grand jury subpoena to provide information regarding Della Torre and the Swiss accounts. Hutton officials promptly notified a Della Torre associate in Switzerland of the subpoena, despite specific requests by the government that no such disclosure be made. The firm's attorneys requested immunity for Hutton officials. Since no charges had been filed, the government's question naturally was 'immunity from what?'

Hutton's actions remained under intensive review. What the firm did, according to one Treasury agent, was 'right on the knife-edge [between legal and illicit conduct] and, depending on the intention, could amount to an obstruction of justice.'[12]

New initiatives

As a result of the Bank of Boston revelations, US banks appear to be increasing internal controls to guard against money laundering, including greater emphasis on training programs, revised policies, and improved computer software. Training programs teach tellers to identify launderers. New policies make cashier's checks available to regular customers only. Data processing software has become available that produces daily lists of accounts with cash transactions of more than $10,000.

The US Treasury carried forward its offensive against money laundering, beginning in July 1984, with a broad set of proposals that would require banks to supplement the already mandated disclosure of international currency movements in excess of $5,000 with:

- all credit card charges received or shipped by financial institutions, including date, amount of charge, and submitting merchant;
- all travelers check transactions, overseas checks and drafts, including the names of payee and payer, names of enforcers, date and amount; and
- all transfers of securities, certificates of deposit, commercial paper and wire funds transfers.

Such far-reaching disclosure requirements were immediately condemned as overkill by bankers, raising possible constitutional questions and violating the spirit of the Right of Financial Privacy Act: '... the Fourth Amendment to the United States Constitution prohibits not only illegal search and seizure but also protects individuals from unreasonable invasion of legitimate privacy interests at the hands of the Government.'[13]

The government did initiate a series of meetings with the American Bankers Association to increase awareness of the money-laundering problem and is seeking a consensus on how to combat it. Amendment of the Financial Privacy Act is being sought so that bank employees will be encouraged to report any suspicious behavior.

The Treasury also brought gambling casinos under the CTR reporting requirements. The common strategy had been to take, for example, $100,000 in cash to a licensed casino and buy chips. The next step was to gamble away $5,000 or so. The rest of the chips would be turned in at the cashier's window for a $95,000 credit, which the launderer instructed the casino to wire to another casino abroad. The launderer then needed only to hop a plane to pick up his money and deposit it in a foreign bank.

Another US unilateral initiative would involve establishing an ad hoc federal commission whose functions would include accumulation and dissemination of information, coordination of inter-agency and inter-governmental activities, and provision of personnel and support to countries seeking to improve their bank supervision and control arrangements, and to provide a financial investigative service. The United States has had very little in the way of a truly coordinated approach to these problems, although there is a general consensus among government agencies that cooperation is needed to improve investigation of offshore criminal activities. As yet, however, there are no guidelines as to possible procedures, nor is there an accessible inventory of work done by the various government agencies. In the State Department, for example, attention to Caribbean matters has always been of low priority. The Internal Revenue Service did publish the Gordon Report on tax havens in 1981,[14] while the Customs Service was among the first to recognize the role of banks in laundering narcotics money. However, there has clearly been inadequate use of the Currency Transaction Reports and the Currency & Monetary Instrument Reports for control purposes.

The President's Commission on Organized Crime, for its part, concluded that banks, brokerage houses and casinos are either unwittingly or knowingly involved in the laundering of criminal funds, which it estimates at $5–15 billion in 1984 from narcotics trade alone – two-thirds traveling through US financial institutions. Its proposals for stricter surveillance and fines of up to $250,000 or twice the value of the laundered money and imprisonment for up to five years on first offense ($1 million, five times the amount of the laundered money and up to ten years' imprisonment for subsequent offenses) were strongly opposed by the American Bankers Association. The President's Commission has also proposed a 'Financial Institutions Protection Act' that would make money launderers criminally liable if they use financial institutions to launder money.

Incensed at the apparent role of US-based money laundering specifically in the drug trade operating out of Mexico – and the indifference shown by the managements and shareholders of financial institutions accused of money laundering – columnist William Safire offered the following suggestions:

> Step one: pass legislation now before Congress to make money laundering a criminal act, with the punishment running to individuals as well as institutions. Step two: raise the limit on fines to banks that break the law, thereby penalizing and awakening the stockholders of the launderers. Step three: change the color of U.S. currency, requiring an exchange of all the old bills. The hidden cash illegally socked away will lose much of its value, and the sacks of bills in the laundering pipeline will cost organized crime and its unsullied financiers a bundle.[15]

It is in this spirit that US legislators, discouraged by what they see as regulators' lack of interest in money laundering, have moved to approve a bill that would empower the Treasury to subpoena bank records on its own when it suspects money laundering, rather than wait for cooperation from bank regulators or the impaneling of a grand jury. The bill would also increase the potential fine for violations to the full amount of the illegal transaction. Other legislation being considered provides that bankers who deliberately ignore the laundering of currency be subject to prison sentences of up to 10 years.[16]

135

The US courts have also contributed to the attempted diminution of money laundering. In the 1983 trial of money launderer Eduardo Orozco Prada, discussed in Chapter 3, two new legal precedents were established. First, the prosecution convinced the jury that Orozco was himself a 'financial institution', and was therefore required to file Currency Transaction Reports. This means that if a launderer is discovered to have bought 20 cashier's checks of $5,000 with an original $100,000, he could be held in violation of the Bank Secrecy Act for not having filed reports for the whole amount, with penalties set accordingly.

Second, the prosecution secured the conviction of Orozco as a co-conspirator who was 'aiding and abetting' drug traffickers, even though Orozco had a policy of never dealing directly with anyone who had a drug conviction. Previously, money launderers could work with impunity as long as they kept their operations separate from their drug-dealing counterparts.

Despite all of these initiatives, money laundering remains relatively easy in the United States. A 1985 estimate put the volume of illicit currency laundering through US financial institutions every year at $100 billion, of which $40–80 billion is attributed to drug money (compared to $4 billion in 1974). Although it is more time-consuming, launderers can go to several banks and buy relatively small money orders, for which CTR reports are not required. Because tellers have become more suspicious of transactions just under $10,000, the size of the launderer's deposits have been declining steadily, to $7,000 or even $5,000. The 'smurfs' (couriers who make the deposits) have proved to be remarkably prolific. 'On a good day, working in teams, they can do 30, even 40 transactions at $5,000 to $7,000 a shot,' commented an FBI agent. Most smurfs operate in cities where banks have short lines at teller's windows. Hence, New York City is out because it would take too much time to buy the cashier's checks. Money laundering remains hottest in Miami, Jacksonville, San Francisco, El Paso, Los Angeles, Nashville, Philadelphia and San Antonio.

Other countries than the United States, of course, have also made unilateral efforts to come to grips with the underlying causes of secret money flows, and with the flows themselves – even countries that are among the beneficiaries.

In 1984, after the assassination of the Colombian Justice Minister, Rodrigo Lara Bonilla, the government declared a state of siege and began its first serious crackdown on the drug trade with potentially far-reaching consequences for the national economy. Roughly 75 per cent of the cocaine, 50 per cent of the marijuana and 50 per cent of the methaqualone consumed in the United States originates in Colombia, with drugs estimated to exceed both coffee and cut flowers in export value as the country's largest earner of foreign exchange. The effects of the crackdown were felt immediately in the black market exchange rate, where the dollar quickly appreciated in response to the projected decline of currency inflows attributable to drug export cuts.

In Italy, a 1982 law allows the tax police to inspect the bank accounts and other financial holdings of anyone suspected of having Mafia links. In effect, the suspect is guilty until proven innocent.[17]

Other efforts to control laundering include a Council of Europe 1985 meeting on 'financial assets of criminal organizations', a UK parliamentary proposal to expand government wiretapping authority to include currency transactions, and Interpol's design of model banking legislation for the Caribbean.

No cash transactions reporting rule such as exists in the US has been applied in Canada, even though three of the five major Canadian banks (Bank of Nova Scotia, Canadian Imperial Bank of Commerce, and Royal Bank of Canada) have extensive branch networks in the Caribbean. However, the Bank of Nova Scotia case (discussed in the following section) and the Bank of Boston revelations in the US increased pressure in Canada for some sort of initiative to address the money-laundering issue. In March 1985, the Inspector-General of Banks in Ottawa asked financial institutions to strengthen 'know-your-client' rules and to alert their branches both in the Caribbean and on the US border against cash purchases of large-denomination drafts, major swings in daily cash balances, and conversions of large amounts of US dollars into other currencies.[18]

Banking authorities in other major financial centers such as London, Hong Kong and Frankfurt do not monitor large cash transactions. And many international bank managers appear to want things to stay that way. 'Top management is less worried about snuffing out unsavory depositors and more worried about preserving Frankfurt's role as an international financial center', commented an officer at a major West German bank.[19] Political factors also complicate international regulatory efforts abroad. The head of the City of London's fraud squad reportedly must go through slow diplomatic channels every time his inquiries lead to the Continent. It is not unusual for the wait to be more than a year.

Patterns of cooperation and external pressure

Given the apparent limits on the effectiveness of unilateral attempts to deal with flows of secret money, much effort has been devoted to securing cooperation from countries around the world that serve as secrecy havens. Occasionally this leads to intergovernmental friction – with the financial institutions caught in the middle.

Historically, probably the most common form of cooperation is bilateral tax treaties. However, the US House Ways and Means Committee has found that some tax treaties, while having as their objective the

137

elimination of double taxation, are often abused by third-country residents to avoid paying either US or third-country taxes. This kind of abuse is commonly known as 'treaty shopping'. Two treaties that have been extensively used by 'treaty shoppers' are those between the US and the Netherlands Antilles, and between the US and the British Virgin Islands. The US elected to cancel the latter at the end of 1982.

Certainly the most visible efforts at cooperation have taken place between the United States and Switzerland. Despite tenacious efforts by Swiss officials and banks to uphold rigid disclosure limits, some compromises have been reached. Limited mutual assistance treaties are the primary vehicles, and the Swiss government has been cooperative in devising methods of assistance.

The bilateral assistance efforts between the US and Switzerland began in 1951 with the ratification of the Swiss–American Tax Convention. In 1973, the Swiss–American Treaty on Mutual Assistance on Criminal Matters was ratified. This treaty broke new ground in that the Swiss agreed to pierce the veil of bank secrecy in criminal cases that do not involve crimes in Switzerland – for example, the activities of US organized crime. This waiver of the principle of mutual penal liability was an important breakthrough for the American authorities, and eliminated some of the protection previously afforded US organized crime figures by Switzerland. The treaty came into force in 1977.

Despite some difficulties in coming to agreement, the treaty has been successfully used in over 200 cases of criminal prosecution brought in the United States. In 1983, a law on International Mutual Assistance on Criminal Matters extended the bilateral treaty's provisions to all other countries. The line between tax evasion and tax fraud is a problem that remains to be clearly defined.

Although Switzerland only registers Swiss companies, the law does allow the beneficial owner to be hidden behind offshore companies. As noted in Chapter 4, Swiss attorneys can routinely purchase companies in Liechtenstein, Panama, the Cayman Islands or elsewhere without leaving their offices. The 'layering' of secrecy is achieved through complex arrangements involving nominee companies and accounts, and this complicates any attempts to achieve disclosure through cooperation.

Moreover, contrary to the official views of the Swiss government, some Swiss bankers insist that it is silly to forgo the potential profits involved since the funds will simply go somewhere else instead. Consequently, there has long been tension between the business community and the authorities when it comes to deciding what banking information is to be provided to foreign authorities. The bankers continue to maintain that they should certainly not be pressured to police tax evasion and violations of exchange controls in other countries. This, they argue, is the responsibility of national authorities that often change the rules and, in any case, are responsible for punitive taxation that gives rise to evasion in the first place. According to one source,

> If the U.S. can provide us with information about criminal funds sources and the Swiss lawyers or banks they use, then we can act. Unless the U.S. tells us, how can we know? Is it not easier to learn in the U.S. who the criminals are and how they export funds, than to come here after the black has been dyed white? If the U.S. genuinely wishes us to take action against their criminals, then transmit to our Minister of Justice the list of names and their companies. We will act. It is that simple.[20]

Nevertheless, Swiss banks have taken some cooperative steps to curb abuses of financial secrecy. The *Vereinbarung* discussed in Chapter 4, and its application, is one example. One Swiss bank, Union Bank of Switzerland, reportedly requires that any account opened by someone recognized as a politician from another country must be notified to senior management. It is said that such accounts have indeed been refused on occasion. Despite the resounding defeat of the 1984 bank secrecy referendum by the Swiss voters, revision of the Swiss banking law has proceeded apace and there were a number of indications that it would contain tougher provisions on the abuse of secrecy, enforcement, and the closing of loopholes in the law.

Meantime the Pope, on a 1984 visit to Switzerland, cautioned its citizens to insure that its banking system not be used to promote war and injustice throughout the world. 'As a democratically constituted society you must watch vigilantly over all that goes on in this powerful world of money ... The world of finance, too, is a world of human beings – our world, subject to the consciences of all of us. Ethical principles apply to it, too.'[21]

A US–Cayman Islands disclosure pact was negotiated with the help of British authorities in 1984. Under the agreement, the Cayman Islands government will release financial information regarding drug cases within about two weeks of receiving a request from US authorities, making a major potential dent in the estimated $20–30 billion in illicit funds laundered annually through the Caribbean countries. The request must be certified to be drug-related and necessary for the prosecution of the case, and the records are to be accompanied by an affidavit attesting to their authenticity. The agreement was considered a possible model for comparable arrangements with other countries in the region.[22] Nevertheless, it was negotiated without the fanfare that might ruin the Caymans' image as a secrecy haven.[23] Indeed, a number of such initiatives seem to have had significant competitive effects, some of which have especially favored Panama. According to one US Justice Department official, 'You just don't get records out of Panama. They probably have the tightest secrecy laws. I know of [no subpoenas] that have been successful.'[24]

In response to an increase in drug smuggling from the Caribbean and South America through the Turks and Caicos Islands, the US Drug Enforcement Administration in 1983 asked the Islands' government to help reduce the flow of narcotics. The British protectorate agreed, and indeed invited Federal agents to the Islands to assist in the effort. It was suspected that Colombian drug smugglers were flying large amounts of cocaine to the Islands, where the cargos were broken up for delivery to South Florida by fast, small boats island-hopping through the Bahamas.[25]

An ironic twist to the cooperation between the two governments was that undercover operations led to the arrest of three high-ranking Turks and Caicos Islands officials. On 5 March 1985, the highest elected official, Chief Minister Norman Saunders, the Minister of Commerce and Development Stafford Missick, Legislator Aulden Smith, and businessman André Fournier, were arrested in Miami and charged with plotting to use the Islands as a base to smuggle narcotics into the United States. A British Embassy spokesperson said that the officials did not have diplomatic immunity because they were in the US on 'private business'.

Given the potential economic costs of proceeding against financial secrecy in a cooperative manner at the request of another government, it is little wonder that most international efforts to attack secret money have involved a good deal of diplomatic and economic pressure, as well as outright arm-twisting.

Take the case of a US grand jury's investigation of a criminal fraud in the early 1980s. Relevant bank records were subpoenaed from the Bahamas branch of the Bank of Nova Scotia, headquartered in Toronto. Citing the Bahamas Bank and Trust Companies Regulation Act, which prohibits the release of documents to foreign authorities without official authorization, the Bank of Nova Scotia refused to comply. The American judge held that, when the laws of two countries are in conflict, a 'balancing test' should be used to determine whether the interests involved in the investigation or the interests of the foreign country in maintaining secrecy should dominate. In this case, the 'balancing test' weighed in favor of the US investigation. A federal judge in Florida thereupon fined the bank $500 per day on a contempt of court citation in late 1981, fines that were affirmed by a federal appeals court in 1983 and let stand by the Supreme Court itself. Subsequently, the judge increased the fine to $25,000 per day, whereupon the bank turned over the requested documents.

The Bahamian government undertook a criminal investigation of the Bank of Nova Scotia's violation of local disclosure laws, threatening a fine of $15,000 and two years' imprisonment for those involved. It also sent strong letters to President Reagan and Vice President Bush, protesting US legal extraterritoriality and further straining diplomatic relations over the matter of financial disclosure. The US government, meanwhile, announced its intention to continue to press for disclosure in whatever ways seem appropriate in criminal cases where the countries concerned 'fail to reach a reasonable accommodation between bank secrecy and the requirements of bona fide, reasonable law enforcement interests.'[26]

An almost identical sequence of events involved the Bank of Nova Scotia in connection with heroin smuggling into Florida and channeling of the proceeds to Cayman Islands accounts, as well as a number of cases of tax evasion. Again, the bank's US subsidiary was fined $25,000 per day for not revealing subpoenaed account information, which the bank appealed – supported by both the Canadian and Cayman Islands governments. The latter had initially issued an injunction preventing the bank from handing over the documents, but later relented under severe US and bank pressure, and eventually accepted the broader degree of disclosure mentioned earlier. The Bank of Nova Scotia was caught in the middle, with exceedingly high stakes as the largest Canadian bank operating in both the United States and the Caribbean. It continued to appeal the US ruling. And the Canadian as well as the Cayman Islands governments protested bitterly about the extra-territorial application of US law.[27] The bank's fine eventually amounted to $1.8 million. Overall, the Bank of Nova Scotia complained of having been served with 30–40 subpoenas for foreign records.

The Bank of Nova Scotia cases left the use of subpoenas to crack foreign financial secrecy somewhat muddied, although the bank's appeal to the US Supreme Court promised to clarify matters. 'If the Bank wins the case it is likely to establish a more rational way of resolving these increasingly acrimonious disputes. Even if the bank loses, the court's ruling should lay down exactly what the limits are on the use of subpoenas.'[28]

In a 1984 tax evasion action against Gucci Shops, Inc., a US court ordered the Chase Manhattan Bank to turn over Hong Kong financial records. The bank was held in contempt and threatened with a fine of $10,000 per day even though a Hong Kong court ruled that the records in question would remain blocked. Chase was caught in the middle and appealed both orders. Eventually, Chase relented.

The emerging US view has thus been that the information requirements of domestic legal proceedings take precedence over the financial secrecy statutes of other countries, including compliance with a subpoena served on US soil – all to the intense displeasure of governments such as the UK, Canada, Switzerland and the Cayman Islands. In the process the United States has been widely accused of extending the application of its laws well beyond its national boundaries in the effort to crack financial secrecy used for criminal purposes. According to one analysis of foreign reactions to this US extraterritorial reach,

It is critically noted that Americans resort to legislation for all manner of purposes, overusing statutes, lawyers and litigation, not realizing that the problem is not one of legislation but of what people's morals really are as expressed in their deeds. The U.S. optimism about the morally educative function of further law is dismissed. Consequently, the American tendency to seek to expand its legislative approach worldwide is resented and resisted.

The U.S. has the tendency to seek to legalize [legislate for] the whole world. One *must* not assist the U.S. in this wrongful activity. While all nations must assist one another in preventing the use by criminals of havens, and everyone must agree to interfere in crime itself, other nations cannot accept underlying U.S. views, values and exported problems.[29]

Nevertheless, a number of proposals have been made in the United States to try to come to grips more effectively with the problem of secrecy havens abroad in the absence of the desired degree of cooperation from foreign governments. This includes increasing further the responsibility of bank officials to report unusual account activity, notifying US banks of foreign banks against which fraud complaints are pending, prohibiting foreign banks that fail to provide information in criminal cases from doing business in the US, and requiring a new visa of US residents for each visit to a foreign secrecy center.[30]

The Gordon Report to the Internal Revenue Service came up with a series of rather draconian measures against countries declared to be 'non cooperating offshore havens'.[31] These would prohibit US airlines from serving such countries, bar US banks from doing business there, apply a 59 per cent withholding tax on any dividends and interest due to residents of these countries, and tax all loans from their institutions to domestic residents as ordinary income. Other measures would include denial of landing rights to airlines from non-cooperating countries, eliminating customs pre-clearance arrangements, requiring special visas for travel to such countries, denying voting rights on stocks held there, denying purchasing rights to US assets, denying tax deductions for business travel to a haven and associated expenses, denying banks with operations there the right to do business in the United States, and blocking the accounts of non-cooperating banks in criminal cases involving havens.

One hope for the US to penetrate banking and commercial secrecy in the Caribbean has been the Reagan administration's Caribbean Basin Initiative (CBI). The administration proposed that Caribbean countries that participate in the investment tax incentives incorporated in the plan be required to cooperate fully in the US tax investigations involving Americans. Under this proposal, Americans who invest in any of the 30 eligible countries would be entitled to an investment tax credit only if the country enter into a bilateral executive tax agreement with the United States. Furthermore,

> [the CBI agreement] shall provide for the exchange of such information as may be necessary and appropriate to carry out and enforce the tax laws of the U.S. and the beneficiary country, including information which might otherwise be subject to non-disclosure provisions of the local law of the beneficiary country such as provisions respecting bank secrecy and bearer shares.

The Ways and Means Committee of the US House of Representatives, in recognizing that the economies of countries such as Bermuda and the Bahamas are highly dependent upon American tourist dollars, likewise took a carrot-and-stick approach to bring pressure to bear. Instead of the proposed investment tax credit, the Committee substituted an *indirect* incentive to Caribbean tourist countries – tax deductions for Americans attending conventions, seminars and similar meetings in any of the Caribbean countries and Bermuda. Tied to the offer of favorable treatment was the requirement that, before any tax-deductible convention opens, the host country must have in force an agreement with the US to exchange tax information. At this writing, Jamaica is the only Caribbean country where the convention deduction applies. In return for the deduction, Jamaica made substantial concessions in anti-treaty shopping provisions, and promised to negotiate a mutual assistance treaty concerning criminal matters in general.

As is true of most other countries, the British view of the regulatory implications of international financial secrecy is far more relaxed than the official US position. While the authorities generally acknowledge that the regulatory/supervisory situation in some countries is corrupt, inefficient and inept, and that others see it in their own interest to supply secrecy services, they consider that the fundamental problems lie in the home countries themselves. These include dysfunctional tax systems, inadequate domestic law enforcement, confusion and conflict among the responsible agencies, and similar factors that either create incentives to take advantage of international financial secrecy or minimize the disincentives.[32]

The problem of insider trading

Certainly in no area of the secrecy business has the effort to use intergovernmental cooperation and pressure to enhance the degree of disclosure been pursued more consistently and vigorously than insider trading – identified in Chapter 3 as perhaps the principal source of secrecy demand emanating from illegal activities in the securities markets.

Historically, when foreign entities have been involved in questionable securities transactions under review by the Securities and Exchange Commission (SEC) in the United States, comity (mutual respect for the laws of foreign countries) was weighed heavily by judges in deciding on the enforcement of subpoenas. Under well-established principles of international law, a US court has no authority to enforce domestically issued subpoenas against a foreign national in his own country. Thus, even after the allocation of staff time and expense in compliance actions of this type, the SEC could still face defeat, since efforts to pry open foreign bank secrecy usually prove fruitless. This has clearly defined the limits of the SEC's enforcement power in insider trading cases involving foreign financial institutions and foreign nationals.

Foreign financial secrecy laws and blocking statutes were thus alleged to contribute a lack of symmetry to the rights and obligations of participants in US financial markets. These markets are among the most important in the world, and attract borrowers and lenders globally within the growing interlinkage of financial centers.

> The dollar and the integrity of our capital markets stand at the center of the world economic order. Stock and bond purchases in the United States by foreign persons or institutions have more than doubled in four years, to $53 billion in 1982. Our markets are also a source of capital for foreigners. About 250 foreign issuers and 25 foreign governments have securities registered with the SEC.[33]

Yet, while all players assumed they had the right to gain access to these markets, not all acknowledged an obligation to comply with regulations designed to prevent their abuse.

Foreign individuals and entities were thus considered to have the best of two worlds – the participation in US capital markets and the cloak of foreign financial secrecy – which in effect enabled foreigners to engage in securities transactions illegal under US laws and avoid American sanctions. A double standard was alleged to prevail – a strict standard of conduct for persons effecting transactions domestically and a lesser enforcement standard for foreigners or for persons or entities employing a foreign intermediary:

> Clearly, participants who place orders for financial assets through a secrecy jurisdiction may be able to escape their obligations under U.S. financial regulations. Similarly, players who maintain records in jurisdictions that apply blocking laws can do likewise by seeking to have their disclosure to U.S. authorities prevented.[34]

One problem with the development of truly global, 24-hour securities trading is that investments by foreign institutions in US securities would doubtless increase, including those from countries with secrecy laws. Already US securities firms have reportedly felt leery about trading with Swiss and some other foreign banks because they cannot be sure the banks' customers aren't trading on inside information.[35]

In an attempt to restore symmetry to the rights and obligations of participants in US financial markets the SEC initiated a plan to negotiate individual disclosure agreements with each of the 25-odd countries that have secrecy or blocking laws, a slow and laborious process and one that encountered stubborn resistance and little real success. Instead, the SEC has used individual cases to try and crack foreign bank secrecy used to shield individuals violating American securities laws.

A new trend seems to be emerging, however. According to a 1981 decision by Judge Milton Pollack in a case involving the St Joe Minerals Corporation, 'It would be a travesty of Justice to permit a foreign company to invade American markets, violate American laws, if they were indeed violated, withdraw profits and resist accountability for itself and its principals for the illegality by claiming their anonymity under foreign law.'[36] Moreover, the US Supreme Court has upheld the view that persons who purposefully avail themselves of the privilege of conducting activities in US securities markets should be subject to the full enforcement *and* protection of its laws.

Specifically, the SEC charged that an Italian investor used privileged merger information to purchase St Joe Minerals Corp. stock and options through the Banca della Svizzera Italiana in Lugano. The privileged information involved plans to merge with the Santa Fe International Corporation. The SEC also found evidence of substantial purchases of stock and call options in Santa Fe International just before its merger with Kuwait Petroleum Corporation, by individuals acting through Swiss intermediaries. Insider trading clearly seemed to be involved, but Swiss secrecy laws immediately barred disclosure of the purchasers' identity.

In 1977, Faisal al Massaoud al Fuhaid, a Kuwaiti businessman with close ties to Kuwaiti government officials, was allegedly tipped off about an impending bid by the Kuwait Petroleum Corporation to acquire Santa Fe International for $2.5 billion. Fuhaid then allegedly passed the information on to several others, who evidently made over $5.2 million on the inside information, activating their transactions and secreting their profits through Swiss banks. One of the insiders, Darius Keaton, eventually consented to 'disgorge' his profits without admitting guilt, but the others remained shielded by Swiss bank secrecy. At the SEC's request, a US federal judge froze the profits that were determined by the courts as having been illegally channeled through Swiss accounts. The SEC traced the proceeds to a bank account in the New York offices of Banca della Svizzera Italiana and persuaded a federal judge to freeze $2 million of the bank's assets pending the outcome of the subsequent negotiations. Without information identifying the investors, the investigation became arduous and time-consuming. The Swiss Federal Tribunal rejected the SEC's request for access to financial information in 1981 on the grounds of insufficient evidence.

In a subsequent case, from October 1981 to mid-1984, the Swiss-based stockbroker Ellis AG was alleged by the SEC to have purchased common stock and options in over 40 US companies in advance of takeover announcements by principals charged with acting on inside information. A number of the defendants evidently obtained advance information on pending deals from materials at a major New York law firm, and used it as the basis for illegal trades through the Swiss brokerage firm, coupled to a tax evasion scheme designed to protect the ill-gotten profits. The SEC made strenuous representations to the Swiss authorities to obtain disclosure pertinent to the case, but 'received nothing'.[37]

In addition to these cases, a separate SEC action also paved the way for an accord between the US and Swiss governments on insider trading. This involved allegations that John Seabrook, former chairman of IU International Corporation, had raided the company's treasury and deposited the proceeds in Swiss accounts. Switzerland's highest court ruled that the SEC was entitled to information regarding Mr Seabrook's account in the pursuit of its investigation of fraud charges.

Bilateral efforts between the US and Switzerland to curb insider trading began in March 1982 over the St Joe Minerals request for information. Swiss officials resented the pressure imposed on its banks by US authorities, but agreed to draft temporary measures to combat insider trading until appropriate legislation could be passed. Independently, the Swiss commercial banks indicated their willingness to cooperate with SEC officials by requiring their foreign customers to sign waiver forms permitting disclosure of information identifying clients when evidence is presented by enforcement authorities showing a possible violation of US securities laws.

After months of debate and negotiation, an agreement was reached between the Swiss government and the SEC establishing a procedure permitting the SEC to make a formal request for customer information from Swiss authorities. In an eleven-article convention thereupon drafted by the Swiss Bankers' Association – the so-called Memorandum of Understanding and Private Agreement – the institutions committed themselves to provide information requested by the SEC to a three-member Commission appointed by the Association. The Commission's members were not to hold executive posts in any banking establishment. The Commission was given authority to refuse SEC requests for information if it felt that the evidence of illicit conduct was insufficient. Complaints immediately arose from customers of Swiss financial institutions, reflecting the fear of possible disclosure to US tax authorities.

Perhaps as a *quid pro quo*, Swiss bank officials required a rather strong showing of proof before information could be released.

In May 1984, after almost three years of US pressure, the Swiss Federal Tribunal in Lausanne reversed its earlier decision and ordered Crédit Suisse, Swiss Bank Corp., Lombard Odier and the Swiss branches of Chase Manhattan and Citibank to turn over to the SEC certain account-information and order tickets regarding the Santa Fe International insider trading case. Whereas the SEC's original complaint to the Swiss court had been thrown out because it failed to prove that the alleged securities law violations represented a crime in Switzerland, a second SEC attempt successfully linked information by the Kuwaiti tipster to the illegal transactions in a way that constituted a violation of Article 162 of the Swiss penal code (disclosure of business secrets to third parties).

In 1985, Switzerland finally dispatched further documents sought by the US in the Santa Fe International case. The Swiss Justice Ministry said the government had rejected a plea by unnamed individuals who had asked that assistance not be granted. The release of these documents ended the three-year dispute over disclosures in the Santa Fe case. The SEC planned to use the same techniques in moving ahead its case against Marc Rich and Pincus Green (see Chapter 3).[38]

Both the SEC and the Swiss banks claimed victory. The SEC argued that cooperation had won over confrontation. According to a Justice Department official, the case '... will signal to those who would trade on the basis of inside information that Swiss bank secrecy is no longer available as a shield from SEC investigations.'[39] The banks argued that the duration and cost of the legal proceedings would effectively discourage any further US incursions into Swiss bank secrecy in pursuit of securities law violations except under the most egregious of circumstances. Looming in the background, however, were continued rumblings in the US Congress to severely curtail Swiss banks' access to American securities markets unless effective cooperation continues.

In the fall of 1984 it was announced that the Swiss government would submit a bill to parliament that would remove banking secrecy in cases of suspected insider trading on Swiss or foreign securities exchanges, thereby potentially removing a major cause for Swiss–American friction in this area. It would broaden the definition of insiders to include informants, and provide penalties, fines and imprisonment for up to three years. The law would take effect in 1986. In the meantime, Swiss banks agreed not to take orders for securities trading to be executed on US exchanges unless the customer agreed to disclosure of his identity, should an insider trading case be established against him.

A more confrontational effort to attack the use of foreign banking secrecy and blocking laws was undertaken by the SEC in 1984. In order to avoid the cumbersome and conflict-prone approach of filing suit in US courts to compel foreign banks to release documents and identities of individuals linked to insider trading, a different approach was suggested by the SEC. This so-called 'waiver by conduct' approach would consider US securities trading tickets and confirmations as implied consent on the part of traders to waive any and all secrecy rights. The intent is to apply the same disclosure standards to both foreign and domestic traders who are active in US securities markets.

The waiver by conduct proposal was introduced by John Fedders, former chief of the SEC's Enforcement Division, in the light of the fact that almost all of an estimated $79.8 billion in foreign purchases of stocks and bonds on US exchanges in 1983 originated in countries that have either secrecy or blocking statutes. As expected, the 'waiver by conduct' proposal elicited serious objections. The possibility was raised that such action would drive securities trading offshore – for example, to London, where over 150 US corporations are already listed on the stock exchange. Another consideration was that such an approach would again be viewed as extraterritorial application of US law, and hence a hostile act, by at least some of the two dozen countries maintaining secrecy or blocking laws. Indeed, a Swiss spokesman noted that any such a waiver '... has to be governed by the laws of the country with secrecy statutes. Swiss citizens or foreigners who use Swiss banking secrecy aren't compelled to honor U.S. laws.'[40] The Swiss reaction, although not official, was hardly unexpected, given the position of Swiss banks as the largest foreign purchasers of US equities.

According to one perceptive analysis of Swiss views,

> ... we have seen that there is reticence to serve the U.S. as an outpost for its 'detour' approach to criminal prosecution. Any demands for further reductions in bank secrecy strike at the heart both of commercial interests, where secrecy is seen as essential for business success and for Swiss bank primacy in commerce, and of Swiss sentiments that individual privacy must take precedence over the interests of the state.
>
> If one respects freedom, as protected by financial privacy, one does not wish to know, nor encourage others to be able to know, about how people earn or handle their money. This is a Swiss view. The Americans have no respect for freedom or for privacy. They encourage government interference in citizens' lives. The price of the Swiss view is that we will not know about criminality. The price of the American view is that the citizen is neither private nor free, for his own government is his enemy.[41]

In addition to such objections, the very effectiveness of a waiver by conduct rule is in question. Violators could thwart the SEC by trading through a long chain of nominees and agents. Countries with blocking laws, which forbid the presentation of documents in foreign courts, would be unaffected since neither the SEC nor the US government has any jurisdiction over the laws of a foreign state. As noted in Chapter 4, not only are there 16 countries with blocking laws, but another 15 have secrecy laws that prevent banks from revealing the names of their clients unless clients agree. If the 'waiver by conduct' proposal passes, countries without blocking laws will probably pass such legislation.

The US Treasury Department has also discussed a plan that would require foreign investors in US stocks and bonds to obtain certification from their governments every time they buy an American security. German and Swiss banks have viewed this Treasury move as part of a broader attack on financial secrecy.

Multilateral approaches

Multilateral initiatives and general behavioral codes have also been suggested to combat secret money. One such initiative would involve the International Monetary Fund. It is felt that, given the reputation of the IMF, any pronouncement of its interest with respect to ethical conduct could carry some weight in the international banking community. Education of banking personnel, expansion of technical competence of local governments to engage in effective supervision, and creation of independent teams to run central bank authorities in problem countries are some long-range suggestions. In any country where the Fund is providing standby facilities, the possibility exists for the IMF to require the central bank to extend its supervision of commercial banks and to intensify deposit diligence. The argument is that thugs and gangsters will cause a country already in difficulty to suffer further losses through fraud and other crime, so that the IMF has a legitimate role to play that is consistent with its broader mandate.

Other methods to create disincentives to secret money flows include a coordinated increase in regulation through central banks in home countries and a rigid imposition of a carefully policed 'due diligence' requirement that would seek to ban criminal monies from the banking system. This would involve an expanded communication network allowing access to certain central files and to the credit, police and banking authorities of any nation for the purpose of inquiry. A disciplined, ethical Bar would be responsible for policing nominees' diligence in screening the clients they represent. It would also be necessary to have a cadre of investigators capable of examining the business aspects of crime. The investigators would be sworn to observe local secrecy laws during their presence 'on assignment' to any national jurisdiction. Flight capital or funds escaping taxes or exchange controls would not be included in the diligence check, although the lack of international consensus on tax policy could make it difficult to enforce effectively any such diligence requirements.

In June 1985 the OECD Fiscal Affairs Committee issued a draft recommendation that asked member governments to amend bank secrecy provisions 'with a view to increasing the availability of information to tax authorities' and to develop 'exchanges of bank information' under double taxation conventions. Although not legally binding, approval would provide moral pressure for cooperation on governments. The Swiss delegation immediately signalled its intention to veto or abstain from voting on the recommendation.

All multilateral efforts suffer from the same basic weakness – the fundamental difference of interest among countries in curbing secret money flows. Discontinuities in tax systems, economic policies, political and judicial arrangements, law enforcement and other factors bearing on secrecy demand and supply virtually doom from the outset any efforts to achieve cooperation beyond relatively narrow confines of mutual interest.

Summary

The problem of controlling secret money is devilishly difficult. People are surely right when they point to secret money as a symptom rather than a cause. But others have an equally valid point when they note that attacking secrecy may do more damage to the underlying illicit transactions than trying to deal with them head-on. Pressuring the 'facilitators' makes their deals more costly, more risky and less attractive, regardless of the kinds of activities that are involved.

Each approach to raise barriers to secret money flows has its problems. Unilateral efforts are necessarily partial and, at least in the US, have suffered from rather severe implementational problems. Pressuring foreign countries to change their policies on financial secrecy runs into extraterritoriality problems, imposes costs on them, and invariably leads to intergovernmental conflict. Bilateral cooperation can make some headway, but is seriously impaired by conflicting views and interests, and by the diversion of secrecy seekers to other, possibly less cooperative suppliers. Multilateral approaches remain well beyond reach.

So apart from spotty successes against egregious uses of secret money, the countermeasures seem rather ineffectual, taken as a whole. We can expect the flows to change in form, in direction and (from time to time) in size. But unless there are some underlying changes in the motivating forces, business will continue to thrive.

Notes

1 Permanent Subcommittee on Investigations, Committee on Governmental Affairs, United States Senate, *Crime and Secrecy: The Use of Offshore Banks and Companies* (Washington, DC: US Government Printing Office, 1983).

2 Penny Lernoux, 'The Seamy Side of Florida Banking', *New York Times*, 5 February 1985.

3 'Drug Smugglers Say Hard Part is What to Do with Money', *New York Times*, 29 November 1984.

4 Richard A. Gordon, *Tax Havens and their Use by United States Taxpayers* (Washington, DC: Internal Revenue Service, 1981), p. 82.

5 Lernoux, *op. cit.* (n. 2).

6 Fox Butterfield, 'Bank of Boston Reiterates Denial on Employees', *New York Times*, 28 February 1985. Fox Butterfield, 'Boston Bank Calls Misuse of Cash Unwitting', *New York Times*, 22 February 1985, p. 1. Bob Davis, 'Bank of Boston Currency Moves Foundation in Probe', *Wall Street Journal*, 10 February 1985. Alex Beam, 'Bank of Boston: A Public Relations Nightmare', *Business Week*, 4 March 1985, p. 38. Nathaniel C. Nash, 'Bank of Boston Officer Says He Erred on Rule', *New York Times*, 13 March 1985. Bob Davis, 'US Says Bank of Boston Unit Was Told It Broke Law 2 Years before Compliance', *Wall Street Journal*, 28 February 1985, p. 16. Fox Butterfield, 'US Says Boston Bank Know of Rule On Cash', *New York Times*, 27 February 1985, p. 1. Fox Butterfield, 'U.S. Jury Reported Investigating 2 Ex-Employees of Boston Bank', *New York Times*, 25 February 1985, p. 1. 'Bank of Boston', *The Economist*, 23 February 1985, p. 87.

7 Fox Butterfield, 'Boston Bank Cites "Systems Failure"', *New York Times*, 12 February 1985. Fox Butterfield, 'Statement by Boston Bank Due', *New York Times*, 10 February 1985, p. 1. Fox Butterfield, 'US Clarifies Letter on Bank', *New York Times*, 2 March 1985. 'When Banks Launder Dirty Money', *New York Times*, 16 February 1985.

8 James Rowe, 'Bank Regulators Track Paper Trails in Seach of Laundered Transactions', *The Washington Post*, 3 March 1985. Nathaniel C. Nash, '41 Banks Studied on Cash Rules', *New York Times*, 5 March 1985.

9 Lois Therrien, Blanca Riemer and Daniel Moskowitz, 'An All-Out Attack on Banks That Launder Money', *Business Week*, 25 February 1985, p. 30.

10. Alex Beam, 'Two Brokerages Get Tangled in the Money Laundering Net', *Business Week*, 11 March 1985, p. 37. Blanca Riemer and Lois Therrien, 'Money Laundering: The Defense Gets a Star Witness', *Business Week*, 28 March 1985, p. 27. James Sterngold, 'Boston Bank Cites More Violations', *New York Times*, 29 March 1985. 'More Banks Say They Didn't Report Transfers Totalling Millions of Dollars', *Wall Street Journal*, 28 March 1985. Robert A. Bennett, 'Two Banks Broke US Cash Rules', *New York Times*, 28 March 1985. Daniel Hertzberg, 'Chemical Bank Says It Failed to Report $25.9 Million in Cash Moves Since 1980', *Wall Street Journal*, 27 March 1985. Fox Butterfield, 'A Second Bank in Boston Says It Didn't Report Big Cash Transfers', *New York Times*, 9 March 1985. David Wessel and Monica Langley, 'Boston Banks Didn't Report Cash Transfers', *Wall Street Journal*, 11 March 1985.

11 Nathaniel C. Nash, '4 New York Banks Face Fines by U.S. in Cash Violations', *New York Times*, 18 June 1985.

12 Roger Cohen, 'Laundry Service: How the Mob is Using Financial Institutions to Disguise Its Gains', *Wall Street Journal*, 12 March 1985, p. 1. In May 1985, E. F. Hutton pleaded guilty to criminal fraud charges involving a massive scheme to overdraw checking accounts with US banks, involving 200 counts of felony, See 'E. F. Hutton: It's Not Over Yet', *Newsweek*, 20 May 1985, and Nathaniel C. Nash, 'E. F. Hutton Guilty in Bank Fraud; Penalties Could Top $10 Million', *New York Times*, 3 May 1985.

13 David Burnham, 'Treasury Wants More Foreign Data from Banks', *New York Times*, 3 July 1984. See also David Burnham, 'Money-Laundering Bill seen as Privacy Threat', *New York Times*, 23 June 1985.

14 Gordon, *op. cit* (n. 4).

15 William Safire, 'Mote in a Gringo's Eye', *New York Times*, 25 March 1985.

16 Sarah Bartlett, G. David Wallace, Carla Anne Robbins, Lois Therrien, Ronald Grover, Blanca Riemer and John Rossant, 'Money Laundering', *Business Week*, 18 March 1985, p. 74.
17 Cohen, *op. cit.* (n.12), p. 1.
18 Bernard Simon, 'Canadian Authorities and Banks Act to Curb Money Laundering', *Financial Times*, 26 March 1985.
19 Anne B. Fisher, 'Money Laundering', *Fortune*, 1 April 1985, p. 34.
20 Richard H. Blum and John Kaplan, 'Offshore Banking: Issues With Respect to Criminal Use', Mimeo., The Ford Foundation, 1979, p. 28.
21 'Pope Reminds Swiss About Ethics', *The Times* (London), 15 June 1984.
22 Robert Taylor, 'Cayman Islands Could be Erased as Haven for Drug Profits Under Pact, U.S. Says', *Wall Street Journal*, 13 September 1984.
23 Martha Brannigan, 'Courts Aid Officials' Efforts to Get Offshore Bank Data of U.S. Firms', *Wall Street Journal*, 24 July 1984.
24 *Ibid.*
25 Jon Nordheimer, 'Head of Isles near Bahamas Accused of Drug Plot', *New York Times*, 6 March 1985.
26 Robert Taylor, 'Bank of Nova Scotia Quietly Complies with U.S. Subpoena of Bahamas Records', *Wall Street Journal*, 22 September 1983.
27 'No Secrets, Please, We're American', *The Economist*, 23 November 1983.
28 'Permission to Peek', *The Economist*, 20 October 1984.
29 Blum and Kaplan, *op. cit.* (n. 20), p. 30.
30 Shirley Hobbs Scheibla, 'Where Hot Money Hides', *Barrons*, 11 July 1983.
31 Gordon, *op. cit.* (n. 4).
32 'Tax Havens and Funk Money', *International Currency Review*, Vol. 15, No. 2, 1983.
33 John M. Fedders, 'Foreign Secrecy: A Key to the Lock', *New York Times*, 16 October 1983.
34 *Ibid.*
35 Sarah Bartlett, 'Another Threat to Foreign Bank Secrecy, *Business Week*, 28 January 1985. Scott McMurray, George Anders, E. S. Browning and Bruce Ingersoll, 'As Global 24 Hour Trading Nears, Regulators Warn of Market Abuses', *Wall Street Journal*, 10 February 1985.
36 SEC v. Banca della Svizzera Italiana and Certain Call Options for the Stock of St. Joe Minerals Corporation, 81 Cir. 1836 (MP), 16 November 1981.
37 'Eight Men Are Indicted in Insider Trading Case', *New York Times*, 20 September 1984.
38 Margaret Studer, 'Swiss Release Data to SEC in Probe of Insider Trading,' *Wall Street Journal*, 21 February 1985. 'Swiss to Aid Insider Inquiry', *New York Times*, 21 February 1985.
39 Bruce Ingersoll, 'SEC Hails Ruling by Swiss Court Forcing Banks to Help in Inquiry', *Wall Street Journal*, 18 May 1984.
40 Bruce Ingersoll, 'SEC Urges Plan to Extend Disclosure Rules Abroad', *Wall Street Journal*, 1 June 1984. See also 'The Fedders Proposal Won't Go Away', *Euromoney*, April 1985, and 'The Epidemic of Insider Trading', *Business Week*, 29 April 1985.
41 Blum and Kaplan, *op. cit.*, (n. 26), p. 29.
42 'Swiss Bankers Fight OECD Attempt to Ease Bank Secrecy', *Financial Times*, 17 June 1985.

6

Theory of International Financial Secrecy

The previous chapters have attempted to describe, to the extent possible, the phenomenon of international financial secrecy based on bits
and pieces of available evidence. The approach has basically been an
economic one, presupposing that financial non-disclosure is something
that has value and that can be bought and sold. This approach suggests
that it ought to be possible to develop a reasonably coherent conceptual
framework using conventional tools of economics, which can then be
applied to an analysis of observed secrecy phenomena and to predict
their causes, course and consequences. This framework can be constructed from models of secrecy-oriented behavior that make it easier to
explain what is really going on and perhaps to reach reasoned, defen-
sible judgments about the probable behavior of people and institutions
under a wide variety of circumstances.

Economists are fond of developing more or less elegant models of
human behavior, intended both to interpret observed events and to
suggest the probable course of future change. These models are invariably simplifications, based on assumptions that keep things within
reasonable limits of complexity but that can later be relaxed in order to
move closer to the real world. They require a focus that is confined to
the framework specified, often involving the analysis of a single market
but sometimes extending to the behavior of entire economies. Used
judiciously, models of economic behavior can be quite instructive in
coming to grips with observations that may otherwise be extraordinarily
difficult to interpret.

This chapter attempts to lay out such a model by examining the
tradeoffs that exist between secrecy, risks and returns, the determinants
of the real value of secret money, and the characteristics of markets for
financial secrecy. Inevitably, the discussion is difficult in spots, and
readers with a limited interest in (or tolerance for) theory are advised to

153

skip to the concluding section of the chapter (pp. 173–4), which contains a summary in plain English.

Secrecy versus expected returns

Secrecy is rarely 'free'. It must be purchased by an individual intent on non-disclosure by putting together a portfolio of assets (or a single asset) that yields the desired level of confidentiality. One 'cost' of secrecy to the individual is thus the difference between the expected yield on his secrecy-oriented portfolio and the yield on a 'benchmark portfolio' put together by the same individual when secrecy is not a consideration. The tradeoff involved is depicted in Figure 6.1.

A portfolio of assets that contains no secrecy has an expected market return of R_0 in the diagram. This could be a composite of interest or dividend returns, rents and royalties, expected capital gains, and the like, all in real terms. As the secrecy consideration mounts, it is probable that the expected return on successive portfolios displaced from the completely 'open' mix of assets will decline – possibly to zero and perhaps even to negative real values – along line RESE, the return/ secrecy rela-

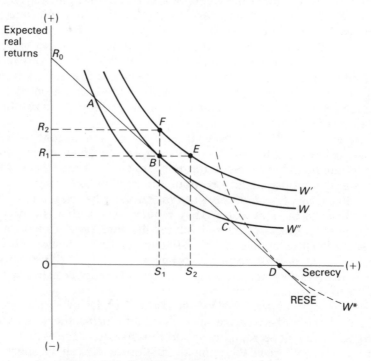

Figure 6.1 *Secrecy versus expected real returns*

154

tionship depicted in Figure 6.1. That relationship may not, of course, be linear. In addition it may not be stable as different secrecy vehicles shift in terms of expected real returns.

The preference for expected yield compared to the level of secrecy for an individual is given by the shape of welfare contours W in Figure 6.1. Their shape indicates a diminishing marginal rate of substitution of portfolio returns for secrecy. When the secrecy content of the asset portfolio is already very high, for example, the individual would want to add still more secrecy only if the 'price' in terms of further erosion of expected real returns is rather low. As the degree of secrecy *and* expected returns increase from W'' to W to W', the individual is successively better off. The optimum mix of expected yield and secrecy is point B (R_1 and S_1) in Figure 6.1. Combinations A (high expected yield, low secrecy) and C (low expected yield, high secrecy) are both inferior because they lie on curve W'', which is lower than W. Similarly, points such as F (S_1 and R_2) as well as E (R_1 and S_2) cannot be attained with the available secrecy-bearing assets, even though curve W' represents a level of welfare that is superior to W.

The optimum level of secrecy the individual would want to purchase is S_1, with an expected real return on the portfolio of assets held being R_1, and a 'cost' of secrecy equal to $R_1 - R_0$. This cost would then have to be balanced against the benefits of secrecy (the probability and disutility of disclosure), which are imbedded in the position and shape of the welfare contours W. For example, if the cost of disclosure in Figure 6.1 rises (perhaps, because of increased competitive disadvantages attributable to disclosure), the welfare contours shift to the right perhaps to W^*. As a result, the desired amount of secrecy purchased rises substantially, expected yield in this example drops to zero and the 'cost' of secrecy increases to $0 - R_0$. The cost could, of course, increase still further if the expected real returns on the assets held became negative, as when currency is buried in the ground during a period of inflation, or if intermediaries charge heavily for their services.

Secrecy versus risk

Besides the cost of secrecy imbedded in the expected real returns on assets, there is also the matter of risk. It seems likely that portfolios of assets containing greater degrees of financial secrecy are also more risky. For example, assets may have to be held abroad, resulting in foreign exchange risk and country risk. Or they may be forced into configurations that are susceptible to increased interest-rate risk. Various ways of hedging risk, including the ability to diversify portfolios and shift risk by means of futures and options markets, may not be available to the secrecy seeker. One could argue that the degree of risk (defined in terms of the covariance of expected future returns on the assets contained in the portfolio) tends to increase with the secrecy content of the portfolio. Again, we have a tradeoff line such as SERI in Figure 6.2. As it is drawn, the figure suggests there is some degree of risk associated with *any* conceivable portfolio of assets, no matter how well hedged or diversified – that is, SERI cuts the vertical axis somewhere above zero. As secrecy requirements increase, which in turn may limit asset selection, availability of hedging vehicles, etc., the covariance in the expected returns on these assets tends to increase as well.

The position and shape of SERI, whether linear or not, can be argued at length. For example, it may be that at very high levels of secrecy the asset-holder is forced into a tightly restricted portfolio selection (perhaps a single type of asset in a single location), and the SERI curve at those secrecy levels may well become increasingly steep.

In conjunction with the tradeoff between the degree of risk embodied in asset portfolios and their built-in level of secrecy, there is an interplay between the preference for risk and the preference for secrecy on the part of the asset-holder. If we assume such individuals are normally risk-averse, then they tend to prefer portfolios that incorporate lower rather than higher covariances in expected future real asset returns, all else equal, although, of course, the attitude toward risk may differ enormously among individuals. Similarly, the assumption of a positive value on secrecy results in welfare contours such as M in Figure 6.2. The shape

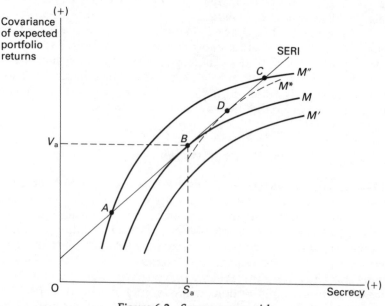

Figure 6.2 *Secrecy versus risk*

of M indicates how much additional risk the individual is willing to accept in return for additional financial secrecy, yet still be equally well off. The shape of M in Figure 6.2 implies that the tolerance for increased risk decreases once very high secrecy levels have already been attained and, conversely, that very substantial reductions in risk would be necessary to induce acceptance of lower financial secrecy once these are already at minimum levels, all under the presumption that the individual is no better and no worse off than before.

If the market makes available a risk/secrecy tradeoff depicted by SERI in Figure 6.2, and the individual's risk/secrecy preferences are given by the shape of M, a level of risk indicated by a covariance in expected returns V_a would be accepted in return for level S_a of secrecy. A lower level of risk *and* secrecy, such as A, or a higher level of both (C) would be worse in view of the individual's preferences – it would leave him on welfare level M'', which is clearly inferior to M. In much the same way, while the individual would be better off with risk level V_a *and* greater secrecy than S_a, or with secrecy level S_a *and* lower risk than V_a (for example, a move onto M', which is superior to M), he cannot achieve either one, given the tradeoffs available in the market.

If the individual's desire for secrecy increases, it is logical that he would be willing to take on an increased degree of risk. This might be represented by the new family of preference contours M^* in Figure 6.2, which induce the individual to seek greater secrecy *and* accept greater risk at a point such as D.

Risk versus returns with secrecy

Conventional views on the creation of 'efficient' portfolios do not take financial secrecy considerations into account. But they can easily be made to accommodate them. An efficient portfolio is one that maximizes investor returns, subject to a risk constraint, or minimizes risk given a particular return target. Both the individual's attitude toward risk, or risk preference, and the measurement of risks and returns available in asset markets are important elements in the design of efficient portfolios.

Consider Figure 6.3, where the horizontal axis measures the expected real return on a portfolio of assets, and the vertical axis measures the covariance of those returns. RR is the risk/return relationship provided by the market. Even at zero risk, there will be some positive return. As the risk rises, so does the expected return. The individual's risk/return preferences are indicated by a family of welfare contours such as N. The way they are drawn assumes the individual is normally risk-averse – that is, he will accept more risk only if he expects to receive a higher return in order not to sacrifice in terms of welfare. More risk with a given expected return means reduced welfare (a move from N to N'' for example). So does a lower expected return with a given level of risk.

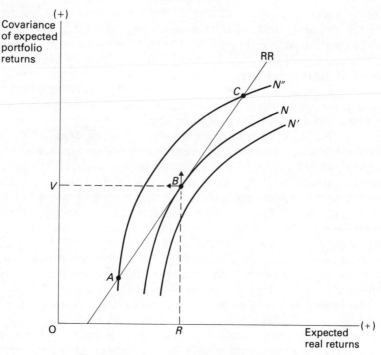

Figure 6.3 *Secrecy and the efficient portfolio*

An individual will maximize his welfare with an asset portfolio such as *B*, with a risk level of *V* and a return of *R*. A portfolio characterized by higher expected returns *and* higher risk, such as *C*, would leave the individual on a lower level of welfare *N"*. So would a portfolio that combined a lower level of risk and lower expected returns, such as *A*. The individual would, of course, be better off (*N'*) if he could obtain higher expected returns with a given level of risk, or obtain a lower risk level with given expected real returns. Unfortunately, the market's risk/return tradeoff given by RR in Figure 6.3 precludes that.

Now what happens when we incorporate an individual's desire for financial secrecy? From the earlier discussion, he should be willing to accept a reduced rate of return and/or be willing to expose himself to a higher level of risk. Here, it would tend to displace the efficient portfolio represented by point *B* in the direction of the arrows. That is, the individual will have to make do either with a reduced expected return or increased risk, or both. And so, from a risk/return perspective, he will be worse off and the level of welfare attained may shift from *N* to, say, *N"*. Does this mean he is really worse off in terms of his total welfare? Certainly not, because the welfare gains from the enhanced secrecy may well outweigh the welfare losses in the risk/return dimension.

158

An overall view

We now have three different dimensions under discussion – risk, return and secrecy. Between any two of these dimensions, there are clearly tradeoffs presented by the markets for various types of assets – between risk and returns, between returns and secrecy, and between secrecy and risk – as discussed in the preceding sections. At the same time, we have seen that there are tradeoffs between each *pair* of objectives as perceived by the individual asset-holder. In each case, an optimum combination can be defined once the individual's preferences and the market's tradeoffs are known – one that optimizes the individual's welfare under the constraints imposed by the market.

All of this can be put together quite neatly in Figure 6.4. For convenience, we alter the 'risk' axis to represent 'safety', with a risk-free portfolio being represented by some maximum safety point on the axis and asset covariance rising (safety declining) as one moves along the scalar away from that point. From our earlier discussion, we know that the asset markets present the individual with a risk/return tradeoff (here

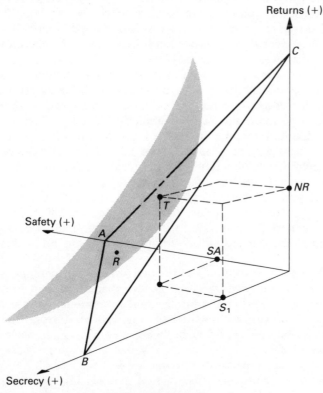

Figure 6.4 *Welfare maximization under secrecy*

line *AC*), with returns rising with increasing risk, or decreasing safety. We also know that these markets present a return/secrecy tradeoff (here shown as line *CB*), with *C* being the maximum net real portfolio return when secrecy plays no role whatsoever, and returns declining with increased secrecy, perhaps eventually resulting in negative net returns (not shown). Finally, we have discussed a secrecy/risk tradeoff, under the presumption that the acquisition of greater secrecy forces the individual into a more risky selection of assets or closes off options for portfolio diversification or risk shifting. This tradeoff is shown by *AB* in Figure 6.4 – increased secrecy has to be 'purchased' by asset portfolios that embody reduced levels of safety.

If we assume that all three market-determined tradeoffs are linear, we can define the plane *ABC* in a three-dimensional diagram such as Figure 6.4. The individual can choose any asset mix yielding a combination of safety, returns and secrecy that lies on the *ABC* plane. For example, if secrecy plays no role whatsoever in the individual's objectives, he will want to operate along line *AC* at the 'left edge' of the plane. Similarly, if returns are an immaterial consideration compared with safety and secrecy, he will want to operate along the lower (*AB*) 'edge' of the plane. If all three considerations are to be taken into account, he will want to position himself somewhere on the inside of the *ABC* plane. But where?

This will be determined, as we have seen earlier, by the individual's relative preferences for the three objectives. We can depict the relative preference for safety versus returns by the shape of convex contours as in Figure 6.3, which show that the individual is willing to accept reduced safety for increased returns, but at a decreasing rate – that is, the individual is normally risk-averse. Similarly, the convex contours show that the individual is willing to trade lower returns for increased secrecy, again at a decreasing rate, as in Figure 6.1. And he is likewise willing to trade lower levels of safety for higher levels of secrecy along a third set of convex contours, as in Figure 6.2. The shapes of the three sets of contours depend on the 'marginal rates of substitution' between each pair of objectives. The better the two objectives substitute for one another, the more the contours approximate straight lines. The less they are regarded by the individual as substitutes, the more convex the contours.

We thus can envisage a set of bowl-shaped 'preference surfaces' among the three objectives (such as the shaded area in Figure 6.4), which defines the nature of an individual's preferences at a given level of welfare. If the surface lies 'higher' – farther away from the origin – he will obviously be better off by being able to avail himself of more secrecy *and* safety *and* returns. Conversely, a 'lower' bowl-shaped preference surface represents a lower level of welfare.

We can now complete the picture by placing the individual's preference pattern for secrecy/safety returns, and the market's 'supply' pattern, ABC in Figure 6.4, together. Given the tradeoffs dictated by the market, the individual may want to obtain S_1 of secrecy, which requires a portfolio of assets yielding SA of safety and earning NR of net real returns – at point T in the diagram, where the bowl-shaped preference surface is *tangent* to the supply plane ABC, and where the individual will maximize his welfare given the various assets available in the market. Of course, he could also operate with any other mix of secrecy/safety/ returns defined by the ABC plane, such as point R. But any such mix would leave him worse off – that is, on a *lower* preference surface – and consequently would make no sense. Nor could he reach a higher preference surface under existing market conditions, so that point T is indeed an optimum.

How can the individual become better off, and move to a higher preference surface? One way is for the market to throw off higher expected real returns, as when global credit conditions tighten – point C moves upward. Another is for the cost of secrecy to decline, as when there is increased competition among secrecy vendors – point B moves to the left. If new, less risky types of assets become available, or greater opportunities for diversification or risk-shifting present themselves, point A moves to the left. Any of these developments will raise the level of the ABC plane and permit an increase in the individual's level of welfare – a move to a higher welfare surface. Unless all three increase proportionately, however, the *shape* of the ABC plane will change as well, and hence the *mix* of safety, returns and secrecy will likewise be altered (the relative location of point T). Conversely, factors affecting reduced yields, secrecy and portfolio safety will leave the individual worse off, on a lower welfare surface.

Now suppose the ABC plane remains unchanged, but the individual's preferences shift. For example, for a reformed tax evader who no longer needs secrecy to escape from the fiscal authorities, point T would move onto line AC – he would end up better off in the risk/return dimension. If, on the other hand, the perceived benefits from secrecy increase, point T would move in the direction of greater secrecy to reflect a preference surface that is more 'biased' in that direction than before. Similar changes in the mix would reflect an alteration in the relative preference for safety versus returns.

Marginal costs and benefits

The discussion can be joined by using a cost–benefit framework – always keeping in mind that costs and benefits to the individual need somehow to be established, especially in an incremental sense for the development of reasonably robust conclusions. In Figure 6.5, the vertical axis is intended to measure the incremental cost and benefit

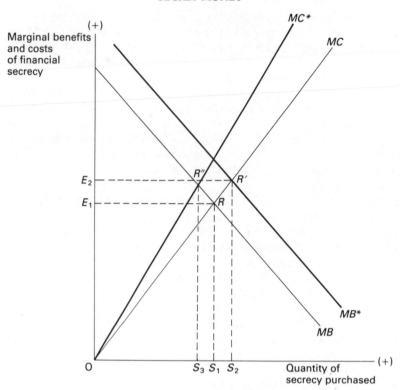

Figure 6.5 *Cost–benefit analysis applied to financial secrecy*

associated with the acquisition of one additional unit of financial secrecy, measured along the horizontal axis.

If the marginal benefits associated with acquisition of various levels of financial secrecy are as depicted by curve MB in Figure 6.5, then increased secrecy throws off successively lower marginal benefits. We know from Chapter 3 that the MB curve has imbedded in it a set of motives driving the individual's preferences – whether they are related to normal business or financial confidentiality, prospective divorce proceedings, tax or exchange-control evasion, bribery and corruption, or conventional criminal activities ranging from drug trafficking to securities fraud. These motives will determine both the shape and the position of the MB curve. As we have also discussed earlier, the incremental acquisition of financial secrecy entails incremental costs, either in the form of reduced real expected returns on assets or increased portfolio risk. This is shown in the position and shape of the MC curve in Figure 6.5, and is the result of factors prevailing in the market for secrecy that faces the individual concerned – a market that may itself be highly segmented. The optimum amount of secrecy acquired will be

S_1, associated with a marginal cost and benefit level of E_1. Given MB and MC, levels of secrecy lower than S_1 mean that the incremental benefits of increased purchases would exceed the incremental costs, and more should be acquired, while levels in excess of S_1 represent an excessive acquisition of financial secrecy under existing cost–benefit conditions.

Clearly, a shift in benefit or cost factors will alter the behavior of the individual. Increases in tax rates, in political instability or in personal security concerns, for example, will cause a shift in MB to the right – perhaps to MB^*. The individual would then be willing to pay more for the existing level of secrecy, and to acquire more (S_2 in Figure 6.5), at a marginal cost of E_2. Similarly, a change in market conditions might increase the marginal cost (MC^*) of secrecy. This might be attributable to government measures to crack down on domestic secrecy vendors, institute tighter exchange controls, reach agreements with foreign governments on access to offshore financial records, and the like – thus forcing the individual into higher-cost vehicles or into vehicles that expose him to greater risk. With unchanged marginal benefits, therefore, he could be expected to acquire less financial secrecy (S_3).

The acquisition of financial secrecy can thus be thought of as a rational process, one that balances costs against benefits and in which a change perceived in either one is likely to change behavior of individuals in rather predictable ways.

Value of secret assets

How much are secret assets really worth? As the foregoing discussion has implied, it all depends on risks and net returns, benefits and costs. The value of any asset depends in part on the returns the asset is expected to generate during future time periods, the costs associated with bringing in those returns, and their variability in relation to the returns variability associated with the market as a whole, as a measure of risk. In the case of secret assets, it also depends on the probability of being found out, the penalties that may be imposed, and the individual's attitude toward risk (both asset-related risk and discovery/ punishment risk).

This can be stated very simply as follows, where NPV_t represents the net present value of a secret asset portfolio to the individual:

$$NPV_t = \sum_{t=0}^{n} \frac{(ER_t - EC_t)\dfrac{1}{(1+i^*+B_t)^t}}{P_t(1+a^*)^t}.$$

ER_t represents the expected return flows on the assets concerned. Earnings may be zero in the case of domestic currency or demand balances,

163

or positive in the case of interest-bearing assets or equities expected to pay dividends or undergo capital appreciation. Expected returns on assets denominated in foreign currencies, gold, other precious metals and collectables also depend on changing market values anticipated for the future. All values include expectations regarding the return of principal.

EC_t represents the expected costs associated with holding the assets. These might include warehousing and insurance costs (as in the case of gold or other valuables), payments to third parties (e.g. trustees), possible costs of legal or enforcement actions, etc. Consequently, $(ER_t - EC_t)$ represents the *net* expected returns on a portfolio of assets over successive future time periods.

Of course, virtually all assets are subject to certain risks. There are exchange-rate risks, transfer risks, default risks, market risks, and risks of theft. Therefore, the net expected returns have to be discounted appropriately. In the equation above, i^* represents the risk-free rate of return – for an American that might be represented by the Treasury bill rate. Clearly, if i^* rises, the net present value of other assets (e.g. fixed-rate loans and gold) will tend to decline as reflected either in market prices or in opportunity costs. This loss may be limited if the assets held throw off returns that move in tandem with the risk-free rate, such as floating-rate financial instruments.

The term B_t represents the risk associated with the assets held. If only one asset is held, that risk is driven by the variability of the expected future net returns on that asset in relation to the variability of all assets in the market. The higher the variability, and the more risk-averse the individual, the larger will be the value of B_t and the lower the net present value of the secret asset to the individual. If a diversified portfolio of assets is held, B_t is affected by the covariance among different assets in the portfolio, in addition to market variability and the attitude of the individual towards risk. The more risky the portfolio of assets, and the more risk-averse the asset-holder, the lower will be the value of those future streams of expected net returns to the individual.

However, risk-adjusted net returns are only part of the story if secrecy is a motivation. It is also important to look at the denominator of the above equation. P_t represents the disutility (or pain) of punishment that would befall the secrecy seeker should he get caught. The greater the value of P_t, the smaller will be the present value of the assets. For example, if punishment is death and complete confiscation of assets, the value of those assets in the event of discovery is likely to be low indeed. Lesser punishments might include jail terms of varying durations, back taxes, fines and penalties, a nagging spouse, or loss of control over personal or business affairs.

Of course, it is not at all certain that the individual will be exposed, and the whole purpose of secrecy is to prevent this from happening. The

164

term a^* in the equation indicates the probability of getting caught associated with a particular set of secrecy-containing assets, as modified once again by the indvidual's attitude towards the risk of being found out. The smaller a^*, the larger will be NPV_t, either because the chances of getting caught with the assets are smaller, or because the asset-holder has a sanguine view about the likelihood of being found out.

Given a certain attitude of a secrecy seeker toward risk, the equation clearly points to a number of tradeoffs that have been shown diagrammatically earlier. Specifically, a reduction of a^* may have to be 'purchased' with an increase in B_t (the risk associated with the secrecy-containing portfolio), a decrease in ER_t (a reduction in expected returns on a secrecy-containing portfolio) or an increase in EC_t (the associated costs). The rational secrecy seeker will obviously want to maximize the net present value of his assets, NPV_t, and this will require that careful attention be paid to these tradeoffs.

One would be tempted to argue that, in terms of their investment behavior, secrecy seekers should be a conservative lot. Since they are already substantially exposed to risk in terms of the origins of their need for secrecy, they ought to have relatively little tolerance for risk in their asset portfolios. One would conclude that they therefore want a high degree of secrecy *and* a high degree of safety. Given the tradeoffs provided by the market, they would thus be willing to pay a very high price, in terms of earnings forgone, for the dual attributes. This may not be quite so true if taxation is taken into account. Since secrecy seekers may well operate entirely or largely free of tax in the financial markets they use, the after-tax return comparisons may not look quite as bad in comparison with those of (taxed) investors not concerned with secrecy. Moreover, the absence of tax on income as well as on assets, estates and capital gains may increase the secrecy seeker's interest in somewhat more risky assets, since the expected returns are effectively higher. In the real world, it appears, a significant proportion of secrecy seekers are not particularly risk-averse at all.

The principal-agent problem

An investor on the open market walks into a brokerage firm or the trust department of a bank and enters into an asset-management relationship with the investment manager. As the 'principal', he explains his interest in capital appreciation, dividend or interest income, tax exemption, or other investment objectives, as well as his attitude toward risk. The investment manager, in turn, takes on a fiduciary responsibility to carry out that mandate as faithfully as possible, in return for commissions and fees that presumably reflect the value of services rendered. He is to manage the portfolio in accordance with the investor's wishes, and in this role he becomes the investor's 'agent'. Interpreting and fulfilling the investor's objectives are an example of what has become known as the 'principal–agent problem'.

An agency relationship exists whenever an asset-holder delegates some decision-making authority to the manager of a discretionary account. If such a relationship exists, there will be positive monitoring and bonding costs, which can be monetary or non-monetary in nature. In addition, there will often be some divergence between the agent's actual decisions and those decisions that would in fact maximize the welfare of the principal. The principal will thus incur a 'residual loss', which is yet another cost of the agency relationship. Usually, contracts between principals and agents provide appropriate incentives for the agent to make decisions that will maximize the principal's welfare, given existing market uncertainties.

Financial secrecy in an international context raises some unique agency issues. Ordinarily, the agent will have to interpret the investor's wishes and carry them out as best he can. But interpretation of these wishes may not be easy, and can lead to serious disputes down the road. Or the investor's objectives may change, either explicitly or implicitly, with the agent being uninformed or poorly advised. Or the investor may psychologically reposition his objectives after the fact, if the value of his assets has underperformed an alternative portfolio, with undeserved blame assigned to the agent. Or the agent himself may abuse his mandate by 'churning' the portfolio to bolster commission income, for example, or by 'stuffing' it with substandard securities he wants to be rid of. Or he may simply not be very competent. Clearly, if secrecy is added to the agent's mandate, his job becomes very much more complex. He must do all in his power to safeguard secrecy within the limits of (and sometimes outside of) the law. Violation of his fiduciary role, at least in the eyes of the principal, includes violation of his secrecy mandate, triggering potentially serious disputes between the two parties – with possible damage to the agent through erosion in the value of his secrecy-oriented 'product'.

However, the agent has some leverage on his side as well. Ordinarily, agency-related disputes can be taken into court in civil suits, which then supersede other forms of dispute-settlement that have proven unsuccessful. Still, how can the secrecy seeker take the agent to court when a foreign legal jurisdiction is involved, when that jurisdiction is unclear, or when such an action would compromise the very secrecy he is after – that is, when the suit would itself severely erode the real value of his assets? So the agent acquires a certain immunity from the sort of redress usually available to asset-holders confronted by agent misconduct. Could this not tempt him to abuse his agency function, to enrich himself at the expense of the secrecy-seeking investor? Could he not use his fiduciary position and *de facto* immunity from suit to hold himself harmless as well from other forms of redress, like physical violence, by threat of disclosure?

The addition of secrecy to the conventional principal–agent problem obviously has some interesting implications. The real question is whether the shelter attributable to secrecy influences the behavior of the agent. On the one hand, there is a strong incentive for agents to maximize their own welfare, since they are at least partially protected from retribution. In addition, secrecy seekers are fully prepared to pay any normal agency costs that come with secrecy, as long as there are no large unaccountable losses. On the other hand, the competition a secrecy vendor faces from other sellers, as well as traditions of prudence and competence, tend to impose constraints on abusive behavior.

It may be reasonable to assume that there are relatively few cases where agents seek to maximize their own welfare at the expense of asset-holders, and that any such tendency could be checked by competitive and social pressures. Still, this problem puts a real premium on selection of the agent, who must be depended upon to carry out his fiduciary responsibility with great care and sensitivity to client desires — which themselves are subject to change – yet without succumbing to the temptations that derive from his potential leverage as a 'secret agent'.

Demand and supply

The foregoing discussion implies that the demand for financial secrecy will be a negative function of price. That is, the quality of secrecy-containing assets acquired by the individual will be larger, the lower their assessed cost to the investor. In Figure 6.6, a demand curve for secrecy-containing assets is drawn (D) that is relatively inelastic at its upper end and relatively elastic at lower prices. The suggestion here is that the demand for financial secrecy will be relatively insensitive to price for those individuals for whom exposure would be a very serious matter indeed (e.g. drug traffickers), while less burdened secrecy seekers will tend to have better alternatives available to them or be willing to go without, thus leaving such individuals fairly sensitive to price. Once again, by 'price' we mean the risk-adjusted returns on secrecy-containing assets subtracted from the risk-adjusted returns on non-secret assets of equivalent nominal value.

Various developments could cause the demand curve to shift – changes in income, alterations in asset-related risks, changes in tax rates, increases or decreases in penalties associated with exposure or the probability of getting caught, etc. The curve applies only to residents of a particular country. Both the position and shape of the demand curve may differ substantially among countries.

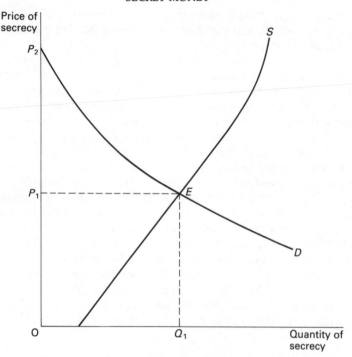

Figure 6.6 *Supply, demand and market equilibrium*

The provision of secrecy-containing assets is represented by the supply curve S in Figure 6.6. The curve starts to the right of 0, meaning that a certain amount of secrecy can be obtained by secrecy seekers at zero cost. This may be rather substantial, with secrecy provided simply by ordinary confidential relationships that are possible in asset portfolios constructed even in the absence of the secrecy objective. However, acquisition of additional secrecy can be undertaken only at successively higher cost (as defined earlier). Once again, the elasticity of curve S is likely to be relatively low at high levels, where the vendors either face substantial incremental costs in shielding their product from prying eyes, or believe that they can extract very high prices for their services.

Once again, a number of things cause the supply curve to shift, including changes in penalties associated with selling secret assets and the probability of being found out, the cost of intermediaries' services, and attractiveness of alternative assets.

Given the demand and supply curves depicted in Figure 6.6, the market price of secret assets of a particular type is P_1 and quantity Q_1 will be bought. Some of these assets would have been bought by individuals willing to pay a much higher price (even P_2), who thus

168

obtain an 'unearned' benefit equal to the amount they *would have been willing to pay* and P_1. This is the 'secrecy seeker's surplus' (SSS), already mentioned in Chapter 1. Here, SSS is given by the area P_1P_2E in the diagram. Similarly, some secrecy vendors would have been willing to sell at a price far less than P_1, and even give it away free. By being able to change the market price of P_1, they therefore receive a 'secrecy vendor's surplus' (SVS) equal to the area $0P_1EQ_1$ in Figure 6.6. Secrecy sales and purchases thus make everyone better off – both buyers and sellers – which is, of course, necessary if exchange in secrecy-containing assets is to take place. What it does to others who are not immediate participants in the secrecy market cannot be determined from this (partial) analysis.

Completing the story, developments that raise the benefits of financial secrecy to purchasers will cause the quantity demanded to rise, while factors that increase the supply of secret assets (e.g. due to the entry of new vendors) will increase the quantity bought and decrease the price. The former will increase SVS, while the latter will increase SSS. Similarly a reduction in the supply of secrecy (e.g. due to a crackdown on vendors by the authorities) will raise the price and reduce quantity (and cut SSS), while a reduction in demand (perhaps due to improved alternatives to secrecy) will reduce both price and quantity (and SVS).

All of this assumes, of course, that secrecy-seekers are a homogeneous group who will all pay the same price. We noted in Chapter 3 that the drug trafficker may be willing to pay far more for financial secrecy than the father intent on keeping financial information from his children. Secrecy vendors may thus be able to discriminate among groups of secrecy seekers (and even among individuals) on the basis of their respective sensitivity to price – thus draining off part of the SSS and enhancing SVS – as long as the secret assets cannot be resold.

Consider Figure 6.7, which depicts a 'market' consisting of two groups with different secrecy preferences. Group A's demand for secrecy (D_A) is clearly less price-sensitive than Group B's (D_B), so it makes sense for secrecy vendors to charge A more than B. M_A and M_B are the corresponding marginal revenue curves associated with sales of secret assets to the two groups. TD and TM are the two groups' respective demand and marginal revenue curves added together, while MC is the marginal cost to the vendor of supplying additional amounts of secret assets. The secrecy seller will want to operate where overall marginal revenue (TM) is just equal to his cost (MC), at point E. Rather than charging both groups the same price, it would make sense to sell Q_A to group A $(MC = M_A)$ at price P_A and Q_B to group B $(MC = M_B)$ at price P_B. That way, vendors can capture a good share of the SSS that the secrecy seekers would obtain if one price applied to all.

Of course, more than two groups of secrecy seekers may exist, and it is possible to set as many prices as there are identifiable groups with

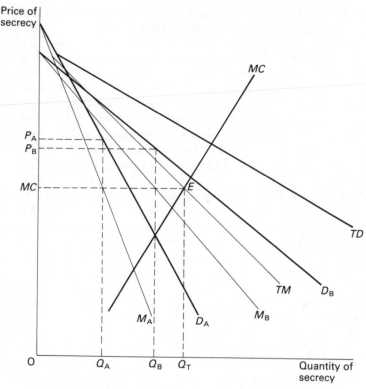

Figure 6.7 *Price discrimination among secrecy seekers*

different demand characteristics. At the limit, where price discrimination is so perfect that each secrecy seeker has to pay the maximum he is actually willing to pay for a given amount of secrecy. SSS goes to zero. Whether this ever happens in the real world is doubtful. But vendors surely are able to 'hold up' individuals from time to time and extract from them substantial secrecy-related profits – particularly when it is possible for those vendors to collude with one another.

The externality problem

The secrecy business clearly has some extremely wide-ranging effects, many of which bear on people other than those directly involved, and which are not directly captured in the economics of the industry. Secrecy seekers gain from the absence of financial disclosure, and are willing to pay for it. Secrecy vendors have a product from which they can extract economic rents, as long as there aren't too many competitors in the game. Both sides win. But others may win or lose as well. International financial secrecy generates 'externalities' that can be both positive (like education) and negative (like pollution).

What about refugees from unjust political or economic persecution around the world, for example? Secrecy offers an opportunity for the oppressed to escape confiscation of assets by capricious or arbitrary actions of governments that may themselves hold power without much claim to political legitimacy. The availability of this avenue may encourage individuals to redouble their economic effort by reducing the risks associated with exposure to possible loss, and others (employees, customers, suppliers, society as a whole) benefit either directly or indirectly. They would, of course, benefit more if the perceived risk were itself lessened and the need for secrecy reduced or eliminated. But half a loaf may be better than none at all. And, if people are ultimately forced to flee, countries in which they seek refuge will be less burdened if some of their financial assets have successfully sought refuge first. Such positive external effects of financial secrecy are magnified whenever human rights, racial and ethnic persecution, and similar non-economic considerations are brought into play.

Positive externalities associated with international financial secrecy have their counterparts on the negative side, of course. The ready availability of secret assets makes possible tax evasion, from which all honest taxpayers suffer. It facilitates bribery and corruption through the maintenance of slush funds and caches for ill-gotten gains. Bribes, in turn, can severely distort resource allocation and income distribution – and the political process itself – to the detriment of individuals and groups around the world. It makes possible organized and unorganized crime ranging from gun running and drugs, to rackets and hijacking, to illegal gambling, smuggling, terrorism and espionage, even contract murder, from which millions of ordinary citizens may ultimately suffer. Not least important, it reduces the commitment of political leaders worldwide, who know that a secret nest-egg abroad may save them from the full consequences of their errors of omission or commission. One could even argue that popular uprisings and the emergence of military dictatorships are often linked to financial secrecy, which encourages the kind of endemic official corruption that eventually leads to revolt and the need to 'clean house'.

None of these benefits and costs is reflected in the market for secrecy itself. Do the negative externalities outweigh the positive ones? Nobody knows. In any case, forcing them back into the secrecy markets – much as is done in pollution control, for example – requires concerted efforts in terms of intergovernmental coordination and enforcement that in today's world stand virtually no chance of coming about.

International trade in financial secrecy

We know that secrecy havens exist. Their characteristics have been explored in detail in Chapter 4. This means that secrecy vendors in some countries supply services that involve value-added to residents of other countries. In other words, there exists a lively international trade in secrecy-related financial services. Why? Obviously, there must be substantial inter-country differences in the demand for, and supply of, financial secrecy. Referring back to Figure 6.6, the supply and demand functions that characterize the market for financial secrecy must differ quite substantially among countries. This is depicted in Figure 6.8.

In Country X, the demand for financial secrecy looks quite impressive compared to Country Y. Why? Perhaps tax rates are higher. Or the economic or political system is rife with corruption. Or the illegal drug business is thriving. As discussed in Chapter 3, market distortions in general create a fertile environment within which a buoyant demand for financial secrecy usually develops. Meantime, the supply of financial secrecy in X looks rather limited, perhaps owing to various governmental enforcement actions, lack of effective legal protection against forced disclosure, or similar factors that constrain its availability and make secrecy very expensive at the margin, as discussed in Chapter 4. In Country Y, on the other hand, the demand for financial secrecy seems

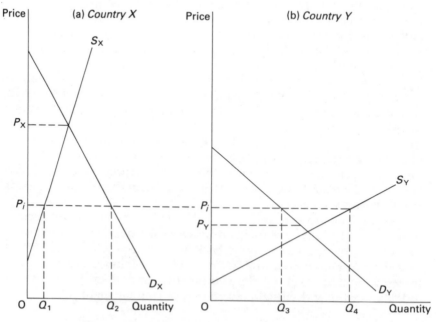

Figure 6.8 *International trade in financial secrecy*

small, probably because many of the factors that give rise to the need for it in X are absent in Y. At the same time, strict bank secrecy laws, ample financial infrastructure and human resources make the supply of secrecy in that country quite robust. If the two markets for financial secrecy remain in isolation it is not hard to predict the outcome: secret money would be expensive (P_X) in Country X and cheap (P_Y) in Country Y.

A perfect opportunity for international trade! We would predict that Country Y (the secrecy haven) will export Q_3Q_4 of secrecy-related services to Country X (the secrecy hell), whose imports are Q_1Q_2. Purchases of financial secrecy-related services will flow from where they are cheap (Y) to where they are expensive (X). In the process, those services will become more readily available (and cheaper) in Country X, residents will gain substantial SSS, and local secrecy vendors will suffer in competition with their foreign rivals. In the secrecy haven (Country Y), vendors will benefit substantially with increased output of secrecy-related services and increased SVS as the price of financial secrecy rises owing to the incremental foreign demand without, however, seriously injuring whatever domestic secrecy seekers are present – price will rise from P_Y to P_i. Moreover, since the production of secrecy-related financial services increases in Country Y, employment, taxation, balance of payments contributions, and various other linked elements – the so called 'external benefits' – are likely to be quite favorable, and will encourage the continuation of government policies that underlie the country's status as a secrecy haven.

Summary

This chapter has attempted to present, within a consistent structure, the conceptual underpinnings of the international market in financial secrecy. Individuals normally try to maximize their welfare in a more or less rational way. This means they try to maximize the returns on asset portfolios within predetermined risk parameters, or minimize risk subject to some target rate of return. The market for financial assets throws up a tradeoff between risk and returns, and individuals try to maximize their welfare (given the strength of their preference for returns and their risk aversion) within this constraint. Financial secrecy adds a third variable to the equation. Now individuals must try to maximize their welfare with a portfolio of assets that combines risk, return and secrecy attributes. Again, however, the market throws up tradeoffs between secrecy and risk, and between secrecy and returns, as well as between risk and returns. The strength of the individual's relative preferences for the three objectives, when coupled to the constraints set by the market, determines the structure of an optimum asset portfolio in the presence of a secrecy objective. Clearly, that portfolio may incorporate many different types of real and financial assets, both domestic and offshore. The true value to the individual of such a portfolio depends on expected future returns, portfolio-related risk, the probability of disclosure, the 'disutility' associated with punishment, and the individual's own attitude toward risk.

The 'market' for secrecy-containing assets was described in this chapter as being relatively 'normal'. That is, the demand for such assets is negatively related to their price, while the supply is positively related to their price. This means that an 'equilibrium' can be identified within a given economy, based on factors such as tax rates, extent of criminal activity, law-enforcement activity, and similar factors, all of which can change over time and affect the nature of that market. We know, furthermore, that these conditions may be vastly different between countries, as are factors affecting the supply of secrecy-containing financial services. Consequently, some countries end up exporting financial secrecy services to the residents of other countries, giving rise to a vigorous flow of international trade in those services.

7

Consequences

Having toured the subject of international financial secrecy in its various dimensions – its character, its roots in both human behavior and complex external pressures – we now come to the consequences. Does it all really matter? Have we been concerned all along with something that is of trivial importance in the workings of global political, social and economic systems? Can it be that secret money is indeed nothing more than a symptom – the result of factors that are themselves much more fundamental in nature? If so, the ebb and flow of secret money can give us some useful guidelines about things that cause it, but not much more. Or does secret money itself permit or facilitate behavior that in turn has real and serious consequences for society? If this is the case, then we are dealing with something that is of far greater interest, and that public policy should address directly.

We have emphasized in this book that the desire for financial secrecy – and the willingness to pay for it – is based on an underlying profile of economic, political and social motives, as well as highly individualistic and personal preferences and attitudes. For example, confiscatory tax policies or measures that affect the convertibility of one currency into others (and into physical assets) can have profound effects on the demand for financial secrecy. However, even in a world completely free of such adversity, demand for financial secrecy driven by economic self-interest hardly disappears, since the need always remains for business confidentiality and personal privacy. So do other motives that have nothing whatever to do with onerous government policies and market distortions. Beyond this, political risk, which can be seen as a matter of uncertainty about future government policies, plays a major role in determining the desire for financial secrecy, as do social pressures, envy, and differing concepts of fairness. Combining economic, political and social factors, we can conclude that the demand for international financial secrecy is largely, but certainly not entirely, man-made.

Within this context, the man-made considerations are by no means predictable in terms of their impact on people's desire for secret money. Some people are simply more secretive than others, just as some people are more averse to risk than others. So a particular set of external factors can result in a wide range of responses with respect to the desire for financial secrecy. Yet the external factors do play enough of a role that one can legitimately talk about a 'derived demand' for secrecy – derived from man-made conditions that determine the environment within which the individual tries to operate in his own best interest.

If various factors in the environment affect the demand for financial secrecy, is it also true that the existence of secrecy vehicles or 'products' affects a range of political, social and economic factors? That is, how might the world look if secret money did not exist? This question begins to get at an identification of the effects of international financial secrecy, and the potential consequences of the kinds of anti-secrecy measures described in Chapter 5.

Economic effects

The economic implications of international financial secrecy are relatively straightforward, but nevertheless highly speculative. There are implications for national income and output, income distribution, savings and investment, fiscal and monetary policies, national balances of payments and exchange rates, and the terms of international trade, among others. And the effects of secret money make themselves felt at the national as well as the international level.

In terms of international payments, we have suggested that there is little doubt that secret money movements are responsible for major inter-country capital transfers – encompassing flight capital, tax evasion and ordinary criminal flows. That these have adverse balance of payments consequences, if a country is trying to maintain a fixed exchange rate, is beyond doubt. Indeed, we have identified overvalued exchange rates brought on by misguided economic policies as a prime cause of international capital flight. A number of countries, including Mexico, Venezuela and the Philippines in the recent past, have found capital flight to be among their most troublesome economic problems. So have their bankers and other creditors, since the capital flight hemorrhage has often been compensated for by massive external borrowing. This, in turn, has certainly exacerbated some of the well-known debt problems that have afflicted developing countries in the 1980s.

In effect, countries borrowed abroad only to see a major part of the proceeds used to feed residents' bank accounts, purchases of real estate, and other asset holdings overseas. It has often been argued that the absence of secret money and its aggressive promotion by bankers and real estate salesmen traveling troubled countries would make their international financial problems a good deal easier to manage. In the words of one US banker embarking on a trip to one of the heavily indebted Latin American countries, 'When I saw my colleagues in the private banking division at the airport and they said they were making a lot of money, I knew that the countries they were coming from were in trouble. When people "vote" with their cash that way you know the end is nigh.'[1] Unable to do anything about the availability of financial havens abroad, governments have tried to clamp down hard on the actual transfers themselves, with mixed success. Tax evasion and criminal transactions involve similar balance of payments 'financing', requiring either a reduction in the country's external reserves or an increase in its external debt if exchange rates are fixed, or a currency devaluation/ depreciation if they are not.

Ultimately, the residents of the country have to pay the piper, through either increased exports or reduced imports of real goods and services, or both, representing a real reduction in levels of living. Those lucky or foresighted enough to have access to foreign assets benefit at the expense of the government and those who have not. According to one authority on the subject,

> There has been an enormous redistribution of wealth from public to private hands. First, these governments sold foreign exchange to the rich. Now that they've run into the external debt problem, they've had to do large depreciations and lower real wages. So Latin American workers are working harder to pay the interest on debts that have enabled the rich either to invest abroad or to consume luxury imports.[2]

The story is somewhat different if the country has maintained a realistic, market-oriented exchange rate from the outset. In that case, the secret money outflows will cause its currency to depreciate in the foreign exchange market and produce an adverse shift in the country's terms of trade – the local-currency price of imports will rise and the foreign-currency price of its exports will fall. In international trade transactions, the country will thus be 'poorer', in the sense that its exports will buy fewer imports. Moreover, the adverse terms of trade shift will tend to trigger changes in international trade flows. Since exports are now cheaper for foreign buyers, they will tend to rise. And since imports are now more expensive for domestic buyers, they will tend to fall. Once again, the secret money outflows will be 'paid for' by more exports and fewer imports, leaving a smaller amount of goods and services available for absorption by domestic residents in their consumption and investment activities.

On the other hand, in economies with substantial unemployment one could even argue (though probably only with tongue in cheek) that, by

177

causing the domestic currency to weaken, secret money outflows may actually stimulate domestic economic activity by causing a favorable swing in the balance of trade and increased production for export as well as the home market.

In fact, the kinds of effects of secret money flows under flexible exchange rates just described may well apply mainly in the case of tax evasion and criminal flows, since a realistic exchange rate and continued currency convertibility under relatively free-market conditions should help reduce or altogether eliminate the motivation for capital flight. However, this argument was not entirely credible after the 1980 election of President Mitterrand in France, where *expectations* of future economic and political conditions played a major role in triggering capital flight.

Beyond balance of payments and exchange-rate effects, there are a number of mainly domestic economic consequences that might be traced to secret money flows. For one thing, capital formation financed by domestic savings is likely to be smaller than would be the case without capital flight – particularly troublesome in countries that are already starved for capital. Consequently, the rate of national economic growth will tend to be slower. There may also be adverse consequences for economic growth in terms of the quality of the labor force (human capital), and for the pace of technological change as skilled manpower and entrepreneurs depart, sending their money abroad ahead of them. Secret money flows associated with tax evasion may sap the government's ability to invest in economic and social infrastructure, thus compromising a prerequisite to economic development in many countries.

Secret money outflows thus appear to be unambiguously adverse to the process of economic growth. But it is too easy to confuse cause and effect. Most probably it is the bleak growth outlook *itself* and the questionable economic policies that are ultimately responsible for the gloomy prospects that may be the source of much of the capital flight. Countries with bright economic prospects based on a solid and consistent record of responsible economic management are rarely hit by capital flight. And there may be a few (perhaps arguable) 'offsets', such as the use of secret money to pay for education or medical treatment abroad for people who will later return home to become more productive citizens.

Then there is the matter of income distribution. Free markets for goods, services, land, labor and capital create a particular market-driven income distribution. In the absence of monopoly power by business firms or labor unions or landlords, this tends to result in an optimum allocation of resources in the national economy. Most of the time, governments do not regard such a market-driven distribution of income as being inherently 'fair', and usually apply some sort of progressive structure of taxation and transfer payments to redress the alleged inequities produced by the free market for capital, labor and land.

178

Income taxes, welfare payments, death duties, wealth taxes, even confiscation of property are all ways of addressing the fairness issue. People who do not regard the government's definition of 'fairness' as being fair have the option of resorting to international financial secrecy. By being able to do so, they can bring about less equality in the distribution of wealth and income. For some people, indeed, any taxes at all are considered excessive and unfair. Stories circulate discreetly about fleet-footed people who pay no taxes to any political jurisdiction, and even about people who cannot recall any members of their families who have ever paid taxes to anyone for generations.

Regardless of the level or structure of taxation, what is not paid by some must be paid by others, so that tax evasion always redistributes the burden of financing the public sector. The fact that some people are getting away without shouldering a 'fair' share of the tax burden – with 'fairness' defined politically – clearly undermines the willingness of others to go along with a system regarded as grossly inequitable, and can result in a wholesale erosion of tax morality. Once tax evasion becomes a national sport, with or without the use of international financial secrecy, it is extraordinarily difficult to rebuild tax compliance, as a number of countries have found out to their great dismay.

For countries that are the recipients of secret money, the economic consequences, by and large, tend to be far happier ones. Inflows of secret money may have beneficial balance of payments and/or exchange-rate effects, which ultimately permit residents to consume more goods and services than they otherwise would have been able to do. In the case of Colombia, secret money inflows have supported the value of the currency, even to the point that it was sold on the black market at an exchange rate that was *above* the official rate from time to time. The national terms of trade will tend to improve as its currency strengthens, although this may not be regarded as beneficial if it prices domestic products out of local and foreign markets, which may lead to an erosion of competitiveness and increased unemployment. A number of countries on the receiving end of secret money flows, notably Switzerland, have had this problem from time to time and have addressed it by offering negative interest rates and other disincentives that may themselves produce certain benefits for the secrecy vendor. On the other hand, the influx of funds can promote domestic price stability via its upward pressure on the exchange rate (and reduced prices of imported goods and services), while at the same time making things quite difficult for the central bank in its efforts to 'sterilize' them – that is, prevent these inflows from causing an unwanted expansion of the domestic money supply and exerting inflationary pressures in the national economy. Properly managed, however, secret money flows can certainly lower the cost of credit to borrowers in recipient countries (including US Treasury borrowings) and aid in financing national budgetary deficits, development of infrastructure, as well as private capital formation – hence promoting economic growth.

At the same time, the secret money industry exports a group of financial services whose 'value-added' can itself promote national economic development, both directly and through a variety of linkage effects. Secrecy seekers who want to 'visit' their accounts have to buy airplane tickets, hotel rooms and restaurant meals – and may want to take a short holiday in the process. The domestic financial services industry and related sectors may end up significantly larger with the secrecy business than without it, and exports of secrecy services may have multiplier effects that ripple through the national economy with favorable implications for income as well as employment.

So, what is an economic and financial plague for some countries is a boon for others. Buyers are poorer and sellers are richer, as the economic consequences of secret money influence national, international and even global economic developments. Unfortunately, in order to quantify its effects one would have to run the world twice – once how it *is* and once how it *would have been* in the absence of secret money. Since this is obviously impossible to accomplish, and since reliable data on the actual secret money flows are virtually non-existent, all we can do is speculate that the economic impact of secret money is indeed rather significant.

Political effects

Beyond economics, secret money can have some important political effects as well. Again, these make themselves felt at both the national and international levels. Secret money may, for example, provide a certain degree of protection from political persecution. Throughout the ages, religious, racial or ethnic groups subjected to popular or government-instigated persecution have had limited options. They could wait it out (if they survived), or they could try to escape to safety abroad.

Political refugees are as much an international fact of life in the modern world as they have been in the past. Many are desperately poor, but others are relatively well-off, having been significant contributors to economic activity back home. The ability to shift funds to havens abroad provides some degree of solace for the victims of political persecution. The trauma of personal flight may be lessened by the availability of start-up capital to begin again somewhere else, and the knowledge that the assets are safe and secure may make political persecution at home a bit easier to bear. Although political refugees often turn out to be long-term economic assets for the host countries that ultimately receive the persecuted, the adjustment burdens are sometimes hard to carry, and

180

may be alleviated by secret money squirreled away abroad before emigration becomes necessary.

However, political conditions do not have to become truly intolerable for secrecy seekers to spring into action. Just the prospect of adverse political change may trigger a perceived need for secret money lodged abroad. Nor does political persecution in the conventional sense have to be involved. The mere possibility of political change may raise the spectre of higher taxes, wage and price controls, or simply a worsening of the way the economy is managed. Or the imposition of exchange controls may appear to be in the offing, or the nationalization or expropriation of business and private assets, or perhaps the perceived threat of execution for 'profiteering' or 'economic crimes against the people', or re-education in the new political line.

All such prospective events have two characteristics. The first is the expected direction of change, its magnitude, and its prospective consequences. The second is the probability of various potential outcomes actually occurring. People who are risk-averse will react to both of these factors. Since some people are more risk-averse than others (and some are more optimistic or pessimistic than others), their responses to prospective political change will be highly individualized. But respond they will, and the politically triggered capital flight that results can be enormous – sometimes even sufficient to alter the nature of the political outcomes that caused them in the first place.

Whether the country is Argentina, Mexico, Israel, Italy, France, the Philippines or Hong Kong, political flight capital has periodically reached very large proportions indeed. And the knowledge that secret money abroad is a readily available option for some of their more affluent and productive citizens may dissuade politicians from going to extremes. Thus, secret money may actually serve as a source of political stability.

What about the political decision-makers themselves? The newspapers are rife with stories of bribers and bribees, with politicians prominently represented among those with open palms. In many parts of the world, bribery and corruption are a way of life. As noted in Chapter 3, bribery requires financial secrecy to work. Big-time bribery, especially, is greatly facilitated by pots of secret money. Slush funds held abroad provide the wherewithal for the briber, the illicit transaction itself has to be kept secret permanently, and then the bribery-proceeds themselves have to be stashed away. Secret money held abroad is clearly more valuable than domestic funds for both sides in the transaction, because it is harder to discover and trace.[3]

So it may well be that the very existence of international secret money promotes bribery and corruption around the world, with possibly serious adverse economic and political consequences – resources are misallocated, income is redistributed to those who haven't earned it,

181

political processes are undermined, and so on. Perhaps more frequently than anyone cares to remember, coups d'état are staged to eject corrupt governments only to install a new management that in short order returns to business as usual. Memories of firing squads are apparently very short. And for those lucky enough to get away, the enjoyment of riches in the fun capitals of the world is tempered by the ever-present threat of sudden retribution by 'hit men' from home.

But is it really justified to blame secret money for the scale of bribery and corruption that appears to exist around the world? There would certainly be a good deal less illicit activity in its absence. But the underlying reasons for bribery and corruption must ultimately be found in government-imposed distortions of market mechanisms, gaps in morality and law enforcement, and imperfections in the political process itself.

Bribery is by definition illegal, but often is considered a 'victimless crime', overlooked by the authorities and the people at large until its consequences have become intolerable and the inevitable crackdown begins. Cleaning house must begin at home, and secret accounts abroad can be viewed more as a symptom than a cause. Countries where secret money is lodged consequently take a rather benign attitude toward the problem – secure in the knowledge that blame cannot rightfully be laid at their doorstep.

Then there is the matter of terrorism. In a world where one man's terrorist is indeed another man's freedom fighter, the use of secret money to support terrorism, insurgency and 'national liberation' movements internationally is probably beyond anyone's control. Again, in the absence of secret money the financing of terrorist movements, the procurement of weapons, and the training and transportation of terrorist cadres would be a great deal more difficult. But the ease of disguising international funds flows and the difficulty of assembling the kind of coordinated effort that is required to ferret out payments destined for terrorists probably means that secret money is a permanent feature of the global terrorist scene.

Finally, there is the issue of international political relations. We know that secret money is used to finance subversive movements, clandestine actions and other political involvements by one country in the affairs of others. It is part and parcel of the cloak and dagger world of international espionage and political intrigue. Occasionally, it can be used to ascertain what the 'other side' is up to, and once the cover is blown the political consequences of disclosure can be quite dramatic, often severely straining diplomatic relations.

We conclude that international financial secrecy plays an important role in the political equation at both the national and international levels. It permits politically sensitive activity of various kinds to go on that would be impossible in its absence. Yet it remains doubtful that secrecy itself is in any sense a causative force in the political affairs in which it is intimately involved. It is a vehicle – a facilitator that makes things possible that would probably go on anyway, though perhaps to a lesser degree.

Social effects

As we have seen in previous chapters, secret money also has a bearing on social phenomena. Most obvious is criminal activity, although it may well be that a certain degree of sophistication has to be reached before international financial secrecy plays a role in fostering crime. Small-time criminals have little need for such services. But running drugs or guns, where the criminal is sophisticated and the amounts involved can be enormous – and where the long arm of the law can be equally sophisticated — international financial secrecy may be a useful weapon in the criminal's arsenal. The volume of funds movements involved in money laundering, to the extent that guesses can be made, is as enormous as the channels are complex. Would the drug trade grind to a halt in the absence of secret money laundries? Probably not. But law enforcement may well be able to proceed more effectively against the launderers than against the drug runners themselves simply because bankers are more concerned with the consequences of discovery and prosecution, are more risk-averse, and have more to lose than hardened criminals. By closing some of the money laundries, the criminal element may be forced into increasingly narrow financial channels that are perhaps more costly or more risky (or both) and may be easier to monitor and choke off.

There is also the social problem of 'white-collar' crime, such as financial fraud or infractions of the securities laws like insider trading. Again, in many cases these need international financial secrecy to work, and for the criminal to escape from the jurisdiction of national law-enforcement authorities. Disclosure and prosecution, as we have seen, require a great deal of cooperation among countries, cooperation that is not always forthcoming.

Besides its link to crime, does international financial secrecy have any other major social consequences? One could argue that privacy and confidentiality are important attributes of any free society, and that privacy indeed can be regarded as an important 'right' in non-totalitarian states. Abrogation or infringement of this right may be viewed as a matter of grave importance for the character of the social order. Yet we have seen that the execution of a variety of social functions, such as law enforcement and taxation, requires a certain abridgement of that right. The question is one of balance. Where do the social costs of secrecy begin to exceed the social benefits? Every society has to answer this question for itself, and the answers will differ widely between countries. This is where international financial secrecy comes in, by allowing non-disclosure to continue that would be prohibited domestically. The 'optimum' degree of disclosure prevailing at home may thus be short-circuited. On the other hand, the actual degree of disclosure permitted may not in fact represent a social optimum, but rather one that is imposed on society by non-democratic means. In such cases, international financial secrecy can actually move society toward an optimum level of financial disclosure. The question of social optima is an exceedingly difficult one, and weighing the social costs and benefits of international financial secrecy remains a rather thankless task.

All individual freedoms, of course, have come under attack in various places at various times throughout history. But it may well be true that financial privacy has been more thoroughly and permanently eroded than any of the others. As governments have grown to take successively larger shares of real income and output, the definition of 'abuse' of financial confidentiality has changed. It always was an abuse of financial confidentiality to employ it in the commission of a crime, and society has the right to defend itself against such behavior. The same has traditionally been true of acts of treason and related political offenses aimed at the overthrow of the state or its defeat in time of war. But it has been the encroachment of the public sector on the allocation of resources in society, accompanied by higher tax burdens, that has probably led most dramatically to a redefinition of financial confidentiality. With it has come a commensurate erosion of individual freedom.

Personal effects

We have seen in Chapter 6 that individuals value secrecy, and that personal behavior reflects this fact, although the precise value people place on financial secrecy – and the reduced returns or increased risk they are willing to trade-off for it – is a highly personal matter. That is, the value of secret money will differ widely among individuals and over time. Secrecy is certainly critical to the drug runner, and without it he would be out of business. But it is marginally important to the middle-income, honest wage-earner who simply wants to keep his financial affairs to himself.

As noted, financial secrecy conveys a certain degree of freedom to the individual and, as such, it could be regarded as a fundamental human right and an important factor in determining the quality of life. Over the centuries this right has been abridged, often virtually supplanted by the supremacy of the state over the individual. Yet people try to hang on to whatever financial secrecy they are able to retain, and are willing to pay for it and sometimes take chances in order to obtain it. If it involves assets held abroad, they are willing to subject themselves to the rules of the game that exist abroad, even in expensive places like Switzerland and risky places like Panama.

They are also willing to put part of their wealth in the hands of agents, which raises principal–agent and moral hazard problems. Is the agent honest? Can he be trusted to carry out the principal's wishes with respect to asset deployment? Can he be trusted to keep his mouth and his ledgers shut? And what recourse is open to the secrecy seeker in the event of serious problems with the agent's execution of his fiduciary responsibilities? Legal redress may have to be sought in foreign courts of law, under foreign rules of the game, and always under threat of disclosure. If the penalty associated with disclosure is sufficiently severe, redress may be impossible to obtain, and this puts an enormous premium on the selection of the agent in the first place – and may be reflected in the price the agent can extract for his services. All this may still be very worthwhile if it retains for the individual his security, safety and mobility, asset values, and personal freedoms that would not otherwise exist.

Summary

We have broken down the effects of international financial secrecy into four more or less distinct but highly interrelated dimensions – economic, political, social and personal. Its implications for the national economy and international economic linkages can be very significant indeed, whether the frame of reference involves the actual level and growth of economic activity, the exchange rate and the balance of payments, or the distribution of income. The political implications are no less important, involving political stability, the integrity of governmental systems and structures, and the ability to carry out political goals at the national and international levels. Bribery and corruption, the abuse of drugs, and erosion of the fabric of society are some of the social dimensions of secret money, while at a personal level there are equally important consequences for the quality of life.

Would the world be better off without international financial secrecy? The issue is sufficiently complex that such a question is impossible to answer. Some people, some groups and some countries would clearly be better off, while others would sustain serious damage. And since there is no useful frame of reference for deciding whether the world as a whole would be better or worse off, the highest level on which this question can be addressed is the national state – and even then there are serious problems in reconciling the national interest with the interests of groups and individuals. It is probably best to be selective. Aggressive pursuit of money laundering connected with drug running may well lead to improvements in social welfare, but this conclusion is far less clear-cut in the case of tax evasion or capital flight.

Secret money is a product of human nature. People lie. People cheat. People commit crimes. People are driven to protect what they regard as theirs. People elect or tolerate governments that foster political and economic adversity and uncertainty. People take advantage of the misery of others. A true international market for secret money is the inevitable result : a market that itself is appropriately cloaked in secrecy. While it may change form and substance over the years, human nature will insure that this market will continue to thrive.

Notes

1 Lenny Glynn and Peter Koenig, 'The Capital Flight Crisis', *Institutional Investor*, November 1984.
2. *Ibid*, p. 305.
3. See Thomas N. Gladwin and Ingo Walter, *Multinationals under Fire* (New York: John Wiley & Sons, 1980), Chapter 5.

8

The Outlook

How does the future of international financial secrecy look? Probably very positive. The industry will continue to survive and prosper. It will also change in the years ahead, as it has done in recent decades, with mostly gradual but sometimes abrupt shifts in the underlying demand and supply factors.

On the demand side, for example, only decriminalization of the production, trade and use of drugs will lead to an erosion of the associated secret money flows. Decriminalization did in fact occur in the United States with the lifting of prohibition of alcoholic beverages in 1933, as well as the legalization of off-track betting on horse racing in various localities and the introduction of state-sponsored lotteries in more recent times. Other countries have had similar experiences. But the socially debilitating effects of mind-altering substances like heroin, cocaine, Quaaludes, even marijuana, are unlikely to lead to widespread decriminalization in today's environment. Whereas such a measure would certainly reduce prices, expand consumption and eliminate the need for associated secret money flows, it would also produce an unknown series of social consequences. Some of these, such as under-cutting resources available to organized crime, are fairly certain and undoubtedly positive. Others, like the prospects for reduced vagrancy, muggings, burglaries and other individual criminal activities, as well as the loads they place on the criminal justice system, are much more debatable. Still others, such as the incidence of 'driving while under the influence', labor productivity, military preparedness, and the quality of life for those who refuse to indulge, are almost certainly adverse. And the experience of countries such as the Netherlands that have experimented with decriminalization hardly seems encouraging. So countries will remain highly risk-averse with respect to the issue of decriminalization of drugs, and indeed many have stepped up enforcement efforts, ranging from mandatory death penalties for possession in parts of Southeast Asia to the application of sophisticated military hardware in the war on drug smuggling in North America.

187

All of this has implications for the secret money business. On the one hand, demand for secret money vehicles and the willingness to pay for them will remain strong and perhaps grow. On the other, in their war on those who deal in drugs, the authorities will increasingly target people, institutions and countries that handle secret money, forcing greater innovation, greater complexity, and higher costs. They doubtless will achieve some successes, perhaps even some dramatic ones, but as long as the underlying economic motivations exist they will never entirely succeed. People are too ingenious, too quick, too greedy. Difficult as it is to observe this war dispassionately, without cheering for the good guys and booing the social parasites, its collateral damage to financial confidentiality could be substantial as the authorities strip away legal safeguards for ordinary people in their pursuit of culprits.

True criminal demand for secret money in other dimensions will be equally durable in the years ahead. Prostitution, protection, labor racketeering, larceny, fraud, auto theft and the like will continue to be blemishes on the fabric of society, as they have been in the past. All will continue to require secret money. Nobody in these businesses will file tax returns, even if for some reason they feel so moved. The money will stay underground, and through various organizational layers will often find its way from the 'retail' level to the 'wholesale' level of organized crime. This is where international financial secrecy comes in. Again, with a few exceptions (perhaps 'victimless crimes' like prostitution and illegal gambling), decriminalization is out of the question. So the demand for secrecy will remain intact, and again will ebb and flow with the intensity of criminal activities and the exertions of law enforcement authorities motivated by political pressure based on public outrage.

For example, in the wake of the Bank of Boston revelations (discussed in Chapter 5), a coordinated approach to bank fraud was initiated by federal law enforcement and banking regulators in the United States during April 1985. Investigative procedures were altered, uniform enforcement guidelines were adopted, training programs were stepped up, and government-wide sharing of information was initiated, all supported by senior regulatory and enforcement officials including the Attorney General, the FBI, the Federal Reserve Board, the Federal Home Loan Bank Board, and the Controller of the Currency, among others. According to a US House of Representatives report, 'criminal activity by bankers has been a major factor in US bank failures. ... Losses to the two major federal deposit insurance funds because of failures linked to fraud were estimated to be more than $1 billion [in 1984].'[1]

Significantly, a major proposal contained in this initiative involved legislative and regulatory changes in US financial privacy laws in order to permit banking authorities to provide prosecutors more easily with confidential information. A side-effect of this initiative against financial

188

secrecy aimed at criminal activities may thus be an erosion of financial confidentiality for ordinary citizens.

With respect to such patently criminal uses of international financial secrecy, one is on relatively safe ground. One can predict that robust demand will continue because the underlying incentives will remain intact, but that the shape and structure of that demand will shift as countries alter the legal and judicial framework and the mechanics of law enforcement. Things get a bit more fuzzy once one moves beyond the realm of unambiguous criminality.

Take the politically motivated demand for secret money involving terrorism, insurgency, illegal political contributions and government-sponsored covert activities. Again, there is no evidence that demand emanating from such sources is ebbing, although periodic crackdowns, domestic political scandals, and restoration of political tranquility in one country or another may change the location and nature of that demand. But the criminal nature of the associated secret money flows is rather ambiguous. Authorities in Luxembourg may be legitimately unconcerned about financial transactions that ultimately are used in support of a particular political party in Algeria despite violations of local laws. Authorities in Switzerland may legitimately feel it is none of their business when funds are routed through local financial institutions in support of technology acquisitions in the US by operatives acting on behalf of Albania.

So, while crackdowns on secret money flows associated with activities that are unambiguously criminal in nature can expect at least some degree of international cooperation and even coordination, flows related to politically motivated activities cannot. Coordination will continue to have a spotty record at best, and even cooperation and comity among national authorities will (perhaps legitimately) continue to be extraordinarily difficult to achieve. It certainly does not help matters when a government seeks international assistance regarding one type of politically driven flow of secret money, while at the same time initiating, aiding or abetting others. Since political needs for secret money are accompanied by the willingness to pay for them, middlemen quickly emerge and the economic incentive structure falls into place. Unless one is able to predict the dawning of a golden age of domestic and international political tranquility, this source of demand for secret money will continue to be a vibrant one indeed.

Things get even more difficult in prognostications about the use of secret money for purposes like insider trading in the securities markets, smuggling, evasion of exchange controls and taxation.

As discussed in Chapter 3, there is a great deal of controversy about the justification for barriers to insider trading, in terms of their economic and social consequences. Improved information flows should limit opportunities for insider trading, but again will never entirely eliminate them. Political concerns about the inherent fairness of capital markets to all participants will keep markets heavily policed. Perhaps, over time, the two forces together will gradually erode this particular demand for secret money even as the global integration of financial markets enhances the potential significance of this issue. The fact that most financial centers around the world have a vested interest in continued access to all of the world's premier financial markets makes cooperation and coordination all the more likely.

Smuggling and evasion of exchange controls are always the products of market distortions. Trade barriers to protect domestic industry, price controls and unrealistic exchange rates invariably create incentives to evade. There are risks to be taken and money to be made, often staggering amounts, which must subsequently be hidden – preferably abroad. There is some evidence that governments are increasingly convinced of the futility of some of these distortions in terms of their long-range damage to the process of national economic growth. Observed differences in economic performance between countries that have piled on distortions and those that have followed relatively free-market principles have begun to sink in.

The financial difficulties of many countries in the early 1980s have provoked some serious thinking about the efficacy of trade and financial distortions, sometimes promoted from the outside by institutions like the International Monetary Fund. It may be that we have entered a period of liberalization of market mechanisms, and with the erosion and dismantling of distortions will come a reduction in this particular source of the demand for secret money. Still, political decisions will continue to dominate market decisions in many cases, and so the incentive to evade and the role of secret money in making evasion possible will hardly disappear. Nor will international coordination and cooperation in combating this type of secret money flow get very far, in some cases perhaps fortunately so from the standpoint of global market efficiency and economic development.

Things get even more difficult with respect to tax evasion, certainly the largest single factor underlying the demand for international financial secrecy. It is easy to predict that secret money demand from this source will remain strong, as governments continue to lay claim to large shares of national income and output and are forced to raise the necessary financial resources in various ways that are more or less easily subject to evasion. Certainly the need to fund defense, infrastructure and social programs will continue to put pressure on fiscal resources, but the size and shape of that pressure will surely continue to change over time.

On the one hand, there has been a powerful movement around the world to reassess the efficacy and efficiency of government expenditure and the claims of various interest groups on the public purse. The need

190

for the public sector to live within its means is increasingly recognized politically, painful as it may be, particularly given the inflationary impact of debt monetization (as an alternative to taxation) on national economic performance. This has placed limits on spending and upward pressure on taxation. It has also run up against equally widespread recognition of the damage that can be done by excessive taxation, which has triggered an effort in many countries to ease tax burdens in order to stimulate economic incentives to work, invest and innovate. The result is an energetic search for public-sector economies, including greater efficiency in the provision of government services, more careful defense procurement, denationalization of government-owned enterprises and the like.

Unfortunately, the restoration of sensible public policies in the tax area is exceedingly difficult. There are too many vested interests built into the existing arrangements, and taxes are too tempting as a tool of social tinkering for politicians. Yet only major tax reform can begin to attack the incentives to evade, and there always remains the question whether tax morality, once lost, can ever be completely restored.

So, in the United States as in other countries, the demand for financial secrecy arising from tax evasion seems destined to continue unabated. The same goes for the underground economy, which itself is driven in part by tax evasion. This includes an enormous volume of cash transactions ranging from skimming of profits by owners of small businesses, to workers engaging in services transactions 'off the books', profits of street vendors, and the like.

To the extent that a commitment to fiscal responsibility can be coupled with a reasonable balance between the claims of the private and public sectors on economic resources, growth of the tax-evasion demand for secret money nevertheless may be eased somewhat. But since there will always be at least *some* incentive to evade taxes, and since countries will differ vastly in terms of the level, structure and incidence of taxation, that demand will persist. Again, not much can be expected in terms of an effectively coordinated attack on tax evasion. Countries differ too much in terms of their perceptions of tax issues. And many are genuinely scornful of what they regard as other countries' dysfunctional tax systems. So the most important single demand for international financial secrecy may enjoy a rosy future.

It is possible, of course, that the increasing integration of financial markets and increasing concerns about political risk will change the nature of secret money flows related to tax evasion. We know from Chapter 6 that the tax-motivated secrecy seeker (or any secrecy seeker, for that matter) is always interested in three things – secrecy, return and risk – and that he is caught in a constant balancing game among these three considerations. Assets held in the US may be viewed very favorably with respect to returns and risk, but flawed with respect to secrecy. Assets held in Panama may look good from a secrecy and return point of view, yet may be quite risky. Of course, different elements can be put together in order to obtain more of all three elements – assets placed with a good US or British bank in Nassau, for example. But it may be that secrecy seekers'concerns with the rapidly growing flow of financial information and the increasing need to trade actively in volatile financial markets, and increasing worries about political risks, will encourage even the most fleet-footed among tax evaders to establish a tax home in a respectable country and pay at least some taxes. Secrecy seekers, too, need allies, and a legitimate tax home is one way of obtaining them. By paying this price, it should be possible to operate essentially in the open and take advantage of market opportunities as well as assets held in politically secure locations. Individuals may well find that they are much better off. If this realization takes hold, some of the tax-linked demand for secret money may ease, although certainly not for US citizens who are fully subject to all American taxes (except for an exempt amount) no matter where in the world they establish tax residence. Yet even they get value for money – after all, how many people actually renounce their US citizenship in order legally to escape US taxation?

Things are even more complex with regard to demand for secrecy driven by capital flight. People's expectations and uncertainties about future political or economic conditions, which give rise to flight capital, will continue to emerge from time to time. There is little to suggest that either the political or the economic management of countries will systematically improve or stabilize on a world scale in the years ahead, and so spurts of secret money will continue to flow. More so than even in the case of tax evasion, efforts by countries to stanch those flows will meet with little cooperation abroad, even in anti-secrecy bastions such as the United States.

In short, the things that drive the demand for secret money today will prevail in the years ahead. Some will weaken, while others will strengthen from time to time as the underlying forces change and as government action narrows some options and forces secrecy seekers to use others.

Similar currents will affect the future of secret money on the supply side. The players will be as heterogeneous as the secrecy seekers are complex in their motivations. As we have seen in Chapter 4, individuals, institutions and countries have found that it pays to sell secrecy-oriented products. For individuals and institutions there is money to be made and market niches to be exploited. Crooks will always have their bankers in a rough and furtive game of mutual exploitation against the ever-present backdrop of legally and morally reprehensible behavior; so will tax evaders and those on the run from political and economic adversity around the world.

To serve the needs of capital fleeing from foreign taxation and political instability, up-market institutions around the world will continue to stand ready – usually without moral or ethical burdens to worry about – to serve their needs alongside businesses and individuals who have no need for secrecy. Competition among these institutions is as severe as the potential profits are high, and the players are continually confronted with the need to distinguish between those secrecy seekers whom they wish to attract and those they must avoid like the plague. As the Deak & Co. case discussed in Chaper 5 shows, errors in judgment or wilful misconduct can be exceedingly costly for the institution, and perhaps 'terminal' for the managers involved. Little can be worse for an institution than to be under investigation for involvement with crooks. Ordinary, morally outraged clients will turn to the competition for a cleaner environment, while other secrecy seekers will head for the hills in a scramble to avoid the chance that the spotlight will accidentally fall on their affairs as well. Once contaminated in this way, it seems doubtful that an institution can regain its previous position within any reasonable time-frame.

Indeed, one can argue that this rather severe sanction of the marketplace is sufficiently strong to make sure that the major financial institutions that sell financial secrecy remain relatively free of crooked money – with 'crookedness' being defined legally and politically in their home countries and in the host countries in which they operate. Of course, errors do occur, but employees involved in such errors can expect to find themselves in the job market almost immediately.

Down-market institutions and individuals have less to lose and more to gain from contaminated money, so that the niches they seek may be a good deal less scrupulous. Some are smaller financial institutions caught in a web of severe competition with the majors, who feel driven toward more risky business, are poorly managed, or are owned and controlled by investors who are not particularly risk-averse. And some are individual lawyers, accountants and financial advisers who are happy to make hay while the sun shines and then run for cover when foul weather strikes. They are happy to catch whatever funds abandon the up-market institutions. The hapless secrecy seeker, meanwhile, finds that costs and risks alike rise dramatically as he moves successively down-market.

The heterogeneous structure of market supply facing the secrecy seeker will prevail, both within and between countries. Like the automobile market with its Subarus, Nissans, Chevrolets, Buicks, Volvos, BMWs, Jaguars, Mercedes Benzes and Rolls-Royces, there are different products for different needs. Competition is severe, and the choice is sufficiently wide that an appropriate product selection can usually be made.

We have seen that individuals and firms are not the only secrecy vendors. Countries are too. Their gain comes from the industry itself as well as from linkages to other sectors in the form of jobs, incomes, growth, and foreign exchange earnings. Their role as suppliers of secrecy services is doubly important, because they set the legal and regulatory structures within which the direct vendors of secret money operate and compete with each other. They too face costs and risks, ranging from increased international tension and imported criminal elements and corruption that may accompany the acceptance of tainted funds, to the financial shocks that accompany abrupt runoffs of internationally mobile funds. But for some, especially small, underdeveloped countries with few other resources the potential benefits even of operating close to (or beyond) the edge will often outweigh the risks.

Individuals, institutions and countries will thus continue to stand ready to supply a rich variety of secrecy services into the foreseeable future. Just as secrecy seekers are prepared to pay, the vendors are prepared to profit, and they will.

What can we conclude? On an economic plane it seems clear that international financial secrecy is indeed an important phenomenon that can be and should be examined, interpreted and evaluated in a rational way and that has wide-ranging effects on the performance and structure of national economies as well as the international economy as a whole. It can also have profound effects on the formation and execution of economic and financial policies, and the information on which they are based. Economics permits a relatively value-free examination of these effects, including the external benefits and costs that lie beyond the secrecy business itself.

It is when we move beyond economics into the realm of politics and social values that things become far more complex. The signals are not nearly as clear. There are virtually no absolutes, even with regard to what many regard as blatantly criminal use of secret money. Nor are the social and political costs and benefits easily identifiable or measurable. Consequently, the public policies that emerge are often confused, ambiguous and ineffectual. They will undoubtedly remain so, ensuring lasting prosperity for the secret money industry around the world.

So the international market for financial secrecy promises to continue to thrive, each segment with its own structure of demand, supply and competitive performance. Its costs and benefits form an enormously complex web. But would the world really be better off in its absence? Would governments not be subject to even fewer checks and balances than they already are? As with much of international financial secrecy, the answers to such questions remain shrouded in mystery.

Notes

1 Andy Paztor and Leon E. Wynter, 'US Sets War on Bank-Industry Fraud', *Wall Street Journal*, 2 April 1985.

Appendix

CATALOG OF US CASES INVOLVING BANK OR COMMERCIAL SECRECY

Case name	Type of case	Foreign country involved	Date*
I LAUNDERING OR ILLEGALLY SECRETING PROFITS			
In the Matter of Arawak Trust Co.	Laundering kickbacks via foreign corporations	Cayman Islands	1980
Bank Saderat (Iran) v. Marashi	Misappropriating bank funds through foreign trust	Liechtenstein	1982
Dennis Carlson	Laundering drug profits through foreign entities	Cayman Islands, Liechtenstein	N.A.
James Cross	Secreting embezzled funds in foreign accounts	Bermuda	N.A.
Francisco Fernandez & Guillermo Hernandez	Laundering drug profits through foreign accounts	Colombia, Cayman Islands	N.A.
Rogelio A. Fernandez	Concealing source of drug profits through foreign contract	Mexico	N.A.
Firestone Rubber, Inc.	Secreting legal and illegal profits through foreign accounts	Switzerland	N.A.
John D. Fox	Laundering drug profits through foreign accounts	Ecuador	N.A.
Eduardo Garcia & Alfredo Garcia	Secreting illegally obtained funds in foreign accounts	Panama, Puerto Rico	N.A.
Michael J. Grassi	Laundering drug profits through foreign accounts	Cayman Islands	N.A.
Hughes Tool Co. v. Meier	Secreting diverted corporate funds in foreign accounts	Netherland Antilles	1977
Ostrer v. US	Laundering embezzled funds through foreign casinos	Bahamas	1977
People v. Wilson	Secreting pornography profits in foreign accounts	Cayman Islands Switzerland	1982

195

Case Name	Type of Case	Foreign country involved	Date
Carlos R. Porro	Laundering drug profits through foreign accounts	Several offshore countries	N.A
Derek Price	Laundering drug profits through foreign accounts	Cayman Islands	N.A.
SEC v. Certain Unkown Purchasers of Santa Fe Stock, SEC v. Martin	Secreting securities fraud profits in foreign accounts	Switzerland	1982
SEC v. Zolp	Secreting securities fraud profits in foreign accounts	Bahamas	1982
US v. Beltempo	Laundering drug profits through foreign accounts	Switzerland	1982
US v. Dichne	Secreting embezzled funds in foreign accounts	Switzerland	1980
US v. DiStefano	Laundering kickbacks through foreign accounts	Bahamas	1973
US v. Eimers	Laundering prostitution profits through foreign accounts	Bahamas	1982
US v. Enstam	Laundering drug profits through foreign accounts	Cayman Islands	1980
US v. Erwin	Secreting embezzled funds in foreign accounts	Cayman Islands	1982
US v. Friedland	Secreting kickbacks in foreign accounts	Cayman Islands, Switzerland	1981
US v. Garfield	Laundering drug profits	Bermuda, Panama	1981
US v. Garfield Bank	Laundering drug profits via US accounts	Bermuda, Panama, Liberia	1981
US v. Govern	Laundering drug profits through US accounts	Cayman Islands, Netherland Antilles	1982
US v. The Great American Bank	Laundering drug profits through US accounts, secreting drug profits in foreign accounts	Switzerland, Panama, Peru	1982
US v. Long	Laundering drug profits through foreign accounts	Bahamas	N.A.
US v. Rittenberg	Laundering drug pro-	Lichtenstein,	1980

Case Name	Type of Case	Foreign country involved	Date
	fits through foreign accounts	Switzerland, Bahamas	
US v. Sand	Laundering drug profits through US accounts	Bahamas	1976
US v. Scotto	Laundering kickbacks through foreign and U.S. accounts	Switzerland	1980
US v. Sonal Corp	Laundering drug profits through U.S. accounts	Colombia	1981
US v. Sterling	Laundering drug profits through foreign accounts	Switzerland, Liechtenstein, Cayman Islands	1982
US v. Toombs	Laundering drug profits through foreign corporations	Cayman Islands, Bahamas	1982
Chester Zabik	Secreting kickbacks in foreign accounts	Switzerland	N.A

II SECRETING LEGITIMATE ASSETS FOR ILLEGITIMATE PURPOSES

Case Name	Type of Case	Foreign country involved	Date
Roy G. Anderson	Secreting funds in foreign accounts to facilitate tax evasion	Bermuda	N.A.
John Berkey and Phillip Weinstein	Diverting corporate receipts to foreign accounts	Belgium	N.A.
Bronston v. United States	Secreting assets from creditors in foreign accounts	Switzerland	1973
CBS Imports, Inc.	Using foreign subsidiary to make illegal payoffs	Hong Kong	N.A.
Victor M. Divivo	Diverting corporate receipts, secreting in foreign accounts	Switzerland	N.A.
Ralph D. Franks	Secreting funds in foreign corporations to facilitate tax evasion	Bermuda	N.A.
Margarito Garza	Concealing unreported receipts through foreign bond purchases	Mexico	N.A.
Don H. Lloyd	Secreting funds in foreign entities to facilitate tax evasion	Cayman Islands	N.A.
Phillips Petroleum, Inc.	Secreting funds for illegal payoffs in foreign accounts	Panama	N.A.

Case Name	Type of Case	Foreign country involved	Date
William I. Rials and Stanley E. Galkin	Diverting corporate receipts, secreting in foreign accounts	Cayman Islands	N.A.
Paul L. Rioux	Secreting funds in foreign accounts to facilitate tax evasion	Canada	N.A.
Schlensky v. Dorsey	Secreting corporate funds for illegal campaign contributions in foreign subsidiary's accounts	Bahamas	1978
In the Matter of Harry L. Sears	Secreting corporate funds for illegal campaign contributions in foreign accounts	Bahamas	1977
Charles W. Sizemore	Secreting funds in foreign accounts to facilitate tax evasion	Bahamas	N.A.
Frank J. Tuseck	Secreting funds in foreign accounts to facilitate tax evasion	Cayman Islands	
US v. Aita	Secreting funds in US accounts to facilitate tax evasion	Italy	1982
US v. Baskes	Secreting funds in foreign corporations' accounts to facilitate tax evasion	Cayman Islands	1980
US v. Carver	Secreting funds for kickbacks in foreign accounts	Liberia, Switzerland, Liechtenstein, Cayman Islands	N.A.
US v. Crawford	Illegally bribing foreign officials for business purposes through foreign accounts	Mexico	1982
US v. Hajecate	Secreting funds in foreign accounts to facilitate tax evasion	Cayman Islands	1982
US v. McPartlin	Illegally bribing city officials through foreign accounts	Liechtenstein, Switzerland	1979
US v. Phillips Petroleum Company	Secreting funds for illegal campaign contributions in foreign bank accounts	Switzerland	1977

III USE OF OFFSHORE AND FOREIGN ENTITIES AS AN INTEGRAL PART OF AN OVERALL CRIMINAL SCHEME

CFTC v. US	Conducting boiler-	Luxembourg	1979

Case Name	Type of Case	Foreign country involved	Date
Metals Depository	room operations through foreign bank		
Oran W. Cotton	Deducting costs, eventually returned through foreign accounts	Cayman Islands	N.A.
Karl L. Dahlstrom	Participating in sham 'double trusts' in foreign countries	Belize, Turks & Caicos Islands	N.A.
Billie Sol Estes	Concealing US transactions through foreign accounts	Liechtenstein	N.A.
Calvin Eisenberg	Deduction costs, eventually returned to foreign accounts through foreign entity	Bahamas	N.A.
Robert Falvo & Richard D. Smith	Taking false deductions involving foreign tax shelters	Colombia	N.A.
Fidenas v. Compagnie International pour L'Informatique, Honeywell Bull, SA	Using foreign corporations to defraud	Bahamas, Switzerland	1979
John S. Howell	Secreting funds in foreign accounts to facilitate tax evasion	Belize, Puerto Rico	N.A.
IIT, an International Investment Trust v. Cornfield	Using foreign subsidiary to defraud	Canada, Panama	1980
Index Fund Inc. v. Hagopian	Using foreign mutual fund to commit securities fraud	Bahamas	1976
Schact v. McCollum	Accepting kickbacks through foreign entities	Lebanon, Mexico	N.A.
Lea J. Marks v. Harold J. Marks	Taking false deductions involving foreign tax shelters	Liechtenstein, Switzerland, Cayman Islands	N.A.
James M. Moran	Taking false deductions involving foreign corporations	Bahamas, Cayman Islands	N.A.
Benjamin Mudd	Concealing foreign account	Switzerland	N.A.
New York County v. Firestone	Using foreign account to establish fraudulent tax shelters	Bahamas	1982
Virgil Ogletree	Secreting property	Bahamas	N.A.

Case Name	Type of Case	Foreign country involved	Date
	ownership in foreign country to evade taxes		
Gerald Rogers	Participating in fraudulent tax shelters involving foreign country	Panama	N.A.
Leonard Rosen	Secreting funds in foreign accounts to facilitate tax evasion	Bahamas	N.A.
Robert M. Saunders	Taking false deductions involving foreign entity	England	N.A.
SEC v. Bank of Credit and Commerce International, SA	Using foreign entities to violate securities regulations	Kuwait, Saudi Arabia, Luxembourg	1978
SEC v. Banque de Paris es des Pays-Bas (Suisse)	Using foreign banks to violate securities regulations	Switzerland	1977
SEC v. Cayman Islands Reinsurance Corp., Ltd.	Using foreign corporation to violate securities regulations	Cayman Islands	1982
SEC v. Diplomat National Bank	Trading in violation of securities regulations on behalf of foreign nationals	Korea	1977
SEC v. Everest Management Corp.	Using foreign accounts to commit securities fraud	Switzerland	1971
SEC v. General Refractories Co.	Using foreign corporations to commit securities fraud	Several in Europe	1975
SEC v. Kasser	Using foreign corporations to commit securities fraud	Canada, Switzerland	1977
SEC v. Katy Industries	Using foreign subsidiary to commit securities fraud and make illegal payoffs	Cayman Islands	1978
SEC v. Vesco	Using foreign corporations to commit securities fraud	Bahamas, Luxembourg, Costa Rica	1972
State of Arizona v. Williams	Using foreign corporations to commit securities fraud and evade taxes	Panama, Mexico, Montserrat	1981
US v. Becker	Using foreign banks to defraud investors	Bahamas	1978

Case Name	Type of Case	Foreign country involved	Date
US v. Brinlee	Using foreign accounts to defraud	Antigua	1981
US v. Courtois	Using foreign accounts to commit securities fraud	Bermuda, Bahamas, Luxembourg, Switzerland	N.A.
US v. Crosby	Using foreign banks to honor worthless checks	St Vincent	1982
US v. Federbush	Using foreign banks to defraud	St Vincent	1980
US v. Firestone Rubber	Using foreign subsidiary to circumvent US regulations	Switzerland	1981
US v. Jaeger	Using foreign accounts to commit currency exchange fraud	Turks & Caicos Islands	1979
US v. Kelly	Using foreign trust to commit securities fraud	Liechtenstein, Switzerland	1965
US v. Kelly	Using foreign fund to defraud	Panama	1978
US v. Kilpatrick	Using foreign banks and corporations to establish fraudulent tax shelters	Cayman Islands	1982
US v. Krown	Using foreign banks to establish fraudulent tax shelters and defraud	St Vincent	1980
US v. McDevitt	Using foreign corporations to establish fraudulent tax shelters and defraud	Anguilla, Bahamas	1982
US v. McDonnell Douglas Corp.	Using foreign corporations to bribe foreign officials	Guernsey, Cayman, Islands, Bermuda, Belgium	1979
US v. Newman	Using foreign banks and trusts to commit securities fraud	Bermuda, Bahamas, Luxembourg, Switzerland	1981
US v. Osserman	Using foreign banks to establish fraudulent tax shelters	Cayman Islands	1980
US v. Palm State Bank	Using foreign accounts to defraud and evade taxes	Cayman Islands	1980
US v. Parker	Using foreign corporations to establish fraudulent tax shelters	Switzerland Cayman Islands, Italy, Germany	N.A.

Case Name	Type of Case	Foreign country involved	Date
US v. Rodriguez	Using foreign accounts to defraud	Antigua	1982
US v. Sarault	Using foreign banks to honor worthless checks	Bahamas	1982
US v. Twombly	Using foreign corporations to bribe foreign officials	Bermuda, Puerto Rico	1980
US v. Sindona	Using foreign banks to commit securities fraud	Switzerland, Italy	1980
US v. Vetco, Inc.	Using foreign subsidiary to circumvent US regulations	Switzerland	1981
US v. Whipple	Using foreign corporations to establish fraudulent tax shelters	Cayman Islands, Andorra	N.A.
US v. Wolfson	Using foreign banks to promote worthless checks	Bahamas	1971
US v. Wolfson	Using foreign bank to promote worthless checks	St Vincent	1980
Alfred I. Willett	Concealing commodities fraud through a foreign corporation	Libya	N.A.
Herbert M. Wolstencraft	Aiding in false representations to IRS involving activities in foreign countries	Bahamas	N.A.

IV DISCLOSURE OF FINANCIAL RECORDS IN SUPPORT OF CRIMINAL INVESTIGATIONS

Case Name	Type of Case	Foreign country involved	Date
In the matter of Arawak Trust Co.	Complying with grand jury subpoena of foreign bank records	Cayman Islands	1980
Application of Chase Manhattan Bank	Complying with subpoena for bank records in light of possible violation of foreign law	Panama	1962
Ings v. Ferguson	Complying with subpoena for bank records in light of possible foreign law violations	Canada	1960
Ryan v. Commission of Internal Revenue	Complying with subpoena for bank	Switzerland	1975

Case Name	Type of Case	Foreign country involved	Date
	records in light of possible foreign law violation		
SEC v. Banca della Svizzera Italiana	Complying with subpoena for bank records in light of possible foreign law violation	Switzerland	1981
SEC v. Minas de Artemisa, SA	Complying with subpoena for bank records in light of possible foreign law violation	Mexico	1945
Société Internationale pour Participation Industrielle v. Rogers	Complying with subpoena for bank records in light of possible foreign law violation	Switzerland	1958
Trade Development Bank v. Continental Insurance Co.	Mandating secrecy waivers at court discretion	Switzerland	1972
US v. Bank of Nova Scotia	Complying with subpoena of bank records in light of possible foreign law violation	Bahamas	1981
In re Grand Jury Proceedings US v. Field	Complying with subpoena of bank records in light of possible foreign law violations	Cayman Islands	1976
US v. Loften	Liability for substantive legal violations of attorneys representing racketeers	Various	1981
US v. Payner	Complying with subpoena of bank records in light of fourth amendment constitutional challenge	Bahamas	1980
US v. Quigg	Complying with subpoena of bank records of possible foreign law violations	Bahamas	1980

*N.A. = Multiple years or not available.

Source: Senate Committee on Governmental Affairs, Permanent Subcommittee on Investigations, *Crime and Secrecy: The Use of Offshore Banks and Companies* (Washington, DC US Government Printing Office, 1983).

Bibliography

Achleitner, Paul M. *Das Bankgeheimnis in Österreich,Deutschland und der Schweiz* (Vienna: Österreichisches Forschungsinstitut für Sparkassenwesen, 1981).

Adams, Stanley, *Roche versus Adams* (London: Jonathan Cape, 1983).

Aliber, R. Z., 'Monetary Aspects of Offshore Markets', *Columbia Journal of World Business*, Fall 1979.

Asheshov, Nicholas, 'Will Hot Money Spoil Miami?', *Institutional Investor*, September 1981.

Barrass, Alice, 'Clipping the Wings of Swiss Bankers', *The Banker*, August 1978.

Bawley, Dan, *The Subterranean Economy* (New York: McGraw-Hill, 1982).

Blum, R. H., 'Offshore Money Flows: A Large Dark Number', *Journal of International Affairs*, Spring/Summer 1981.

Blum, R. H. and Kaplan, John, 'Offshore Banking: Issues with Respect to Criminal Use', Mimeo., The Ford Foundation, November 1979.

Bok, Sissela, *Secrets* (New York: Pantheon, 1982).

Braun, David, W., 'The Swiss Base Company: Tax Avoidance Device for Multinationals', *Notre Dame Lawyer*, April 1975.

Browne, Harry, *Harry Browne's Complete Guide to Swiss Banks* (New York: McGraw-Hill Book Company, 1976).

Business International, *Investing, Licensing and Trading Conditions Abroad: Switzerland* (New York: Business International Corporation, 1983).

Chambost, Eduard, *Bank Accounts: A World Guide to Confidentiality* (London: John Wiley, 1983).

Clarke, Thurston and Tigue Jr, John J., *Dirty Money* (New York: Simon & Schuster, 1975).

Columbia Broadcasting System Television Network, 'The Castle Bank Caper', *Sixty Minutes*, Vol. XII, No. 47, 3 August 1980.

Columbia Broadcasting System Television Network, 'Safe Haven', *Sixty Minutes*, Vol. XII, No. 33, 2 December 1979.

Cornwell, Rupert, *God's Banker* (London: Victor Gollancz, 1983).

Crédit Suisse, *Banking Secrecy in Switzerland* (Zurich: Crédit Suisse, 1978).

Crédit Suisse, *The Truth about Swiss Banking* (Zurich: jointly published, 1972; reprinted 1975).

Diamond, Jeffrey M., 'Foreign Bank Secrecy and the Evasion of United States Securities Laws', *New England Law Review*, Vol. 14, No. 18, 1978.

Dufey, G. and Giddy, I. H., 'The Unique Risk of Eurodollars', *The Journal of Commercial Bank Lending*, June 1978.

Economic Research Counselors, *An Investor's Guide to Inflation Hedges* (Vancouver: Economic Research Counselors Publications, 1980).

The Economist, *Quarterly Economic Review of Switzerland*, Intelligence Unit Limited (London: EIU, 1983).

el Hadj, Elie, 'The Economics of an Offshore Banking Center', *Euromoney*, September 1979.

Fehrenbach, J. R., *The Swiss Banks* (New York: McGraw-Hill Book Company, 1966).

Gladwin, Thomas and Walter, Ingo, *Multinationals under Fire* (New York: John Wiley & Sons, 1980).

Gordon, Richard A., *Tax Havens and their Use by US Taxpayers — An Overview* (Washington, DC: Internal Revenue Service, 12 January 1981).

Greenawalt, Kent, and Noam, Eli, 'Confidentiality Claims of Business Organizations', in Harvey J. Goldschmidt (ed.), *Business Disclosure: Governments' Need to Know* (New York: McGraw-Hill, 1979).

Guggi, Bruno B. *Forms of Companies and Taxation in the Principality of Liechtenstein* (Vaduz: The General Trust Corporation, 1972).

Guttentag, Jack and Herring, Richard, 'Disclosure Policy and International Banking', The Wharton School, University of Pennsylvania, 1984 (summer).

Gutmann, Peter M., 'The Subterranean Economy', *Financial Analysts Journal*, November/December 1977.

Handelsbank N.W., *Swiss Bank Secrecy: Fact and Fiction* (Zurich: Handelsbank N.W., 1975).

Hanselman, Guido, 'Mutual Understanding between Switzerland and the USA in the Field of Banking', Speech delivered before the Swiss Society of New York, 21 April 1981.

Kelder, James, 'A Swiss Bank Primer', *Personal Finance*, 28 May 1980.

Kelder, James, 'Austrian Banks', *Personal Finance*, 27 May 1981.

Kelder, James, *How to Open a Swiss Bank Account* (New York: Thomas Y. Crowell Company, 1976).

Kelder, James, 'Swiss Charge-Cards', *Personal Finance*, 3 September 1980.

Kronholz, June, 'Swiss Bank Secrecy Faces Attack', *The Wall Street Journal*, 23 June 1980.

Lernoux, Penny, *In Banks We Trust* (New York: Doubleday, 1984).

Leutwiler, Fritz, *Swiss Monetary Exchange Rate Policy in an Inflationary World*, translated by Dr Herbert Zassenhaus (Washington, DC: American Enterprise Institute for Public Policy Research, 1978).

Levine, Theodore *et al.*, 'Insider Trading: A Forty-Eight Year Assessment', *Corporate Law and Practice Course Handbook Series*, No. 402, Practicing Law Institute B4-6634, B6-6626, 1982.

Mack, J.A., *The Crime Industry* (Lexington, Mass.: D. C. Heath & Co., 1975).

Matter, Alfred, 'Swiss Banking Secrecy', *Prospects* (published by Swiss Bank Corporation) No. 155/2, 1975.

Mendelsohn, M. S., 'BIS Stresses Euromarket Supervision', *American Banker*, 18 April 1979.

Mendelsohn, M. S. 'Switzerland Cracking down on Violators of Bank Code', *American Banker*, November 1980.

Meyer, Bernhard F., 'Swiss Banking Secrecy and its Legal Implications in the United States', *New England Law Review*, Vol. 14, No. 18, 1978.

Meynell, Charles, 'The Problems of Fritz Leutwiler', *Euromoney*, October 1978.

Meynell, Charles, 'Why Swiss Banks Worry about Their Popularity', *Euromoney*, October 1978.

Newcomb, D. and Kohler, A., *Coping with Secrecy and Blocking Laws*, (New York: Shearman & Sterling, 1983).

OECD, *Regulations Affecting International Banking Operations* (Paris: OECD, 1981).

Peat, Marwick, Mitchell & Co., *Banking in Switzerland* (New York: PMM, 1979).

Peat, Marwick, Mitchell & Co., *Finance Companies in Switzerland* (New York: PMM, 1981).

Pick, Franz, *The Numbered Account: Functions, Advantages and Drawbacks* (New York: Pick Publishing Corporation, 1969).

Rankin, Deborah, 'Are Swiss Accounts Worth the Credit?' *New York Times*, 19 February 1984.

Reich, Carl, *Financier: The Biography of André Meyer* (New York: William Morrow & Company, 1983).

Schultz, Hans, 'Banking Secrecy and the Swiss–American Treaty on Legal Assistance in Criminal Matters', *Swiss Bank Corporation Booklet* No. 11, October 1976.

Senate Committee on Governmental Affairs, Permanent Subcommittee on Investigations, *Staff Study on Crime and Secrecy: The Use of Offshore Banks and Companies* (Washington, DC: Government Printing Office, 1983).

Simon, Carl P. and Witte, Ann D., *Beating the System* (Boston, Mass., Auburn House, 1982).

Skousen, Mark, *The Complete Guide to Financial Privacy* (New York: Simon & Schuster, 1983).

Stiglitz, Joseph E. and Weiss, Andrew, 'Incentive Effects of Termination: Application to the Credit and Labor Markets', *American Economic Review*, Vol. 73, No. 5, December 1983.

Sturm, Paul W., 'The Gnomes Are Nibbling', *Forbes*, 16 April 1979.

Swiss Bankers' Association, *The Relations of the Swiss Banks with the USA*, Circular No. 3895 (Basle: Swiss Bankers' Association, 1968).

Swiss Bankers' Association, *Vereinbarung* (Basle: Swiss Bankers' Association, 1977).

Swiss National Bank, *Das Schweizerische Bankwesen* (Zurich: Swiss National Bank, various years).

Switzerland, *Civil Code*, 10 December 1907.

Switzerland, *Code of Obligations*, 30 March 1911.

Switzerland, *Criminal Code*, 8 November 1934.

Tanzi, Vito, *The Underground Economy in the United States and Abroad* (Lexington, Mass.: D. C. Heath, 1982).

Tax Haven Study Group, *Estimates of Levels of Tax Haven Use* (Washington, DC: Internal Revenue Service, 1981).

Union Bank of Switzerland, *Double Taxation Treaties Concluded between Switzerland and Other Countries* (Zurich: Union Bank of Switzerland, 1981).

Union Bank of Switzerland, *Founding a Company in Switzerland* (Zurich: Union Bank of Switzerland, 1976).

Union Bank of Switzerland, *Swiss Federal Banking Law* (Zurich: Union Bank of Switzerland, 1972).

US Department of State, *United States Treaties and Other Obligations*, 2 U.S.T. 1751, 'Tax Convention, United States – Switzerland', T.I.A.S. No. 2316, 24 May 1951.

US Department of State, *United States Treaties and Other Obligations*, 27 U.S.T. 2019, 'Treaty on Mutual Assistance in Criminal Matters, United States –Switzerland', T.I.A.S. No. 8302, 25 May 1973.

Vicker, Ray, *Those Swiss Money Men* (New York: Charles Scribner & Son, 1973).

Wallich, H. C., 'Why the Euromarket Needs Restraint', *Columbia Journal of World Business*, Fall 1979.

Weber, Christopher, 'A Look at the Cayman Islands', *World Market Perspective*, Vol. XIII, No. 10, 16 October 1980.

Ziegler, Jean, *Switzerland: The Awful Truth* (New York: Harper & Row, 1976).

Index

International Fuel Development
Corporation 27
International Monetary Fund (IMF) 20,
46, 149, 188
International Mutual Assistance on
Criminal Matters law (1983) 138
International Telephone and Telegraph
Corporation (ITT) 40–1
IOR 69–78
IOS Ltd 26
IRA 87–8
Ireland *Fig* 2.1, 87–8
Irish Northern Aid Committee of New
York City (NORAID) 88
IRS 16, 18, 27, 29, 31, 41, 49, 52, 54–5,
80, 135, 142
Irving Trust Company 81, 102, 132
Israel 21, 44, 179
Italy 12, *Fig* 2.1, 17, 24, 44, 50, 69–79,
137, 179, *Appendix*
IU International Corporation 146

J. David & Co. 67
Japan *Fig* 2.1, 101, *Table* 4.2
Jetaire, Ltd 28
John Paul II, Pope 77
John W. McGrath Co. 29
joint account 32

Keaton, Darius N. 25, 145
Keats, Richard 105
Kilpatrick, William A. 27, *Appendix*
Korean Air Lines 28
Kuwait Petroleum Company (KPC) 25,
145

La Centrale 72–3, 76
La Fidèle 71
labor market approach 12
Lark International Ltd 120
Latco Development Corporation 29
Latin America 42, *Figs* 3.1 & 3.2, 44–5; *see
also individual countries*
laundering, money 3, 22, 24, 29, 40, 80–5,
88, 116–18, 119, 122, 125, 127–37, 139,
181, 183, *Appendix*
Lazard, Frères & Co. 40–1
Lebanon 24, 44, *Appendix*
Leclerc & Cie 102
legal tax potential approach 12
Lemire, Joseph C. 28
Leoni, Filippo 73
Lesser Antilles Trading Company 29
Liberia 21–2, 28, *Table* 4.1, *Appendix*

Liechtenstein 28, 33, 40, 59, 69, 71–4, 76,
Table 4.1, 99–100, 138, *Appendix*
Linea Aeropostal Venzolana 28
Lockheed Corporation 119
Lombard Odier 147
Luciano Chiarini and Associates 28
Lusser, Markus 108
Luxembourg 5, 74–7, *Table* 4.1, 119, 187

McConnell, Richard 82–3
McDonnell Douglas Corporation (MDC)
28
McPartlin, Robert 29
Mafia 75, 79, 137
Manic S.A. of Luxembourg 73–4
Manufacturers Hanover Trust Company
68, 132
Marc Rich & Company AG (Switzerland)
53–7
Marc Rich International 54
Marcinkus, Cardinal Paul 70, 72, 74–6, 78
Marine Midland Bank & Trust Company
81, 132
Mario Genghini 73
market structure, secrecy 8–9, 151–72
Markowitz, Edward 68
Markowitz, Nathan 83
Marlborough Investments, Ltd 27
Martin, Gary L. 25
Meltzer, Clyde 54, 57
Memorandum of Understanding and
Private Agreement 146
Merrill Lynch 133
Mexico *Fig* 2.2, 16, 20–1, 42, *Figs* 3.1 &
3.2, 44, 46, 174, 179, *Appendix*
Meyer, André 40–1
Microelectronics Research Institute (MRI)
60–1
Milan-Rodriguez, Ramón 115–16
Mobuto, President 46
Montserrat 67, *Table* 4.1, 111–13, *Appendix*
Morgan Guaranty Trust Company 68, 132
Mueller, Richard 59–61

National Graphical Association 41
national income statistics 12
National Union of Mineworkers (NUM)
41
Netherlands 23–4, *Tables* 4.1 & 4.2, 113,
185
Netherlands Antilles *Table* 4.1, 113–15,
120 138, *Appendix*
New York County v. Firestone (1982) 28,
Appendix